# The Battle of Saint-Vith and the Potteau Ambush, December 1944

Hugues Wenkin

Pen & Sword

**MILITARY**

First published in Great Britain in 2024 by
Pen & Sword Military
An imprint of Pen & Sword Books Limited
Yorkshire – Philadelphia

ISBN 978 1 03610 393 4

A CIP catalogue record for this book is
available from the British Library.

Typeset by Mac Style
Printed in the UK by CPI Group (UK) Ltd, Croydon, CR0 4YY.

Pen & Sword Books Limited incorporates the imprints of After the Battle,
Atlas, Archaeology, Aviation, Discovery, Family History, Fiction, History,
Maritime, Military, Military Classics, Politics, Select, Transport, True Crime,
Air World, Frontline Publishing, Leo Cooper, Remember When, Seaforth
Publishing, The Praetorian Press, Wharncliffe Local History, Wharncliffe
Transport, Wharncliffe True Crime and White Owl.

For a complete list of Pen & Sword titles please contact

PEN & SWORD BOOKS LIMITED
47 Church Street, Barnsley, South Yorkshire, S70 2AS, England
E-mail: enquiries@pen-and-sword.co.uk
Website: www.pen-and-sword.co.uk
or
PEN AND SWORD BOOKS
1950 Lawrence Rd, Havertown, PA 19083, USA
E-mail: Uspen-and-sword@casematepublishers.com
Website: www.penandswordbooks.com

# The Battle of Saint-Vith and the Potteau Ambush, December 1944

# Contents

The Poteau ambush was a moment in the Battle of the Ardennes that has become mythicised, mainly because of a series of German photographs captured by the US Army. Understanding what happened at that precise moment was one of the motivations for this book. (*Nara*)

Introduction

# Why Saint-Vith?

The first days of the Battle of the Bulge saw tactical defeats for several formations of the American army, with the Saint-Vith sector being particularly hard hit by the surprise attack that prevailed on the morning of 16 December 1944. Two American units, the 106th Infantry Division and the 14th Cavalry Group, were pummelled in front of this small town of vital importance to the German offensive in the Ardennes. After the war, their men would be accused of cowardice and incompetence. As I write the first lines of this new book, the first question that comes to mind is: did these men really deserve to be remembered? The human aspect is key in a battle, and the stereotypical images of the Battle of the Bulge show the front line retreating and the situation being saved by valiant units moving up the line. The story of the first days of the Kampfgruppe (KG) Peiper breakthrough (*The Breakthrough of Kampfgruppe Peiper in the Battle of the Bulge*, Pen & Sword Books, 2024) has already shown that this was not the case for some front-line units. We shall therefore approach the history of the battle by endeavouring to detach ourselves from preconceived ideas. Historians must reconstruct the facts and present them without judgement, but this does not prevent them from offering analytical conclusions, even going so far as to highlight the responsibilities of some of the parties involved.

Like all battles, the Battle of the Bulge saw some units fight heroically. Thrown into the fray without knowing what to expect, the 7th Armored Division came to the rescue of the defenders of Saint-Vith, just as the 'Screaming Eagles' of the 101st Airborne Division had done at Bastogne. The Battle of Saint-Vith, however, has remained far less famous. By extension, Major General Hasbrouck's armoured division does not occupy as important a place in historiography as McAuliffe and his men. Perhaps the fact that it was ordered to evacuate the Saint-Vith salient and was therefore not encircled in the town is the reason for its lesser celebrity.

In addition, the Battle of Saint-Vith was fought with as much determination and heroism as the Battle of Bastogne. The two towns were of similar strategic importance, and one could almost evoke a form of tactical twinship. Yet the former is rarely mentioned in the American national historiography, while references to the latter are plentiful. This is one of the interesting aspects of this commitment. We will therefore analyse what fundamentally differentiates the situation in Bastogne and Saint-Vith.

The small hamlet of a few houses to the north-west of Saint-Vith is called Poteau. It is well known to military history buffs because of a series of photographs taken by a German propaganda company. These photographs were taken by the US Army and are available at the National Archives in Washington. This institution allows anyone to copy them and use them in publications without charging royalties. Photographs of the German army in the Ardennes sector are rare, so publishers often use this series of images to illustrate any book about the battle. This is no exception, but we will look at the circumstances in which this series of photographs was taken. The first thing that needs to be made clear is that the photographs are actually posed; they are a vulgar staging of a battle for propaganda purposes. Nonetheless, their frequent appearance in history books on the Ardennes offensive makes one wonder what really happened

The 7th AD knew the Saint-Vith sector well, having passed through during the liberation of the area in September 1944. The sign posts give an idea of its strategic importance. (*Nara*)

The Battle of Saint-Vith went through two phases. After having to abandon it on 21 December 1944, the soldiers of the 7th AD returned to take it back a month later. (*Nara*)

in this small village on the border between the Ardennes and the German-speaking cantons of Belgium.

As you can see, evoking the Battle of Saint-Vith means plunging into a multitude of questions. Finding the answers is the real interest of a historian's work!

## The Logistical Importance of Saint-Vith

In the eyes of the commander of the 5. Panzer-Armee, General der Panzertruppen Hasso von Manteuffel, the success of the German offensive in the Ardennes depended on three conditions: the element of surprise; the atmospheric conditions that prevented action by the Allied air force; and a rapid advance beyond Saint-Vith.

The terrain between the Schnee Eifel and the Ardennes is rugged and heavily wooded. Frequent streams and numerous hills with relatively steep sides add to the topological difficulties of the terrain. The area is criss-crossed by few roads of poor quality. But in a mechanised attack, even one carried out by tanks capable of passing almost anywhere, it should not be imagined that communication routes are not of paramount importance.

In the Ardennes, roads are rare and of poor quality in terrain that is difficult to access. (*Nara*)

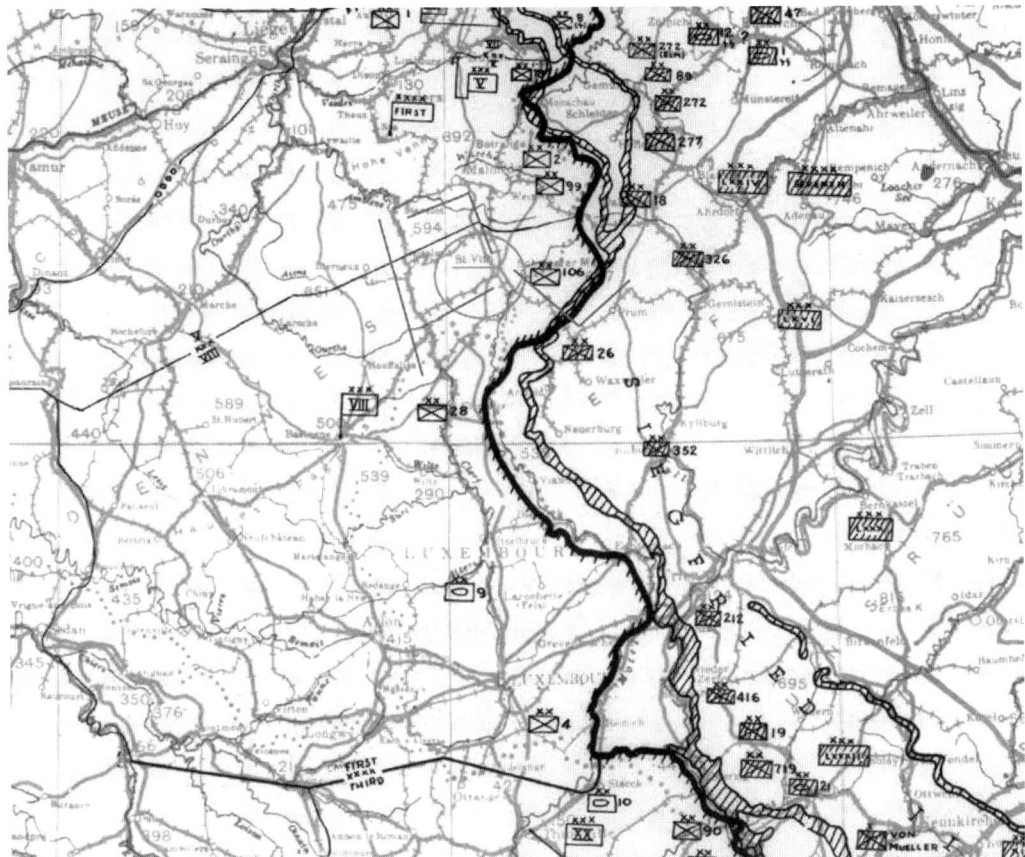

Map of the Saint-Vith sector (position of units known to the 12th Army Group on 13 December 1944). The marked lines indicate the important rail links between the German and Belgian networks. (*Nara* (*mod Hugues Wenkin*))

Quite the contrary! To enable tanks to move forward, with infantrymen to fight and guns to fire, you need petrol, rations and ammunition. This means lorries were needed to transport this freight and even, in the case of the Wehrmacht, horse-drawn wagons. To move this huge volume of traffic, roads were needed. And in the Ardennes, roads were all the more precious for their scarcity. The main routes cross in the medium-sized towns, which have enabled their development since the Middle Ages. These localities are known as road junctions.

However, Saint-Vith is more than just a road junction; it is, strictly speaking, a centre of lines of communication. First and foremost, the town is home to one of the three key road junctions on the entire Ardennes front. From here, roads led to Dinant and Liège in the west, to Malmedy in the north-west, to Stavelot in the north and finally to Houffalize and Bastogne in the south, all linked to the centre of the Reich via Schönburg and Prüm in the east.

Even more important were trains. At the end of 1944, Wehrmacht units had very few organic means of transport. Their logistical support was grossly undersized. To enable an offensive to develop under the right conditions, the Oberkommando der Wehrmacht

Saint-Vith seen from the air after the battle. The small size of the town is out of all proportion to its strategic importance. (*Nara*)

(OKW) knew it was going to need the railways. There were only two single-track lines linking the Belgian Ardennes to the rear bases in Germany. One passes through Malmedy and the other via Saint-Vith. These two towns are linked to the two-track Bastogne –

Liège line. The only east–west railway line stretching from the Rhine to the Eifel and the Ardennes via Prüm also passes through Saint-Vith. It is also worth remembering that petrol was stored in large quantities on the other side of the Rhine, thus making Saint-Vith an unloading point on the main logistics artery; an essential feature that neither Bastogne nor Houffalize had. By holding Saint-Vith, it would therefore be possible for the 5. Panzer-Armee, with its notable lack of lorries, to shorten the road length of its logistical umbilical cord.

## The Operational Importance of Saint-Vith

Von Manteuffel's objective was to cross the Meuse between Givet and Andenne. His armoured forces were then to push on beyond Dinant, towards Namur, where they would cross the Sambre and finally head due north to seize Brussels, located on the main road to Antwerp.

Important though it was, von Manteuffel's armoured army played only a secondary role in this affair. The real German spearhead was further north and involved the

Photograph taken in Eupen on 30 September 1944. The number of signs at the crossroads shows the strategic importance of the towns in the Ardennes and Eifel. (*Nara*)

6. Panzer-Armee led by General der Waffen SS Joseph 'Sepp' Dietrich. The role of von Manteuffel's formation was to protect the SS leader's right flank as it advanced towards Antwerp.

Because of the axis of attack defined to reach Antwerp, a demarcation line was planned between the two German armoured armies. This passed a few kilometres north of Saint-Vith. If von Manteuffel was unable to occupy this town in time, the two armies' advance would be split, forming two smaller salients instead of a breakthrough with a broad base. Two small points of attack that would be easier for the defenders to cut down. This was the worst-case scenario for KG Peiper's armoured point, which could not be joined by the 2. SS-Panzer-Division on its right flank.

Lastly, Saint-Vith is a town where bypasses and link roads (i.e. roads linking the suburbs to the town centre) pass through. The rocades are roads running parallel to the future front, passing through Eupen – Malmedy – Weiswampach and continuing along the 'Skyline Drive' from the Grand Duchy of Luxembourg. Holding this route made it easy to transfer troops on a north–south axis to act on the weak points of the front under attack. In the context of December 1944, this was of crucial importance to the Germans. This communication route, located close to the front line, was ideal for this purpose. It

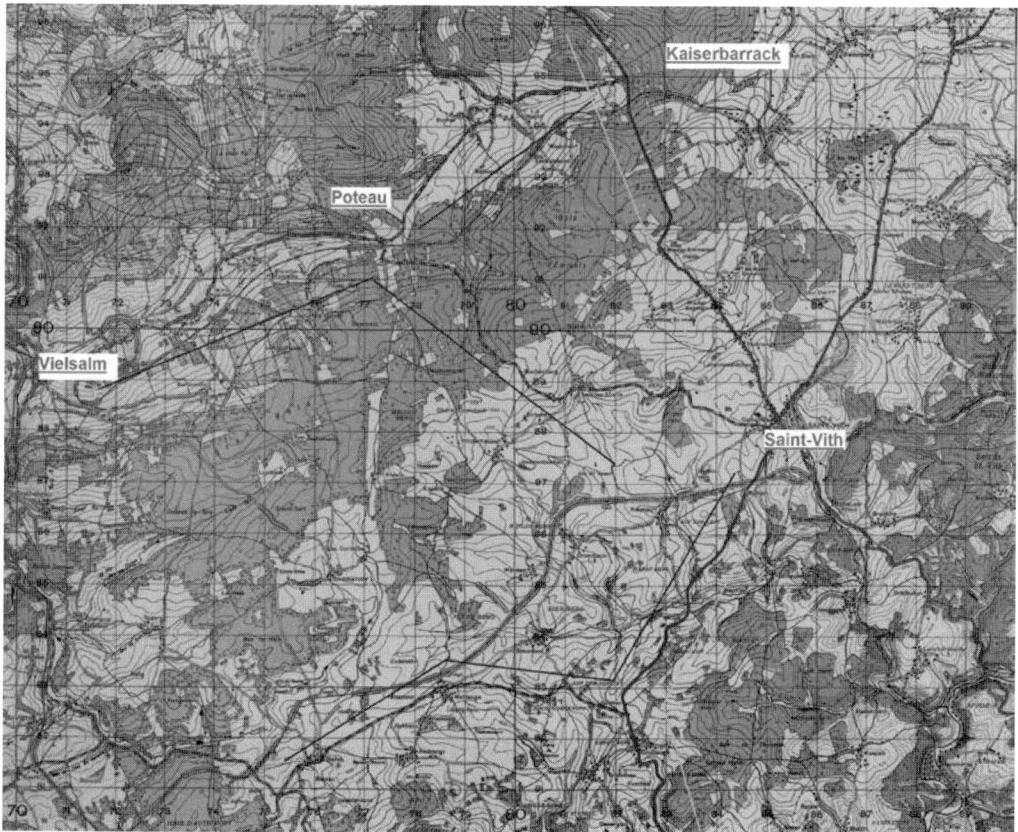

Map of the Saint-Vith sector (US 1943 1/50000). The ring roads can be seen surrounding the villages, while the other lines indicate the link roads. (*Nara (mod Hugues Wenkin)*)

The Battle of the Bulge took place in appalling weather conditions. The OKW relied on this factor to keep the Allied air force on the ground. (*Nara*)

was neither too far away to allow action at key points, nor too close in the sense that it was out of range of enemy artillery. It was perfect for organising the offensive in the sector flexibly, as the German planners had decided, and possibly transferring troops from one side of the front to the other. If the Germans had not had the roads through Saint-Vith at their disposal, the rapid concentration towards Bastogne from 27 December to reduce the corridor that Patton had just opened would have been impossible.

Link roads are privileged communication routes leading from the rear to the front. They provide attackers with routes that enable them to penetrate very quickly and in depth, eventually overtaking troops defending a continuous front. In this sense, Saint-Vith was also ideally placed. The town was an essential crossing point for Malmedy, La Roche-en-Ardenne and Houffalize. These three other medium-sized towns were on the route that would enable the 5. Panzer-Armee to open up its two main axes of penetration: Marche – Namur and Bastogne – Dinant.

Of course, for the American camp, these bypasses and link roads played exactly the same role in the opposite direction. It was therefore clear that possession of the small town of Saint-Vith was crucial for both sides and that the battles to hold it would be fierce.

# Chapter 1

# German Preparations at Saint-Vith

## Von Manteuffel's Plan for Saint-Vith

The 5. Panzer-Armee was made up of three corps: the LXVI. Korps and the XLVII. and LVIII. Panzerkorps. In the south, General Lüttwitz's XLVII. PanzerKorps comprised the 127-strong 2. Panzer-Division and the 84-strong 130. Panzer-Lehr-Division. The centre was occupied by Krüger's LVIII. Panzerkorps under Krüger with the 116. Panzer-Division (Pz-Div) with 107 tanks and the 11. Panzer-Division with 160 tanks, but it would not come online until a later stage.

The German plan called for the Saint-Vith sector to be targeted by the LXVI. Korps, commanded by General der Artillerie Walther Lucht. He commanded two Volksgrenadier divisions: the 18. and 62. Volksgrenadier-Division (VGD) to fulfil his mission. The width of his front was around 26 kilometres. There were four usable link roads in this zone: in the north, the Hallschlag road to Manderfeld; in the centre, the Roth, Auw, Schönberg

General der Panzertruppen Hasso von Manteuffel commanded the 5. Panzer-Armee. (*Rights reserved*)

The German artillery prepares to shell the US positions. (*Rights reserved*)

axis and the Prüm, Bleialf, Schönberg road. And finally, to the south of the system, the road leading to Saint-Vith via Pronsfeld, Habscheid, Winterspelt and Steinebrück.

When, after the war, von Manteuffel went back over his plan, he explained:

*After encircling the Schnee Eifel in a pincer movement, the Lucht troops were to charge towards Saint-Vith. The rapid capture of this communications hub (to which three railway lines and five roads converge) was of vital importance, not only for my 5. Panzer-Armee, but also for the whole of Heeresgruppe B, so that armoured engagement, lateral links, flank protection and the arrival of supplies could be achieved. Here, too, speed was the essential corollary of surprise. Here, too, there was a serious obstacle: the Our river. It was therefore vital that the troops should be able to take the bridges at Steinebrück, Schönberg and Andler intact! Any delay in taking these bridges could have jeopardised the entire operation. The Luftwaffe had been unable to provide the aerial photos we had requested; all we had were maps and photos from dusty archives... and the hope that they would still be relevant. The roads leading to the assembly points had been repaired and signposted. All activity was forbidden during the day, so the men had to hide in the woods to escape any aerial reconnaissance. My LXVI. Korps had no panzers, but it had been allocated a brigade of assault guns mounted on self-propelled mounts. They had to cross the rows of Drackenzähne[1] which we could not dynamite without attracting the attention of the Americans; moreover, the vehicles would have risked becoming entangled in the debris. So we made wooden ramps which were brought in during the previous nights, carefully camouflaged and assembled during the night of 15 to 16 December.*

*The Korps artillery was installed to the south-west of Prüm and, at my request, an artillery observation battalion was assigned to it. It was able to provide us with invaluable information on the number and positions of the enemy batteries and their activity (i.e. frequency, number of salvos, targets most frequently fired at). Thanks to all this information, the artillery was able to meticulously draw up its fire plans. Further to the rear, we tried out artificial moonlight, which was intended to enable the assault troops to infiltrate 'like raindrops' through the American lines, seeking out points of resistance to eliminate them silently. 'The bullet is mad', wrote Count Suvarov, 'the bayonet knows what it's doing... and less noisily'.[2]*

Von Manteuffel goes on to explain that to the north, in the sector of the 18. VGD, an infantry regiment and a battalion of self-propelled guns were to break through Bleialf and seize the Schönberg bridge. The other two regiments and around forty assault guns had to pass through the Losheim Gap, where the American position seemed incredibly weak. The German officer would have liked to commit his entire 18. VGD to the north. Unfortunately, as his other division was totally inexperienced, he had to give up. The 18. VGD was therefore ordered to attack the southern sector of the Schnee Eifel. The instructions given to this division stated: *'At 05:30 on 14 December, the 18. VGD will attack, concentrating its effort on the right wing. Its vanguard elements will cross the main line of resistance and advance on both sides of the Schnee Eifel. The initial objective will be to cross*

A Stug III Ausf G is examined by GIs in the Hederscheid sector of Luxembourg. Forty-two assault guns of this type supportted the 18. VGD. (*Nara*)

All the available artillery was assembled. (*Rights reserved*)

*the River Our at Schönberg, after which the division will advance with a mobile force along the road alongside the River Our towards Saint-Vith, which is to be taken by a surprise assault.'*[3]

The 62. VGD was to attack in the Grosslangenfeld – Heckhuscheid region and then advance on a broad front to control the road from Pronsfeld to Saint-Vith. One of its primary objectives was to seize the bridge over the Our at Steinebrück. Two entire divisions threw themselves on the positions of the only American division: the blue 106th Infantry Division 'Golden Lions'.

## Strengths and Weaknesses of the Volksgrenadier-Division at Saint-Vith

The 18. and 62. VGD were two large infantry units of a new type that deserve a closer look. They comprised just under 13,000 men, almost 3,000 fewer than the traditional Infanterie-Division. The core of a Volksgrenadier-Division consisted of three Infanterie-Regimenten with two Abteilunge[4] with three reinforced Volksgrenadier companies. One of the three regiments had an Abteilung whose men were equipped with bicycles to increase their speed of movement. Each regiment was also equipped with two additional

The drop in numbers was offset by the use of the Sturmgewehr 44. This soldier is being trained in the use of the weapon. (*Rights reserved*)

Kompagnien, one for artillery support with a platoon of eight 120mm mortars and a second with four 75mm Leichte Infanterie Geschutz. The second was an anti-tank Kompagnie equipped with fifty-four Panzerschreke,[5] a more effective copy of the American bazooka.

To increase the offensive effectiveness of the manpower and maintain a strike force equivalent to the previous units, automatic weapons such as the MP40 or the new Sturmgewehr 44, the ancestor of the modern assault rifle, were introduced in greater numbers. To find the men needed, the rear services were scoured for the last usable manpower. They were supervised by a few veterans to ensure that they held up well under fire.

As for the 18. and 62. VGD, von Manteuffel's comments on them make it possible to clarify the limits of their real offensive potential:

*Of the divisions definitively placed at our disposal, the 18. and 62. VGD[6] were to be employed as permanent divisions in the future sector of attack under the command of the LXVI. Armee Korps. These two divisions had to defend large sectors and could therefore only detach a small number of local reservists, who were hardly trained, as the tasks of such forces, stationed so close to the front and alerted for action, did not permit this. Reserves were allocated to divisions from replacement battalions in the field.*

*The 18. VGD had a good replacement staff, a sufficient number of young men, many of whom had come from the navy or the Luftwaffe and had not received infantry training.*

The VGD's leadership was not very motivated when it came to getting the units back on their feet.

Experienced officers succeed in making the 18. VGD a quality unit. (*Nara*)

*Most of the subordinate commanders had fought on the Eastern Front, the others had come from various branches of the Wehrmacht or from the reserve army, and very few had graduated from good army schools. The officer corps represented a good average, but some of them had no experience of the front, while the young reserve officers had combat experience.*

Von Manteuffel also pointed out that Hoffmann-Schönborn's 18. VGD also only had heterogeneous elements, but since it had come online a fortnight earlier, its commander had managed to turn it into a coherent unit by sending small groups to the rear (the sector remained quiet) to undergo much-needed training.[7] The division was re-equipped with some of its equipment.

Horses arrived at the unit in poor condition. (*Nara*)

The mobile detachment was partially equipped with bicycles. The horses, which made up a large part of the means of transport, were overworked.[8] In reality, the unit's presence on the front line on 16 December was a real challenge, given the difficulties encountered by its commanders as soon as it was activated on 9 September 1944, near Kolding in Denmark. It brought together a cadre of 2,500 fighters from the 18. Luftwaffe-Feld-Division and 3,000 others from various Luftwaffe and Kriegsmarine reserves. It also received 5,000 men, skilled workers who until then had been considered indispensable in the factories of the Third Reich.

The remaining gaps in the organisation chart were filled by young people from the most recent recruitments. It was therefore made up mainly of middle-aged men, most of whom had never seen action. Its anti-tank artillery consisted of a company of 75mm and a company of 37mm towed anti-aircraft guns. Individual anti-tank weapons were sorely lacking. Nevertheless, the division went into battle fully equipped with ammunition. The morale of its men was not constant. The leadership came from the 18. Luftwaffe-Feld-Division that had experienced defeat on the Seine. Filled with defeatism, the non-commissioned officers did not look after their new recruits. It took all the energy of General Major Günther Hoffmann-Schönborn to give his formation real cohesion, and by the time they had set off on their assault, morale had greatly improved and there were very few desertions; mainly just Volksdeutsche and young recruits frightened by the precision of American fire. After six weeks of training in a quiet sector, the division had become more solid and its chain of command had been strengthened.[9] Its right flank was to hit the 14th Cavalry Group's (CG) position head-on, while its left flank attacked the 106th Infantry Division's (ID) positions to the north. Oberstleutnant Dietrich Moll, the division's chief of staff,[10] explained the circumstances of its activation:

> The lack of experienced men in the division was in itself an indication that extensive training would be necessary, a task that was seriously hampered by the lack of training aids and equipment and by the fact that replacements were slow to arrive. A month after activation, only two-thirds of the division had been assembled, and only a limited stock of weapons was available. Several light machine guns were present, but their mounts had been destroyed in an air raid on the Hamburg ammunition depot. It was therefore impossible to show them how to handle a machine gun. Saddles had been distributed for the artillery horses, but training could not begin because the stirrups were not available. Former members of the air force and navy had to learn how to handle machine guns and mortars. All these difficulties were overcome thanks to the efforts of the division's energetic and experienced commander, who knew how to select and assign competent subordinates. However, almost all the Luftwaffe officers originally assigned proved to be unreliable and had to be replaced.
>
> By 15 October, the division was almost complete and had almost all its equipment. Training had reached a point where soldiers were at least familiar with their weapons and equipment. Field exercises had been organised by all units, and regimental and battalion headquarters had received tactical training through map exercises.

The anti-tank artillery was equipped with 75mm Pak 40s. (*Nara*)

The infantry support weapons only arrived at the last minute, and staff barely had time to familiarise themselves with how they worked. (*Nara*)

> As the division was to be engaged in a quiet area, its commander felt justified in reporting limited preparation for defensive combat, despite the incomplete state of training. However, the divisional commander was fully aware of his unit's shortcomings, particularly its lack of communications training.[11]

With regard to the other infantry unit that was to attack in the Saint-Vith sector, von Manteuffel explained: *'The 62. VGD was a newly activated division whose training was incomplete because of the late arrival of weapons and equipment. It had virtually no live-fire training; its heavy infantry guns did not arrive until the last day. It was fully manned, but only 16% instead of 40% of the personnel were young men. 15% of the men belonged to "Volksturmsgruppe 3"[12] and their orders were given in Polish or Czech.'[13]*

Later, he added that the 62. VGD did not come online until the last night. The division was fully equipped but had no anti-aircraft company. The rifle company (reconnaissance company) was equipped with bicycles. It too had been reconstituted with sailors who had no warships, airmen who had no planes and elements recovered from other units who had obviously received no infantry training. Most of the non-commissioned officers had come from the Eastern Front. As for heavy weapons, they had only arrived on the last day before he left for the front and the soldiers had received no practical instruction in their use.

The only real tanks available to the VGD were, in fact, self-propelled tank hunters grouped together in a Panzer-Jägerabteilung with fourteen Jagdpanzer 38(t) Hetzer. The 62. VGD was equipped with them, while the 18. VGD was better off, however, having instead the Heeres Sturmgeschutz-Brigade 244[14] with forty-two self-propelled

The 62. VGD was just about ready for action. (*Nara*)

Stug-Brigade 244 was equipped with StuGe III Ausf G assault guns manufactured at the end of the summer of 1944, in an industrial effort by the Third Reich to reconstitute its units. (*NAC*)

guns[15] Sturmgeschutz III out of a theoretical total of forty-five. The divisional artillery was represented by an Artillerie-Regiment with four Abteilungen, one incorporating six 75mm guns, two equipped with twelve 105mm guns each and one with six heavy 150mm guns. A Pioneer Battalion was added to the total. Although these units no longer had the offensive value of the Infanterie-Divisionen of 1940, they were still very effective and were no less powerful. However, the lack of experienced soldiers was cruelly felt, as the recruiters of the Third Reich had scraped the bottom of the barrel of the rear units to fill the ranks.

The LXVI. Korps was therefore shaky: a strong division in the north and a weaker one in the south. The 18. VGD inherited the most delicate missions and was divided in two to make up for the weaknesses of its sister division.

## A Second Korps Attacks the US Position at Saint-Vith

It should be noted that the southern wing of the 6. Panzer-Armee also attacked the defenders of Saint-Vith. As already mentioned, the north of Saint-Vith was at the junction of the two Panzer-Armeen going on the offensive. It was defended by the 14th Cavalry Group, attached to the 106th Infantry Division (ID). The cavalrymen therefore had to deal with the 6. Panzer-Armee to the north and the 5. Panzer-Armee to the south. The north of the Saint-Vith sector would therefore find itself facing two different divisions. The Lanzerath sector, to the north, was attacked by the 3. Fallschirmjäger-Division (FJD) and the south by the 18. Volksgrenadier-Division (18. VGD).

The unit of the 6. Panzer-Armee that attacked the Devine positions was the 3. FJD formed in Reims in October 1943.[16] It had been engaged in Normandy and suffered heavy losses at Saint-Lô it in its attempt to halt the advance of the American forces. By July 1944, the division had already lost 35% of its 17,000 men. It suffered further losses in the Falaise pocket, where Major General Schimpf, who commanded it, was seriously wounded. Although severely reduced in numbers, the division proved pugnacious and remained in action until it was relieved in October. It then found itself in Oldenzaal, Holland, where it received many poor-quality replacements, including poorly trained commanders and staff officers. These replacements came from Luftwaffe ground units and airfield support teams, in short, teams with little or no experience of infantry tactics. Veteran paratroopers from Normandy made up for the skill deficit as best they could. The reconstituted 3. FJD was designated to take part in the Battle of the Bulge. It was then amid a major reorganisation, having been engaged in tough defensive fighting west of Düren since 24 November under the command of Major General Wadehn, where it had to contend with American attacks.[17] On 13 December, it was relieved of this defensive front. Two days later, on 15 December, it set off again for its assembly point near Saint-Vith, from where it went on the attack on 16 December. As Major General Schimpff, the division's commander, had not yet recovered from the wounds he had received in Normandy, the 3. FJD remained under the command of Major General Wadehn for the battle to come.[18] As can be seen, the division was a shadow of its former self. It was not at full strength and there were few well-trained and experienced fighters. While

The 3. Fallschirmjäger-Division (FJD) fought hard in Normandy and lost a large part of its elite. (*NAC*)

This Fallschirmjäger belongs to the 3. FJD. The replacement squad was very young. (*NAC*)

parachute units are generally considered to be elite formations, this division was so in name only. Its young, inexperienced recruits were led by officers who, at best, only had staff experience in rear units. The few experienced veterans who remained in its ranks were distinguished by the parachute helmets they wore, which lacked the traditional flared brim of the standard German helmet. The rest wore standard blue-grey overalls and helmets.

The 3. FJD set up in assembly areas near the small town of Hallschlag, 10 kilometres east of Lanzerath. Its men had just walked 30 kilometres to get there on 15 December via Kronenburg and Stadtkyll. As the paratroopers had few motorised vehicles, they transported their essential equipment on handcarts and children's wagons. It formed the southern infantry wing of the 6. Panzer-Armee and was responsible for opening routes D and E for the 1. SS-Panzer-Division Leibstandarte-SS 'Adolf Hitler'. Wadehn could only commit two regiments to the attack, as the 15. Armee,

The Mephisto, captured by the Australian army, was fitted with one-piece Röchling armour and a trestle mount for its 57mm gun. (*Nara*)

which flanked the two Panzer-Armeen leading the assault to the north, needed the third regiment to close a defensive gap further north. Fallschirmjäger Regiment (FJR) 9 was to attack Lanzerath. FJR 5, meanwhile, was in front of Krewinkel.

According to the German plan, once the breakthrough had been achieved, two Kampfgruppen (KG) of the 1. SS-Panzer-Division were to set off towards the Meuse. KG Peiper was to cross Lanzerath and follow route D towards Amblève, Ligneuville and Wanne. On the same route, behind Peiper, KG Sandig followed with the SS-Panzer-Grenadier Regiment 2. On route E, further south, the road was opened by KG Hansen with SS-Panzer-Grenadier Regiment 1, supported by the 1. Panzer-Jäger Abteilung with Panzerjäger IV L/70s. These units were supposed to pass through Manderfeld, Born and Vielsalm, penetrating deep into the American position. Behind them came KG Knittel, comprising the division's reconnaissance troops, SS Aufklärungs-Abteilung 1.

## The Initial Plan for the 18. VGD

Based on the orders received, the 18. VGD was as follows: subordinate to the LXVI. Korps (whose units occupied positions on either side of the division), the 18. VGD would attack on both sides of the Schnee Eifel. After reaching Roth and Bleialf, the two wings would drive inland to destroy the enemy in and west of the Schnee Eifel mountains.

The 18. VGD begins to concentrate on its starting positions. (*Nara*)

After breaking through the main defence zone, the mobile elements would advance through Weckerath to Andler, capturing the bridge near Schönberg and taking Saint-Vith.

The actual operation planned was as follows: two attack groups were organised. The group on the right (main point of effort), made up of Grenadier Regimenten (GR) 29 and 295, was to assemble on either side of Ormont. GR 294, with a strong right wing, was ordered to advance through Weckerath to Auw, with part of the regiment continuing through Verschneid towards Andler and reaching the Our valley. On the left, GR 295, with a strong left wing, was to advance through Roth, branching off towards Kobscheid and securing point 612 (west of Schlausenbach).

The left attack group, comprising GR 293, was tasked with assembling south of Brandscheid, then passing Unterbrandscheid west of Muehlenberg and finally taking Bleialf. Minor elements were to branch off along the Juestenschlag – Radscheid road as far as height 575 (located 0.6 kilometres north of Radscheid), while the bulk of the attack group moved forward to seize the Schönberg bridge.

One of the challenges facing the 18. VGD was to make the best use of its artillery, which was hypomobile. Twelve 10.5cm FH guns were integrated into the VGD. (*Nara*)

The mobile battalion comprising the anti-tank battalion, the divisional support and reconnaissance company and an engineer company was assigned to the Steinberg in the rear of the right attack group. After GR 295 reached Verschneid, the mobile battalion was to advance towards Andler on divisional orders, then secure the Our valley, Saint-Vith and the heights around Wallerode.

The main difficulties encountered in carrying out the attack as ordered lay in the width of the assault zone (19 kilometres wide) and in maintaining communication and links with the two leading groups. From the outset, it was clear that GR 293's commander had the most difficult task, as he would probably have to make independent decisions.

Support units have relatively complicated missions. The artillery was tasked with supporting two different assault sectors. One battalion of the artillery regiment was attached to GR 293, while the rest of the regiment was to support the right attack group and follow its progress. The firing positions in the right sector therefore had to be determined well in advance and the guns moved from the left sector. The area had been relatively bare during the defensive phase. In the eyes of the German command, these measures constituted a necessary violation of the security instructions insofar as they could alert the Americans.

The engineers had to operate in a completely decentralised manner. To achieve this, a pioneer company was attached to the mobile battalion, two platoons to the right attack group and one platoon to the left attack group. Their main task was to enable the division's vehicles to cross the obstacles formed by the dragon's teeth along the main line

The 88mm anti-aircraft guns would take part in the initial shelling of the US positions. (*Nara*)

of resistance. The signals battalion had to establish all the communications necessary for the attack in the areas of main effort, from divisional headquarters to the mobile battalion and above all to the left attack group.[19]

## The 62. VGD's Plan

The report by the commander of the 62. VGD, Oberst Friedrich Kittel[20] does not give many details in his reports about the preparation of his division. He took command on 1 November 1944. His battle plan was relatively similar to that of the 18. VGD attacking to the north of his sector. The division had assembled in the last weeks of November in the Prüm – Schoenecken – Denshorn – Lissingen quadrilateral to be attached to the LXVI. Armee-Korps (AOK). It moved to the front in two stages. Between 13 and 14 December, it moved to the Vatseratt – Pronsfeld – Schoenecken – Nieder Prüm zone. At dusk on 15 December, it took up its initial positions in the Habscheider – Muehle sector, where it relieved the troops occupying the sector. It was inserted between the positions of the 18. VGD to the north and the 116. Panzer-Division to the south. This armoured division depended on the neighbouring LVIII. Panzer-Korps. The artillery fire plan and ammunition supply were defined at corps level, considering the wishes of the 62. VGD headquarters. Links between the various major units were not firmly established.

The division also had to attack at 05:30 and, after taking the enemy's points of resistance, breakthrough in the Gross Langefeld – Gigelscheid-Heckauscheid area in the general direction of Saint-Vith.

The battle plan was simple, not to say simplistic: to attack on a broad front to tear down the American defences and 'clean up' the positions from Hascheid to Steinebrück, then push on to Saint-Vith. The plan was to break through the wooded area from Cigelscheid to Winterspelt, the centre of gravity of the assault. It was also decided to clear the south of Gross Langenfeld and the Heckunscheid plateau to prevent any flanking attack from the road leading to Saint-Vith. The next stage involved capturing the Steinebrück bridge using a specially formed mobile detachment, while at the same time carrying out an assault on Saint-Vith, targeting the railway station and its western exit. Particular attention was paid to capturing the railway bridges leading into the town.[21]

Troops must be concentrated without alerting your opponent's vigilant guard. (*Nara*)

The German intentions could be summarised as follows: to strike a blow to the east of Saint-Vith with the 18. VGD, while the 62. VGD advanced towards the town from the south-east to secure the railway line and the bridges spanning the River Our. The intention of the command was to ensure an efficient rail supply line via the railway junction at Saint-Vith.

## Final Preparations

On 7 December, the offensive was postponed until 16 December. As secrecy provisions prevented the officer in charge of supplies and administration from knowing about the attack, the logistical situation was examined very carefully. The supply regiment's movement plans would obviously depend on how the situation developed.

On 12 December, all unit commanders and key personnel of the 18. VGD were ordered to report to the divisional command post. After a preparatory meeting with the divisional commander, all those present were ordered to sign confidentiality agreements. Company commanders were not to be informed of the attack until 14 December, and their men were not to be informed until the day before the attack. Once the commanders had received their detailed instructions concerning their respective missions, the course of the attack was studied in depth by means of a mapping exercise lasting several hours. This last-minute Kriegsspiel[22] immediately highlighted a series of tactical problems that had not been considered in the plans drawn up at higher levels:

The 62. VGD had Hetzer to support its attack. (*Rights reserved*)

The Kriegsspiel showed that it would not be possible to attack Saint-Vith before 18 December, but the movement of troops on foot meant that this deadline had to be met. (*Nara*)

a. The lack of good roads would make it difficult for combat vehicles and artillery to advance. Strict traffic control would need to be established at vital points and part of the military police unit must be attached to GR 293.

b. Schönberg would not be reached before 17 December due to the difficult terrain.

c. As long as resistance continued in the Schnee Eifel – Andler – Schönberg area, only limited manpower would be available to force the Our valley. Even after breaking through the main line of resistance and the main defence zone, the division could not hope to reach Saint-Vith and the Vellerode hills before 18 December. It should be noted that the corps had not assigned the division any approximate dates for reaching its objectives.

d. Moving GR 294 to the assembly area near Ormont, while leaving behind strong elements to secure the assembly of the adjacent unit on the right (the I. SS-Panzer-Korps), would be a difficult task and might even cause some delay. It was then realised that communications with the command post of the I. SS-Panzer-Korps at Schmidtheim had to be established well in advance to ensure close cooperation in sharing communication lines.

e. Detailed orders were to be given for the movement of personnel from the divisional training school, the relief of GR 293 and 295 and the execution of counter-information measures. These recruits would therefore also be involved in the battle.

The unit commanders assembled at the command post on 10 December were instructed to submit their orders and directives for the attack by 13 December, so that they could be examined first.

All the artillery was in place for the morning of 16 December 1944. This 10.5cm FH would have to move to support the assault on Saint-Vith. (*Nara*)

US air activity was considered low. This P-47 Thunderbolt took off from a base in the north of France on 1 December. Bad weather prevented the allied air force from discovering the German preparations. (*Nara*)

From the outset, the unit that was to assault Saint-Vith understood that it would not be able to complete its mission for very pragmatic reasons until two days after the offensive had been launched. This was far too long to take an American force with excellent communication and transport links by surprise, and as we have seen, Saint-Vith was one of the key objectives for the success of the offensive.

The last days and nights before the attack were devoted to final preparations, with assembly areas identified and approach routes chosen. The artillery batteries were placed in firing positions, and infantry companies withdrawn from the front line one by one to practise attacking with live ammunition. To cross the anti-tank obstacles in the main line of resistance, the engineer battalion built a bridge that was moved close to where it would be used, before being well camouflaged. The assault artillery brigade had arrived the night before the attack and was assembled north-east of Ormont, behind the right attack group, meaning some forty assault guns were now available to the 18. VGD.

The night before the attack was clear and icy. The American units in the sector were quiet, with only routine reconnaissance and combat patrols. Even the air activity of the US Army Air Force was described as low. The cessation of German reconnaissance during the last week before the attack, although it had its drawbacks, was considered necessary to maintain complete secrecy. On the night of 14 December, elements of the 2. Panzer-Division moved to the front westwards along the main road to Büdesheim, 3.5 kilometres west of Gerolstein. The sound of the tanks could be heard for miles around. Although no enemy air reconnaissance was reported following the noise, the 18. VGD commanders doubted that their attack could surprise the enemy in such circumstances. Tensions rose as a result of the preparations.

At noon on 15 December, the I. SS-Panzer-Korps took control of the Neuhof – Ormont sector and prepared to attack to the north of the LXVI. Armee-Korps. These two corps were on either side of the boundary between the 5. and 6. Panzer-Armeen.

On the evening of 15 December, the division moved its command post to a bunker south of Ormont. At 04:00 the next morning, the regiments reported that their assembly was complete. Only a few units from GR 204 were still missing, having had to travel the long distance from their area of assignment on poor quality roads and in complete darkness.

Units of the I SS-Panzer-Korps at Ormont on 15 December. Panzerfaust were distributed to the troops in large numbers. (*Nara*)

At this very moment, every German soldier on the starting line was thinking about his chances of success. Despite the uncertainty, the morale of the troops was considered to be high by the officers. Everyone realised that Germany could still muster reserves, and believed that the end had not yet arrived, despite what the enemy claimed daily in its propaganda leaflets. It is likely that none of those on the front line knew that the attack was a last desperate attempt to turn the tide at the final minute.[23]

A Panther Ausf G commanding the 116. Panzer-Division moves up to the line.
This division attacked south of the 62. VGD. (*Nara*)

The Schnee Eifel Massif was held by an American force stretched to the limit. (*Nara*)

# Chapter 2

## The US at Saint-Vith

# The Thin US Curtain

On the American side, Saint-Vith was at the northernmost point of Major General Troy Middleton's VIII Corps. Middleton reported to General Courtney Hodges, Commander-in-Chief of the First US Army (FUSA), whose headquarters were at Spa. To defend his left wing, Middleton had at his disposal the 106th Infantry Division (106th ID) 'Golden Lions'. Activated on 15 March 1943, this classic infantry unit had a triangular structure, consisting of three regiments with three battalions: the 422nd, 423rd and 424th infantry regiments. Each battalion had three rifle companies and one heavy weapons company. Each regiment also had a canon company, an anti-tank company, a service company and a medical detachment. The regiment was supported by four towed artillery battalions, three of which were equipped with 105mm guns: the 589th, 590th and 591st field artillery battalions (FAB). The fourth, the 592nd FAB, was equipped with longer-range 155mm howitzers.[1] In addition, there was a reconnaissance troop, the 81st Engineer Combat Battalion and traditional service units. The 106th ID was also heavily supported by additional artillery. As well as its three battalions of 105mm and 155mm howitzers, the 275th Armored Field Artillery Battalion (AFAB) was attached to support the 14th Cavalry Group covering the northern flank.[2] Most of VIII Corps' artillery was massed in its sector, with four artillery groups together commanding four of

The 106th ID was a young unit that had not yet been hardened, having just celebrated its transition to operational status. Like all divisions, it had a clique. (*Nara*)

Three artillery battalions of the 106th ID were equipped with 105mm guns. (*Nara*)

The 155mm M3 howitzer was a highly effective weapon with a range of just over 18 kilometres. (*Nara*)

the five 155mm battalions available, two 4.5" and two 8" battalions, totalling ninety-six high-calibre howitzers.[3]

The 106th ID was considered combat-capable in April 1944 and completed its divisional manoeuvres with flying colours. After the landings on 6 June, 60% of its trained personnel were withdrawn to make up for losses in the ranks of the divisions that had been wiped out during the Normandy campaign. Major General Allan W. Jones, in command of the Golden Lions, was therefore forced to reconstitute his large unit by incorporating GIs who had only just completed their basic training. Despite the meticulous preparation it had undergone, the 106th ID was made up mostly of rookies and barely trained infantrymen. Nevertheless, it left the USA on 20 October 1944 and transited through England, being due to land at Le Havre on 2 December.

Then the ordeal began: a storm in the Channel made landing impossible and the GIs were forced to endure four days of battering rough seas, meaning they did not land until 6 December. Jones received his marching orders the next day, specifying that his division was to reach the Saint-Vith sector, so the men set off early to make the gruelling 440-kilometre journey. The unit's history states:

*The next day, in the half-light of dawn, the troops piled into open lorries as a fine, cold rain fell. The men exchanged jokes about sunny France. Others cursed the rain, the cold, the fate that has sent them to a Europe scarred by battle. Others remained silent. [...] The*

As the unit moved up the line, the civilians it encountered exchanged the V for Victory with the soldiers. (*Nara*)

*lorries roared through the crumbling roads towards Saint-Vith, through the towns, the destroyed remains of villages, the carcasses of burnt-out tanks and lorries in the roadside ditches [...]. People came to smile, wave and make V with their fingers. The men smiled and made the V sign in turn. As the long convoy made its way through the mountains of eastern Belgium and Luxembourg, the men saw the fir trees evoking Christmas, which would arrive shortly. Then they stopped thinking about it because they remembered where they were and why they had come. Arriving at Saint-Vith on the night of 10 December, the division moved up to the line the next day.*[4]

The 106th ID was put on the line to gain experience. However, it had trained very well in the USA. (*Nara*)

The GIs of the 106th lined up with their ties on! (*Nara*)

It was a reputedly quiet sector along the border with Germany, where there had been little patrolling activity for ten weeks. This part of the front was specifically allocated to the 106th ID so that it could gain the experience that was sorely lacking in its ranks.

When it arrived on the scene, its rapid-fire weaponry was strictly in line with the official manpower and equipment tables. However, its firepower was less than that of the more experienced units, which were in the habit of increasing the number of machine guns they had by using parts salvaged from previous engagements. The veterans of the 2nd Infantry Division 'Indian Head' were surprised to see the rookies who relieved them go to the front. One of them, Captain James McDonald, described the scene:

*A reconnaissance sent by a companion of a division that three days earlier had landed at Le Havre, France, arrived on 10 December. This confirmed the rumours. For their first experience of combat, the men of this division were delighted to arrive in ideal defensive positions. They expressed no apprehension about the stretching of the lines. [...] The next afternoon, it had begun to snow when the relief appeared. My men were astonished by the appearance of the soldiers in the arriving unit. They were loaded down with all the equipment that only fresh reinforcements from the United States could carry. And horror of horrors, they were wearing ties!*[5]

The men of the 2nd ID left to take up a position further north, taking their surplus automatic weapons with them. (*Nara*)

Official responsibility for the sector was transferred at 19:00 on 11 December.[6] The young US division therefore settled into its positions only five days before the start of the German offensive and did not have time to fully grasp the subtleties of its sector. Officers at all levels of the division were unhappy with the position they had to occupy. The 2nd ID took all its telephones with it; it had many more than the equipment tables allowed after largely equipping itself with captured German sets. Of course, the new arrivals did not have this advantage. As a result, the strongpoints where the new companies took up positions were very poorly connected to each other; the lines existed but were not connected to any terminal equipment.[7] The front the unit inherited was almost 45 kilometres long, twice what it should logically hold. The 424th Infantry Regiment took up positions in the south of the sector, along the River Alf in front of Steinebrück. The lines were so stretched that Major General Jones had to bring his three regiments into line. To have a minimum reserve in case of a major blow, the 1st Battalion of the 424th was kept in the rear, while the 423rd and 422nd infantry regiments spread further north in the Schnee Eifel region. To bolster his defence, Jones received the 820th Tank Destroyer Battalion, which replaced the 612th Tank Destroyer Battalion at the same time as the infantry.[8] Both units were equipped with towed guns.[9] At the time, the American army was facing a shortage of 3-inch anti-tank shells, and the incoming battalion was allocated only six rounds per gun per day. This figure corresponded in fact to the amount of shells fired by its predecessor while occupying its position.[10] Additional field artillery support was provided by Priest M7s, 105mm self-propelled guns from the 275th Armored Field Artillery Battalion belonging to the VIII Corps Artillery and the 634th Anti-Aircraft Artillery Battalion Automatic Weapon.[11] The regiments were organised in the traditional way, with a dedicated artillery battalion forming what was known as a Regiment Combat Team (RCT).

The 32nd CRS operated during the autumn on behalf of VIII Corps. (*Nara*)

## A Cavalry Colonel on the Rules of Engagement

The north of the 106th ID's position was held by a slightly more experienced cavalry formation, the 14th Cavalry Group (CG). Although the front in the Saint-Vith sector had been virtually at a standstill for almost three months, the 14th CG had not been there for very long. Since its formation in February 1901, the 14th CG had taken part in the Philippine and Mexican campaigns, but did not take part in the First World War. On 15 July 1942, the regiment was disbanded, its personnel and equipment transferred to the 14th Armored Regiment of the newly formed 9th Armored Division (AD). On 12 July 1943, the regiment was re-formed as the 14th Cavalry Group at Fort Lewis.

A cavalry group is a cavalry unit corresponding, as it did originally, to the strength of a regiment. It is a corps unit and is therefore not, in theory, part of a divisional organisation chart. However, it is very common in the American army for a formation dependent on this higher echelon to be sent as reinforcements and placed at the disposal of a division, either in its entirety or dispersed under several different commands. The 14th CG was under the command of the intractable Colonel Mark Andrew Devine Jr., the third of Mark and Emma Devine's five sons from San Francisco. A cavalry officer commissioned

A cavalry group is a highly mobile unit with considerable firepower in relation to its manpower. (*Nara*)

Devine was promoted to lieutenant colonel in 1940. (*Rights reserved*)

in 1917 at the University of San Francisco, Devine was considered to be down-to-earth and determined, outspoken and articulate. Of average build, he imitated the dress and mannerisms of a regular army cavalry officer. Appointed too late to take part in the First World War, he spent the inter-war years following a typical *cursus honorum* (succession of office). Promotion was slow in the period following the First World War and it took him ten years to reach the rank of captain and a further nine to finally become a major in 1937. With war approaching and America rearming, the number of places increased and promotions were happening more quickly. As a result, Devine was promoted to lieutenant colonel in 1940.

After the end of the First World War, Devine had joined the American occupation forces in Germany. On his return to the USA, he married the daughter of a former general commanding the Panama Canal Zone and consequently spent many years in Central

America. After graduating from the army's Command and General Staff College in 1937, he voluntarily transferred from the cavalry to the field artillery. In July 1939, he received permission to return to the cavalry branch and was promoted to colonel in January 1941.

Three years later, in May 1944, at the age of 48, Devine took command of the 14th CG; his first combat mission, and proved to be controversial in historiography. He was ordered to take command of the group after one of the squadrons failed a routine field test. It would appear that members of the squadron in question deliberately failed the assessment in the mistaken belief that they would remain at Camp Maxey, Texas, rather than be sent overseas. However, it was a very bad idea that led to them coming under Devine's command, who immediately made his mark on the unit. Assuming that the failure of the assessment was due solely to the incompetence of the small unit commanders, Colonel Devine instituted severe and often brutal disciplinary measures against any officer in the squadron who dared to take a step out of line. A stickler for discipline and cleanliness, he once inspected the fingernails of his men at the front, believing that their cleanliness was an indicator of good order.[12] The colonel's strict military discipline was apparently not much appreciated by his staff. A fervent believer in the 'spit and polish' method, he always insisted that his men, vehicles and equipment be meticulously clean and did not allow officers to smoke when they were in the operations section of group headquarters. He also demanded that civilian staff working in his headquarters stand

Part of the unit's training was carried out at Camp White in Oregon. (*Rights reserved*)

The 14th Cavalry Group was taken over by Colonel Devine. (*Rights reserved*)

up when he entered the camp offices.[13] Such eccentricities earned him few admirers among the officers and troops. However, the result was that the 14th CG no longer failed assessments and earned its ticket to the front. Colonel Devine's methods of command led many to believe that he would 'earn his general's stars', whatever the cost to the unit. Yet others remember him as an individual commanding a unit '*which he cherished, to which he was devoted, put together with men whom he had personally chosen and with whom he would see final victory in Europe*'. Few would dispute that, in addition to his belligerent manner with his subordinates, he rarely ventured forward to see his squadrons in line. When he did step forward, several observers noted that Devine '*never visited one of the squadrons without being escorted by a machine gun jeep*'.[14] Presented by these anecdotes as a man full of himself, he was to be pushed to the wall by the German attack on 16 December. Lieutenant Colonel Levin L. Lee wrote of him:

> *Even before his arrival, Colonel Devine had the reputation of being very demanding, tyrannical and very fussy about discipline. When he went to the front he was, I noticed, extremely shy: he always had an escort. The noise of battle (even at a distance) made him uncomfortable. If he spent the night of 16 to 17 December at the headquarters of the 106th*

Colonel Damon commanded the 18th CRS. (*Rights reserved*)

*ID and not at his command post, I think that apprehension of the fighting and cowardice are the explanation.*[15]

War is an incredible revealer of personalities, and it was not going to do Colonel Devine any favours.

The 14th CG was organically made up of two cavalry battalions called cavalry reconnaissance squadrons (CRS): the 18th was commanded by Lieutenant Colonel Damon. A graduate of West Point in 1933, Damon took command of the squadron in July 1943 and like many other able men, had moved quickly through the wartime promotion system. Unlike Devine, he was promoted to captain in 1940 and major in 1942, becoming lieutenant colonel in August 1943. Damon was a tall, well-dressed man who was totally committed to the welfare of his squadron, with his men remembering him as an impressive officer. Thoughtful, dedicated and knowledgeable, Bill Damon earned their loyalty. In return, his men earned his respect. Colonel Devine and Damon had very different profiles and were often at loggerheads; Bill Damon made no attempt to hide his resentment of the group commander's style of command, and their differences would play an important role in the battle ahead.[16]

The 32nd CRS was under the command of Lieutenant Colonel Paul Ridge, who had taken command of the squadron in October 1944. A graduate of the University of Illinois in 1926, Ridge had previously been the group's executive officer, the deputy to the commanding officer. During his eighteen years of military service, Ridge attended several leadership courses and held various staff positions. At the beginning of the war, he was stationed in what was then the British West Indies (British Virgin Islands) as officer in charge of the postal exchange system. Returning to the United States in July 1943, Ridge underwent refresher training in combat skills before joining 14th CG in England. Commanding the squadron was his first tactical assignment in several years of active military service. Lieutenant Colonel Augustine D. Dugan was the new executive officer. A graduate of West Point in 1924, 'Patsy' Dugan had joined the group's headquarters in November 1944 and was, strictly speaking, an exceptional cavalry officer. After graduating from the Military Academy, he excelled in successive cavalry assignments and was posted for a time to the Philippines then as operations officer of the 2nd Cavalry Brigade at Fort Bliss, Texas, and executive officer of an infantry regiment of the 8th ID, with which he fought in

The fighting north of Saint-Vith revealed the leadership of Lieutenant Colonel Dugan, commander of the 32d CRS. (*Rights reserved*)

Troops A to D were made up of three reconnaissance platoons equipped with M8 Greyhounds. (*Nara*)

Troop E was a support unit made up of two sections of four 75mm M8 howitzers. (*Nara*)

Normandy, where he was awarded the Silver Star. Described as being '*easy to get along with, liked business, was alert and very friendly,*' in the days that followed, Patsy Dugan was to put these fine qualities to good use amid the chaos of battle.[17]

From June 1943 onwards, the Cavalry Reconnaissance Squadron manning table was updated to take account of the lessons learned from the North African campaign. The troop, with an authorised strength of 145 men, was the equivalent of an infantry company. A staff troop was responsible for five or six troops. Troops A to D are made up of three reconnaissance platoons, with Troop E representing the support force made up of two sections of four 75mm M8 howitzers,[18] referred to in the reports as assault guns supported by a supply section. Troop F was equipped with sixteen M5A1 Light Tanks, divided into three platoons of five vehicles, with a total of ninety-seven officers and soldiers. It should be noted that Troop D was only activated by squadrons operating within an armoured division, and therefore did not exist within the two squadrons of the 14th CG.

Troop F was equipped with sixteen light tank M5A1s divided into three platoons of five vehicles. (*Nara*)

The three reconnaissance platoons of a troop had twenty-nine men serving in three M8 armoured cars and six jeeps. (*Nara*)

Each cavalry troop consisted of three reconnaissance platoons with a strength of twenty-nine men serving in three M8 armoured cars and six jeeps. In addition to the .30-calibre machine gun and the .50-calibre machine gun on board each M8, the additional armament included three 60mm mortars and three .30-calibre machine guns. The rest of the personnel was distributed among the support elements and HQ.

It was not until 28 August 1944 that the 14th CG left England for mainland Europe, arriving on 30 September via Omaha Beach. As soon as it was operational in Europe, the group headed for eastern France to take part in the Battle of Metz, where it received its baptism of fire. On 22 October, the unit's two squadrons were temporarily separated: the 18th CRS finding itself reinforcing the 2nd ID fighting in the Saint-Vith sector.

The other squadron, the 32nd CRS, was a former National Guard unit formed from the Black Horse Regiment of Chicago. Most of its personnel were from this region and the surrounding area, with many having been with the unit for more than ten years, particularly the officers, who started their careers at the bottom of the ranks and had been in their current positions for five or six years. All were proud to be cavalrymen and members of their squadron, having long experience of protecting the Panama Canal and then finding themselves in the highly strategic Alaskan sector threatened by Japan.[19] It was only briefly operational under the 14th CG on patrol in late summer 1944 in the Mont Saint-Michel sector, and its first real engagement on the Allied front took place on 25 October when it was attached to the 83rd ID in Moselle. When the infantry division was relieved by the 8th ID, it resumed its duties with it and then with the 28th ID, who it served with in the Clervaux region from 19 November. At the beginning of December, Devine and his staff were at Ettelbruck in Luxembourg.

## The 14th Cavalry Group

On 7 December 1944, the 14th CG, which in reality was temporarily just an empty box, was attached to the 106th ID and arrived in the Saint-Vith sector on 11 December.[20] It was at this point, only five days before the German attack, that Colonel Devine took effective control of the 18th CRS, albeit with the loss of its Troop B. As for the second squadron of the 14th CG, the 32nd, this was not put on the line because its equipment had to be serviced, having been worn out by several weeks of campaigning with the 28th ID. At the beginning of December 1944, its 32nd CRS was still attached to 28th ID at Dasburg on Skyline Drive in front of Clervaux and remained there until 10 December,[21] before returning to the fold of the 14th CG. The 32nd CRS had been in operation for forty-five days in a row and its vehicles were in urgent need of servicing. The squadron was therefore placed in reserve at the rear of the sector, at Rencheuxm,[22] a small village near Vielsalm, where it was surprised by the German offensive in the middle of a maintenance operation.[23] The vehicles were partly dismantled and the radios were removed from the light tanks when the German attack began. On arrival in the sector, the 32nd CRS was informed by the 14th CG that it would have to take over the positions of the 18th CRS. Consequently, Lieutenant Colonel Ridge's troop commanders carried out intensive

The 32d CRS took part in operations in the autumn of 1944 alongside the 28th ID in Luxembourg. (*Nara*)

reconnaissance of the front line. It was planned that each unit of the 32nd CRS would relieve the mirror unit of the 18th CRS, troop for troop. E Troop was the only company of 32nd CRS deployed close to the front line, with its assault guns in position to the west of Manderfeld and Hassenvenn, 1.5 kilometres to the north. They were linked by wire to the fire direction centre of the 275th Amored Field Artillery Battalion (AFAB) at Medendorf. This armoured artillery battalion was officially attached to the 106th ID and supported the 14th CG,[24] equipped with Priest M7B1 self-propelled 105mm guns.

The 18th CRS had been in the area for two months and was deployed on the front line. The enemy had not been aggressive during this period. The positions of the US cavalrymen extended over a little more than 8 kilometres running from the south of Lanzerath – Krewinkel – Roth bei Prüm – Kolbscheid. From the outset, it was clear that the position was not a good one, being opposite a ridge occupied by Westwall bunkers.[25] The lines occupied by the cavalry were nothing more than small pockets of resistance nestling in hamlets, whose thick-walled houses provided good protection against both the harsh climate and enemy fire. These small villages also had the advantage of being crossed by the main roads leading from Germany to the plateau.

After several months of operation, the vehicles of the 32nd CRS needed a complete overhaul. (*Nara*)

Troop E was the only company of the 32nd CRS deployed close to the front in the Manderfeld sector. (*Nara*)

The lines occupied by the cavalrymen were in reality nothing more than small pockets of resistance nestling in hamlets, whose thick-walled houses provided good protection. (*Nara*)

Holding these towns meant blocking the access routes and each of these points was defended by elements the size of a platoon, i.e. around thirty men, in addition to two armoured cars, as many .50 calibre guns and two or three 60 mm mortars. No fewer than 200 different firing positions were planned and studied, with many automatic weapons removed from the vehicles and placed in a battery. Here and there, the twelve 3-inch towed anti-tank guns of Tank Destroyer Company A and two reconnaissance platoons of the 820th Tank Destroyer Battalion attached to the 106th ID[26] hardened the cavalry positions, which were particularly lacking in anti-tank equipment. These elements had only been in the sector since 10 December, having just relieved the 612th TD. A Company of the 820th TD Battalion was scattered throughout the various villages defended by the 18th CRS. Its HQ was in Manderfeld, its 1st Platoon in Merlescheid, with one of its sections in Roth. The 2nd Platoon occupied Lanzerath and was reinforced by the company's 2nd Reconnaissance Platoon. The 3rd Platoon was in Berteradt and the 1st Reconnaissance Platoon was in Krewinkel.[27] Activated on 25 June 1942 at Camp Swift in Texas, it is important to note that the unit had no combat experience and had only arrived in Liverpool on 15 October 1944, landing on the Continent via Omaha Beach two days later. It was equipped with 3-inch towed guns,[28] with each platoon consisting of two sections of two anti-tank guns.[29]

A Company, in the 14th CG sector, was fully manned and had its twelve organic guns. Captain Nash, who commanded it, found himself in a delicate position. On his arrival in the area, he was ordered to replace the guns of A Company 612th TD Battalion piece by piece. The officer was not entirely happy with the set-up. However, he only changed the position of one of his guns to increase its range. Nash nevertheless arranged for most of his other guns to have an alternative location. Colonels Devine and Damon accompanied Nash as he reconnoitred the area before taking up his position on 14 December, just two days before the German attack. Devine did not set up a coordinated defence of his assets, and the cavalry and anti-tank artillerymen worked completely independently. One of Nash's troops alone occupied the extreme left wing of Devine's position, where it had to help elements of the 99th Infantry Division. Nash knew that his guns were well positioned to deal with an armoured irruption, but his guns were excessively vulnerable to an infantry attack. In fact, the enemy had spotted their positions a long time ago and the German infantry were in positions overlooking their own. This meant they were therefore in a position to spray them with mortar shells, against which Nash's men had little recourse. Moreover, the mission given to the anti-tanks was to guard outposts where machine guns played a more important role than cannons. In addition, Devine gave no instructions in the event of an enemy attack having to be parried.[30] The tactical configuration at Saint-Vith was therefore poor, to say the least. Inexperienced units liaised between two army corps with a system that was both distant and inappropriate.[31] To make matters worse, they had just arrived in the sector and were therefore completely unfamiliar with it.

The 99th ID was in position north of the 14th CG. It had two nicknames: Checkerboard and Battle Babies. The chessboard can be seen on this GI's helmet, although the image has been badly censored. (*Rights reserved*)

The strongpoints in the villages were surrounded by barbed wire, while

The positions of the 820th TD's 76mm were not well chosen. (*Nara*)

the open spaces were dotted with minefields of both German and American origin. However, their exact locations were unknown, so Devine immediately asked for others to be installed, but nothing could be done before the German offensive began. The cavalrymen nicknamed their centres of resistance 'sugar bowls', as they considered them tempting for the enemy due to the weakness of their defences. The spaces between these sugar bowls were patrolled regularly to prevent any enemy infiltration. The 18th CRS was aware of its weaknesses and had prepared almost 200 artillery fire coordinates so that it could very quickly request support from the 275th Armored Field Artillery Battalion.[32]

Devine's command post moved to Manderfeld on 12 December and prepared plans for this second squadron to intervene if necessary. According to the official history of the US Army, these plans were ready on the night of the 15th but did not have time to be circulated. Analysis of all these additional measures confirms Devine's reputation as a rigorous respecter of regulations. In fact, the combat manual includes all these instructions in its paragraph on defending an area:

*defending an isolated position requires frequently patrolled approach routes, local security measures, organisation of the terrain for all-out defence, mobile support available to occupy prepared positions or to counterattack. The position is organised to the extent permitted*

Defending an isolated position requires frequently patrolled approach roads, but there is no reason why you cannot combine business with pleasure. (*Nara*)

*by the time available. Rifle positions and automatic weapon emplacements are buried and camouflaged. Weapons are aimed to cover the approaches. Alternative and additional positions are selected and prepared. Close fire plans are studied. Part of the position is occupied. Separate plans are made to reinforce positions, extend them and counterattack.*[33]

Another major flaw in the system was that the cavalrymen were dismounted, having sacrificed the major advantage of their mobility to integrate static positions originally

The riders removed their rapid-fire weapons from their vehicles to provide a static defence. (*Nara*)

designed for conventional infantry.[34] Devine understood his unit barely had the means to put up a defensive screen and delay an opponent who would attack in force. Shortly after his group had taken over the sector, he learned of a contingency plan put in place by the 2nd ID in the event of an assault in force. The contingency plan consisted of a counterattack by an infantry regiment of the 106th ID accompanied by a battalion of tanks. Devine quickly went to divisional headquarters to check the validity of the plan. Major General Jones was too busy with his own unit moving up the line to deal with the problem and in any case, had no resources available to implement the plan. Apart from the fact that his regiments were all on the line, he had no tank battalions attached to his division. Devine was therefore forced to prepare a plan B with the meagre resources at his disposal, which consisted of a delaying action from ridge to ridge to buy time for any reinforcements to arrive. For the moment, however, the only reinforcements he had were the men of 32nd CRS on maintenance rest.

This lack of coordination between the 106th ID and the 14th CG led to a crisis during the defence of the major road junction at Saint-Vith. Another very annoying detail, but one that revealed the lack of coordination in the sector, was the fact the radio officer of the 18th Reconnaissance Squadron had not communicated his frequency plan to the 820th Tank Destroyer Battalion, but as long as the wire links were working, few people seemed to care about this fact. In any case, Devine seems to have spared no effort in preparing for the shock.

In conclusion, the 14th CG system was flawed, to say the least. Strictly speaking, the unit was not new, having been on the line for two months, but had not really had a baptism of fire. Half of its personnel were in a reorganisation phase, several kilometres behind the front line. The cavalry unit's mission was to link up General Gerow's V Corps and Middleton's VIII Corps, with its position extending to the south of the Losheim Gap.

It was a very dangerous mission for two reasons. On the one hand, the 14th CG blocked a traditional invasion route out of the Eifel massif. The German cavalry had

The positions of the 99th ID were to the north of those of the 14th CG. (*Nara*)

already used it in August 1914, and it was also the route chosen by Rommel and his 7. Panzer-Division on 10 May 1940 as they rushed towards the Meuse. With the river once again the target of Hitler's troops, it was hardly surprising that they threatened to use the same routes, with the two roads crossing this area leading to Saint-Vith.

On the other hand, Devine's cavalry group stretched 11 kilometres to the right of this strategic zone. Everywhere, the sector was at a lower altitude than the enemy positions overlooking it to the east. With its limited resources, the unit blocked this too wide gap between the 106th ID to the south and the 99th ID to the north. Both belonged to different corps and the junction of two army corps is always a place where co-ordination is complicated because you have to go up to army level to have a common command. A hinge is always a weak point in the front line, and it is all the weaker the higher up the hierarchy the level of joint coordination. In this case, it was General Hodges' First US Army headquarters in Spa. With the crisis generated by the sudden German attack, it had to be realised that the fate of a cavalry regiment temporarily subordinated to an infantry division did not interest many people.

Finally, we should mention the presence in the region of the only real reserves available in the American system: the Combat Command B (CC B)[35] of the 9th Armored Division, commanded by General William Hoge, stationed at Faymonville. This armoured brigade was detached to the V Corps sector, while the rest of the division remained in the VIII Corps sector.

## Why was the Cavalry Plugging the Hole?

Organically, during the Western European campaign, each American army corps had a cavalry group made up of two squadrons. During offensive operations, this group was intended to be used for reconnaissance or security missions by protecting the flanks of the main battle group. However, in reality, during the Second World War US cavalrymen were used almost as often in defensive missions as in offensive ones. Doctrinally speaking, however, this was not the role for which Washington's military theorists intended them. Nevertheless, there are four objective reasons why US corps generals deploy their cavalry as part of their defensive systems:

Firstly, during operations in the European theatre, the US Army was cruelly short of seasoned infantry divisions. Cavalry units, considered to be very well trained for both mounted and dismounted combat, were capable of taking on the role of infantrymen. This was particularly true of defensive missions, which were considered low-risk in certain specific sectors. With less manpower, but very well equipped with automatic weapons, the firepower of a cavalry reconnaissance troop was far superior to that of a conventional infantry company, and cavalrymen were often very effective in a defensive role.

Secondly, the great mobility of the cavalry means that it can appear to the enemy in several different places, deceiving them as to the real size of the force present. The units appeared larger than they really were, giving them an additional deterrent capability.

Cavalry units were traditionally used for recon missions, but could also be used defensively. (*Nara*)

In a defensive role, the cavalry defended large sections of the front. (*Nara*)

Thirdly, cavalry troops were equipped with high-performance transmission equipment enabling them to be controlled remotely in a much more efficient manner, which considerably increased the offensive performance of these units, despite their small size.

Finally, by deploying his cavalry group in the front line, a corps general could also save conventional infantry units from forming a reserve manoeuvre mass that could move up the line in response to opposing initiatives. The officer who took this decision must, however, bear two factors in mind when designing his system. Firstly, cavalry units were particularly lacking in anti-tank weapons and field artillery. He therefore had to subtract certain units specialising in this role from the conventional divisions to support the cavalry group. This, it should be stressed, caused coordination problems. On the other hand, if the sector held by the cavalry was attacked in force, it had to be reinforced very quickly because the curtain of troops, however valiant and well-equipped, lacked depth and at best was capable of holding back the enemy tide, but could never really stop it.

Major General Middleton, by placing his 14th CG to the north of his VIII Corps, was taking a calculated risk that was common practice. The fact that his sector was considered to be under little threat and was cruelly lacking in reserves amply justified his decision in the eyes of American military orthodoxy. In addition, he benefited from the excellent mobility and communication skills typical of this type of unit, which in theory enabled him to coordinate this pivotal sector as effectively as possible with the V Corps to the north.

# Chapter 3

# The Storm Breaks at Saint-Vith

It was already snowing lightly in places in the Schnee Eifel a few days before the German offensive. (*Nara*)

## The 106th Infantry Division Takes the Full Impact

To break through on the night of 15 to 16 December, the men of the 18. VGD exploited an area left undefended between the lines of the 14th CG and the northern flank of the 106th ID. Surprised in the early hours of the morning, the positions of the 14th CG were quickly submerged and were forced to withdraw, thereby uncovering Major General Jones' northern flank (see below). Encountering virtually no resistance, General der Panzertruppen von Manteuffel's northern pincer developed relatively easily: by mid-morning it had already advanced nearly 5 kilometres.

The 423rd Infantry Regiment also came under fire in the early hours of the morning. Heavy artillery, mortar and Nebelwerfer shelling began at 05:30. The regimental staff immediately put everyone on alert. At 06:00, because of the shelling, the few wired communications linking the unit's position with the anti-tank company of the 820th Tank Destroyer Battalion, Troop B of the 18th Cavalry Squadron and the 590th Field Artillery Battalion were cut off. The radio network took over from the field telephones. The German artillerymen had prepared their attack well; shells rained down on the company on duty. Many vehicles were destroyed and the regimental ammunition depot at Halenfeld was largely blown up, making the supply situation tricky from the outset. Shortly after 06:00, German guns extended their fire and hit Bleialf in the Eifel, forcing

A deluge of fire rained down on the US positions from 05:30. (*Nara*)

the anti-tank gunners to withdraw house by house. The Volksgrenadier then attacked for the first time, only to be repulsed by the resistance of the few remaining American positions. At the same time, another German group moved along the railway tracks to the right of the US infantry regiment. They dislocated the defensive line by destroying a platoon of the anti-tank company, which had the effect of breaking the links between the infantrymen and their support.

At 08:00, the Germans already held most of Bleialf, and the cohesion of the American lines showed signs of weakness. The service company and the heavy weapons company were sent in at 09:30 to regain control of the town. This reinforcement of 100 men, representing all the regimental reserves available, failed to redress the balance. B Company of the 81st Engineer Combat Battalion was sent into the furnace to serve as riflemen. The new arrivals, seventy in number, were employed against the right shoulder of the German penetration without success. It was not until mid-afternoon that a coordinated action supported by artillery succeeded in retaking Bleialf. However, links with the 424th to the south were not re-established.[1]

The German view of the American resistance suggests that it was giving the attackers a hard time:

*Initially, the left attack group also managed to break through the anti-tank obstacles and infiltrate into No Man's Land unnoticed by the enemy. Hesitant resistance developed as*

The reinforcements preparing to go online. (*Nara*)

*the attacking forces approached the enemy line. Heavy infantry weapons could only be brought forward by portage, as the regiment was under flanking fire from the southern Schnee Eifel and the hills just south-east of Buchet, making it impossible to move vehicles along the Brandscheid – Bleialf road. Bleialf was still in enemy hands at nightfall. The central sector of the division's action zone remained calm. A small force from the division's training school was in position there. The enemy tried to break through to the east or launch a decisive attack against the flank of GR 293 and 295. This was a serious mistake, for this inactivity [of RG 293] on the first day of the attack was to have serious consequences.[2]*

In practice, nothing could stop the German pincer which was insidiously developing. To the north, the 422nd IR had its flank in the air because of the retreat of the 14th CG. To the south, the 423rd was isolated from the rest of the position. Major General Alan W. Jones was aware of the danger that threatened two thirds of his infantry. However, his men fought well and, despite their inexperience, held their ground.

## A Rude Awakening for the 424th

Further south, the GIs of the 424th Regimental Combat Team (RCT)[3] were also severely tested. Lieutenant Colonel Charles F. Girand, commanding the 3rd Battalion, 424th Infantry Regiment, explained:

*Assault troops had infiltrated during the night, undetected, in the direction of Winterspelt and Heckhuscheid. At 05:30, for twenty minutes, there was an almost unbearably intense artillery and mortar barrage. The sky seemed to wobble on its foundations, the earth shook, and the men were shaken from head to toe. The woods, it seemed, were full of Germans: they were swarming, swarming! The Grenadiere looked drunk, drugged. The non-commissioned officers were shouting at the top of their voices: 'Schnell! Schnell!' They punctuated these orders with shrill whistle blasts. Howling and vociferating, the first waves became entangled in barbed wire or were torn apart by mines. However, there were so many of them that at about 07:25 a company had to be ordered out. I went with two officers and two men to investigate the situation. Suddenly we came face to face with Germans. Lieutenant William V. Shakespeare 'sprayed' them, and we captured the whole group: a battalion commander, his reconnaissance officer and two soldiers with a 'sulphate gun', which they hadn't had time to use because Shakespeare's reflexes had been so quick. The documents in the commander's briefcase told us that Crombach was the objective for 16 December.[4]*

Despite a good hold by the Golden Lions, the other portion of the 18. VGD also advanced successfully and began to isolate the 424th RCT by taking the village of Bleialf. The GIs of the 423rd counterattacked to retake this locality, and bloody hand-to-hand and house-to-house fighting ensued. The American division's ammunition quickly ran out, but the counterattack paid off; the village was retaken.

The US artillery responded with some effectiveness. (*Nara*)

Small German teams infiltrated behind villages held by the 14th CG. (*Nara*)

Finally, as misfortune never comes alone, to the south of Jones' position, the 62. VGD advanced towards Steinebrück. At the end of the afternoon, the 106th ID was in a very critical situation. Its position threatened to be split in two and its flanks were heavily enveloped. Jones was forced to counter the threat by considering withdrawing to the heights east of Saint-Vith. He referred the matter to General Middleton, his direct superior in VIII Corps, and the latter sent the commander of CC B of the 9th Armored Division, General William Hoge, to assess the seriousness of the situation. The officer arrived in Saint-Vith at around 16:00 and found great confusion in the town:

*On 16 December, at 10:25, new instructions reached my command post in Faymonville: we were to be returned to the VIII Corps, which assigned us to the 106th ID (stipulating, however, that we remained 'attached in place', which meant that General Jones could not, temporarily at least, dispose of my unit, CC B, 9th AD). Shortly after dusk, General Troy H. Middleton ordered me to meet Alan W. Jones. I arrived at St. Vith with a few officers.*

The 9th AD was transferred to the front. Its M7B1 Priest self-propelled guns with 105mm barrels proved to be very effective. (*Nara*)

*There was considerable confusion. None of the staff sections seemed to be working. 'What news have you?' asked the General as soon as I arrived. – Nothing, except that the First US Army has decided that my unit is returning to VIII Corps, and I've been told to contact you. He explained the situation to me; although the intelligence was very confused, one thing was clear from the G-2 map: the division's flanks were in the air, each of the three regiments was only weakly in contact with its neighbours, and the two regiments in the Schnee Eifel were practically surrounded, which particularly worried the general.*

*So I asked: 'What should I do?' – Bring your CC here; I want you to attack at the crack of dawn in the direction of Schönberg.*[5]

The consultation between the two generals led to the urgent need to block the enemy's path through the Losheim Gap by launching the Shermans of CC B of the 9th AD towards Schönberg and Auw to cover the northern flank and prevent the 14th CG from disintegrating.

## A Tough Opening Day for the 18th Cavalry Reconnaissance Squadron

Let us return to dawn on 16 December to understand what was happening north of the positions of the 106th ID. At 05:15 on 16 December, a red flare was fired from the German lines, although there had been no indication of this the previous day. The morning was dark and foggy. At 05:30, just as a V1 flew over the US positions on 'Buzz Bomb Alley,'[6] the GIs came under heavy shelling. The enemy used all his guns: medium and heavy light artillery, mortars and rockets. It very quickly became apparent to the American cavalrymen that the enemy was not very well informed, as artillerymen's shots were aimed more at the buildings than at the foxholes scattered around the villages. A Volksgrenadier company appeared in front of Roth, while Krewinkel was assaulted by Fallschirmjäger. There were around twenty machine guns in each platoon, providing an infernal firepower that managed to repel the first wave. At daybreak, 07:40, a second wave rushed towards the US lines. This time it was more cautious, as the German infantrymen approached in leaps and bounds.[7]

In the sector of the 18. VGD facing the south wing of the 14th CG and north of the 106th ID, the infantrymen responsible for leading the assault had been in place since 04:00. The first contact with the US front line was to be made by an assault company, equipped solely for close combat. Such a unit spearheaded the attack of each Volksgrenadier regiment. Its mission was to disrupt the first line of resistance as quietly as possible and clear the way for the other infantry companies at fixed distances. It should also be noted that from 05:30, artillery support was authorised, but only at the request of the regiments attacking, and so were allocated artillery liaison teams.[8] The regiments all began their assault at the same time and at 05:30 there was a sudden concentration of artillery and anti-aircraft fire from the German lines.

Resistance was organised in the
villages held by the 14th CG. (*Nara*)

The northern sector was attacked by the Fallschirmjäger of the 3. FJD. (*Nara*)

Roth was held by Troop A of Captain Porche's 18th CRS, reinforced by three towed 76mm anti-tank guns and the Reconnaissance Platoon belonging to the 820th TD. These elements bore the brunt of the enemy's pressure. They were engaged by an assault gun and a force of around eighty men, while Krewinkel was attacked by seventy Fallschirmjäger. At 09:00, three Stuge marched out of the woods towards Auw. The village seemed to be quickly occupied, as at 09:30 part of Troop F sent to reinforce Roth was stopped by a dozen German self-propelled guns. By 10:00, the Germans were aware of this first breach, as they sent the equivalent of a battalion of VGDs into the village to exploit the gap in the US position. This vanguard detachment came under heavy US artillery fire, but the Vollsgrenadier nevertheless managed to infiltrate the positions held by elements of the 820th TD. They were ordered to withdraw to Hasenvenu, 1 kilometre north of Manderfeld and in the process lost all their equipment. However, before withdrawing they claimed two German tanks. At 11:00, Porche received an order to withdraw to the Manderfeld Auw line. He replied that the order could not be carried out for the simple reason that his positions were surrounded. This reply reached the 18th CRS HQ at 12:30.[9] The cavalrymen defending the front lines were practically out of ammunition and were supplied from their positions. Porche was advised to try to reach the US lines under cover of darkness, abandoning his equipment.

A brigade of Sturmgeschutz supported the German assaults very effectively. (*Nara*)

Little by little, the horsemen of the 14th CG and the anti-tank gunners supporting them left the villages and abandoned much of their equipment. These 76mm anti-tank guns were captured by the Germans. (*Nara*)

Roth held out to the end. (*Nara*)

Roth fell shortly after 16:30 and the commander of Troop A announced that he was stopping the fight for lack of ammunition after destroying his equipment.[10] The last message from Captain Porche was: '*Tanks 75 yards from my CP firing at point blank range. End of transmission.*'[11]

Kobscheid, further south, was home to the rest of Troop A under Lieutenant Herdrick. The artillery barrage destroyed its wire network, and the radios took over, enabling artillery observers from the 275th Armored Field Artillery Battalion to support the defenders relatively effectively. Despite the small arms fire heard coming from the direction of Rodt, the sector remained calm until 06:30. Private Joseph Gallo was in charge of a light machine gun defending the north-eastern approach to the village and was the first to spot the enemy. He explained: '*It wasn't very light just at daybreak when I saw them. They were only twenty metres from my position, about fifty of them in a pack. I let them go and they fell. Some of them screamed because they'd been hit so badly.*' The Volksgrenadier did not lack courage and advanced under intense fire from American automatic weapons. The first wave of the German assault was decimated. An hour later, the enemy attacked again, this time from all directions. The American cavalrymen refused to estimate the casualties they had inflicted on their enemy, simply agreeing that they had mauled them horribly by firing their automatic weapons in all directions. They also received artillery support, which sprayed the entrances to the village with shrapnel when the Volksgrenadier managed to reach them. They even had the luxury of capturing forty prisoners, mostly wounded soldiers or fighters who had used up all their ammunition. Some engagements were almost hand-to-hand. Private First Class Franck J. Monell, operating a 60mm mortar, used the base plate of his gun to prime his shells and launch them by hand at the enemy, who had come within 20 metres of his position. The village held out all day. At 16:00, Herdrick received the order to take off, which enabled him to avoid annihilation. Surrounded, the officer knew that he had no chance of crossing the lines with his vehicles and therefore gave the order to sabotage them. When night fell, the defenders of Kobscheid split into two groups and headed west out of the cauldron. They marched in single file through their own minefield, managing to reach Lommersweiler, where the positions of the 7th AD were located, with whom they would fire until the end of the Battle of Saint-Vith. Not realising that the village had been evacuated, the Germans prepared a full-scale assault on the village for the following day.[12] This was pointless and wasted additional time for the 18. VGD, which was already behind schedule due to the stubborn US resistance.

Troop C was in the front line from Aft to Krewinkel, with its HQ at Weckerath, and held its sector supported by four 76mm anti-tank guns also belonging to the 820th TD. A platoon under Lieutenant King in a small wood to the east of the Aft – Krewinkel road came under sniper fire at 05:30. Then around twenty shells fell on his position. King's men held firm behind their barbed wire, but they could not prevent the Germans from bypassing them and moving towards Weckeradt, where the Troop HQ would be far too exposed. At 11:00, King received the order to withdraw, abandoning all personal equipment and destroying everything that could not be taken away. The men piled

The 275th AFAB supported the 14th CG, but coordination between these two units was not very effective. (*Nara*)

into M8s and jeeps. The weather was particularly icy and the vehicles had not been driven much since arriving at the position. Consequently, the engines were cold and the grease on the drive shafts was particularly thick, making it impossible to go faster than 20 kilometres an hour. Advancing at reduced speed, King and his men had to follow the route under fire from the Germans. Miraculously, only one man driving a jeep was wounded when his hand and neck were shot.[13]

Further south, Krewinkel was held by the second platoon of First Lieutenant Parens' Troop C, reinforced by a reconnaissance platoon from the 820th TD. They occupied only the north-west corner of the town, from which they had an excellent view of the approaches from the east. A patrol was sent towards Krewinkel following the opening shelling of the German offensive. The patrol reported that the enemy was bypassing the village to the south and advancing towards the rear of the position. When the first light of day began to filter through the pale dawn on 16 December, Parens and his men were presented with a surprising sight: Volksgrenadier from GR 294 marching in ranks of four towards his positions, singing! In reality, however, the Germans had a rather different view of the effectiveness of the American defence than the one given in the various US reports, finding it so inactive that they thought the Americans had abandoned the front line altogether.[14] This explains why the Grenadier advanced in line, unaware that they were in the sights of a plethora of automatic weapons. The American officer obviously took advantage of his opponents' mistake and ordered his men to hold their fire, only opening fire when the first German soldiers approached the first line of barbed wire less than 20 metres from their machine guns. The GIs fired into the

A patrol was sent towards Krewinkel following the shelling that opened the German offensive. (*Nara*)

The US light tanks came up against StuG IIIs against which their 37mm guns had absolutely no effect. (*Nara*)

The thick-walled houses of the Ardennes provided excellent protection for the fighters. (*Nara*)

crowd literally at point-blank range, disintegrating the German ranks.[15] The Americans claimed 200 enemy casualties. Devine sent his Troop F equipped with M5A1s to rescue his surrounded men. The light tanks came up against StuG IIIs, against which their 37mm guns had absolutely no effect, and had to withdraw. Lieutenant King tried to contact the assault guns of Troop E to pound the enemy vanguard, but the telephone lines were cut, and the Germans used Jazz to jam the American radio frequencies.[16] The cavalrymen, deprived of reinforcements, left Krewinkel on the sly after receiving orders to do so, even managing to save some of their rolling stock.

F Company was placed on a slope to the east of Manderfeld to set up a collection line for Troop C and prevent the attackers, who had bypassed the front lines, from advancing towards the 18th CRS HQ set up at Manderfeld. At 12:30, the front lines were ordered to withdraw, with the defenders in the encircled Roth instructed to hold out as long as possible.

A reading of the American combat reports suggests that the Germans paid dearly for an ineffective initial assault on the lines of the 14th CG. The report of the of the 18. VGD's chief of staff gives a rather dissonant version of events:

*Messages from the offensive echelons arrived slowly. In the thick fog, GR 294 had apparently started to march towards Krewinkel instead of Weckerath. RG 295 reported that its main elements had passed north of Roth without coming into contact with the enemy. RG 293 crossed the main line of resistance south of Brandscheid, reaching the woods to the west. Had the enemy recognised the preparations for attack and withdrawn in time, the division would not have reached its main line of resistance before the attacking forces reached the River Our. Some scattered hostile artillery fire was reported at 08:30, but by 09:00 it was clear that the enemy had been taken by surprise.*

*By noon, reports established that the right attack group had broken through the enemy's main line of resistance as planned. With the Divisional Commander personally leading the assault gun brigade, the attack group had successfully advanced into the area north of Roth, with GR 294 crossing a deep valley 1.5 kilometres north-east of Auw and GR 295 passing west of Roth and then turning in the direction of Kobscheid. Strong elements had been left in front of Roth. Most of the fighting was carried out by infantry and assault guns. The infantry's heavy weapons had to be transported because the poor approaches to the bridge over the German tank obstacles had delayed the vehicles.*

He points out, however, that two villages, Auw and Rodt, were still holding out in the evening, although these positions were surrounded. As long as they had not fallen, they considerably hampered links with the left wing of the 18. VGD.[17]

Was there strong resistance or not? Were there heavy losses or not? The truth lies somewhere between these two extremes. In any case, the course of operations clearly showed the inextricable situation in which the 18th CRS found itself. Its sector was far too large, and it was unable to hold a continuous line. Its strongpoints in the villages could not cover the wide gaps through which the Germans were penetrating towards the rear of their positions. One by one, the sugars bowls were surrounded and silenced. The only thing for the US fighters to do was to disengage. Being surrounded, the cavalrymen and anti-tank gunners lost most of their equipment, and Devine had no choice but to bring up his reserves to form a thin line of defence to protect the withdrawal of his outpost line. The morning's resistance in certain villages nevertheless had the effect of hindering the German plans, with repercussions in the German camp well into the next day.

The only thing to do was to stall, and the cavalrymen and anti-tank gunners abandoned most of their equipment. (*Nara*)

## All Hands On Deck for 32nd Cavalry Reconnaissance Squadron

The morning alert naturally had repercussions for the 32nd CRS, which was resting at Rencheux. It was put on alert at 06:00, with equipment undergoing maintenance being rushed back into combat order, and the cavalrymen setting off at 09:30. The first elements arrived in Manderfeld at around 12:00 and were deployed on the heights to the north-west and south of the town. At 15:30, Colonel Devine decided to mount a delaying operation. The 32nd CRS was tasked with protecting the withdrawal of the 18th CRS along the Holzheim – Herresbach line and delaying the enemy's advance westwards along the Manderfeld – Saint-Vith road, while maintaining contact with the 18th CRS on its left flank to the north. Troops A and B of the 32nd CRS took up positions in the Andler area, protecting the southern flank of the 18th CRS, while Troop C of the 32nd CRS took up positions on the northern flank on the Lanzerath – Hassenven road.[18] Devine set up a sort of corridor protecting the wings of the 18th CRS, which was forced to withdraw. At 14:30, he also ordered the formation of a task force under Major Mayes, S3 of the battalion, to infiltrate towards Losheim to reach the towed guns of the 820th TD that were surrounded by the enemy in their positions. At 17:00, the last elements of the 18th CRS evacuated Manderfeld with Troop C as rearguard, taking up positions in

The 32nd CRS leaves to set up a collection position, but first the cavalrymen had to reassemble their equipment in need of maintenance. (*Nara*)

the vicinity of Holzheim. The withdrawal was completed with a new line of defence set up by 22:00.[19]

It is clear from this terrible day that the cavalrymen of the 18th CRS were exemplary in their conduct under fire. On the morning of 16 December, their lines were broken. The Americans were only able to hold the villages, which had been transformed into resistance moles. Lacking manpower, they left large gaps in the surrounding countryside, opening the way for the enemy infantry to bypass their positions. The US positions held out as long as they could, and their withdrawal was by no means a debacle. The fierce resistance cost the German offensive a precious day and caused what seemed to be a significant attrition of German troops. For its part, the 18th CRS suffered two officers killed, twenty soldiers wounded and 134 missing.[20] The movement ordered at 32nd CRS was logical and corresponded to the needs of the time. So far, there was nothing to reproach Colonel Devine for, who took the right decisions to hold his large sector with the limited resources at his disposal. It should also be noted that his HQ, also at Manderfeld, was barely 3 kilometres from his front lines, meaning he came close to death twice that day when shells rained down on his headquarters.

## Slow Start to the Blitzkrieg

The breakthrough had to be achieved by the infantry and the Fallschirmjäger, while the Panzers of KG Peiper were tasked with exploiting the depths. The new Blitzkrieg got off to a poor start, however, with one German veteran describing the chaos:

*On 16 December, the road between Scheid and Losheim was a huge mess. A few months earlier, during their retreat, our troops had blown up the railway bridge east of Losheimergraben. This bridge has not yet been rebuilt. When Peiper arrived at around 14:15, it was to see our troops queuing in front of the level crossing. He was so displeased*

North of the 14th CG, the 99th ID, commanded by Major General Walter E. Lauer, gradually collapsed. (*Nara*)

It is often forgotten, but two schwere Panzer Abteilungen took part in the Battle of the Bulge. The 506 passed through the Loscheim Gap, with the 14th CG in its path. (*Nara*)

*that he ordered his tanks to clear all obstacles and move on. Shortly afterwards, Peiper's column reached the destroyed railway bridge, turned right, went down the embankment, crossed the tracks and went up the other side to reach the main road. By 21:30, Losheim was in sight. At 22:00 the Tigers of the schwere SS-Panzer-Abteilung 501 reached the town.*[21]

It should be noted that Losheim was still within German lines, and the initial front line was not crossed by the first elements of KG Peiper until around 20:00 on 16 December. It then continued north through Bullange, where it refuelled at a US depot on the morning of the following day. The 14th CG's first withdrawal and the collapse of the 99th ID's resistance to the north of its position opened up a first breach, but the US cavalrymen were still in the path of KG Hansen. For the cavalrymen, it was urgent to re-establish the link with the 99th ID to the north.

On the morning of 17 December, the 18th CRS' positions at Werath were attacked by armoured vehicles and infantry. The squadron fell back to Born, where it met the first elements of the 7th AD on their way to Saint-Vith to reinforce the 106th ID and hold the town. At 15:15, the cavalrymen broke contact with the enemy to establish a defensive position on the Poteau heights. This westward movement crossed the 7th AD's north–south route, on roads congested by the withdrawal of units of the 106th ID, which had been badly hit at Saint-Vith. It was now the Americans' turn to suffer the agonies of traffic jams, while the Germans were finally able to speed up their advance.

In the early hours of 17 December, the 32nd's position, severely weakened by the fighting of the previous day, came under attack. Troop B of the 32nd Reconnaissance Squadron was in position at Schönberg and came under attack from Tiger IIs of the 506. schwere Panzer-Abteilung.[22] Needless to say, the 37mm guns mounted in the turrets of the M8s were no better than peashooters against these behemoths. Captain Lindsey, in command of the US detachment, knew his men would be cut down if he did not react, and so asked for permission to withdraw. He did not have time to wait for an answer, however, because his unit had given up and he had already lost nineteen men and several vehicles. On hearing that Bleialf to the south had fallen, he deduced that the line he was on had already been turned. He therefore took the initiative of withdrawing to Heuem, 2 kilometres to the west in the direction of Saint-Vith. For the time being, Lindsey's unit represented the last screen between the important crossroads town and the 18. VGD. The 106th ID south of the gap was not yet in a position to counterattack the German flanks, while the 7th AD had not yet arrived on the scene.

32nd Squadron's HQ, positioned a little to the north at Herresbach, now found itself on the front line. Lieutenant Colonel Ridge was greatly shaken and found an excuse to take refuge in Vielsalm, leaving his command to his deputy, Major John Kracke, who withdrew westwards through the woods on the morning of the 17th. The atmosphere during this withdrawal was truly Dantesque; a mess of vehicles tangled up in potholes. Fortunately for Kracke's men, the Germans were also bottled up. Elements to the south of the 6. Panzer-Armee had chosen to use routes intended for General Lucht's LXVI.

The 32nd CRS bravely went to the front of the line with equipment that lacked the power to counterattack such a powerful opponent. (*Nara*)

The German success on the first day of the attack was largely due to the numerous interventions of the forty-two StuGe of Sturmgeschutz Brigade 244. (*Nara*)

Korps. A huge congestion ensued, considerably slowing down the German advance. As a result, the Volksgrenadier thrust was not very powerful against the retreating cavalry.

In an attempt to save what was left of his group, Devine gave the order to withdraw, thus confirming Lindsey and Kracke's decisions. They were all to move to a collection position north of Saint-Vith between Wallerode and Born. With this instruction, Devine completely opened up the road to the crossroads town to the Germans. It seems that this decision was prompted by the imminent arrival of Hasbrouck's tanks, but be that as it may, the consequences could prove disastrous, especially as Major General Jones was completely unaware of this as at the same time he sent Lieutenant Colonel Riggs, commanding the 81st Engineer Combat Battalion, to reinforce the Heuem position, accompanied by various elements including a platoon from the 820th Tank Destroyer Battalion. Seeing the cavalrymen leaving the village he was supposed to be holding, trailed by the Volksgrenadier, he decided to trade a little space for time. His aim was to give his sappers time to dig in and lay a few mines. Riggs decided to set up his defensive line on the last wooded ridge overlooking Saint-Vith. He knew that if his men gave up, the road junction would come under German artillery fire and would have to be abandoned. As is often the case in the Ardennes, the terrain was favourable to defensive action, which allowed the US engineers to hold their position until the arrival of armoured vehicles from Holland.

The situation at the head of the 14th CG had already deteriorated considerably. In addition, Devine conflicted with Lieutenant Colonel Roy U. Clay, who commanded his artillery support, the AFAB. Clay wanted to shell the Losheim Gap, but Devine

During the day on 16 December, the US lines were infiltrated, but generally held up well. (*Nara*)

The Priests of the 275th AFAB were given fire missions whose targets could correspond to the positions occupied by the men of the 14th CG. (*Nara*)

objected, as he did not know exactly where his men were and did not want to take the risk of US shells falling on them! On the contrary, he ordered him to move his howitzers. Clay refused and referred the matter to General MacMahon, the divisional artillery commander. At divisional HQ, he learned that his battalion had now been assigned to the 7th AD and that it could fire wherever it wished.[23] Returning to his positions, the artilleryman witnessed the 14th CG retreat further west.

On 17 December, at around 13:30, Devine turned up at Saint-Vith at the headquarters of General Jones, commanding the 106th ID. He was visibly overworked and at the end of his tether. He entered the room and said, '*Run for it, I've got a Tiger on my heels,*' even though Jones was in conference with General Clarke supervising the arrival of the 7th AD CC B, who suggested that Devine be seconded to Bastogne to report to Middleton on developments.[24]

Despite their initial resistance, Devine's men were forced to withdraw under intense pressure from their opponents. It was a withdrawal that left a providential path of penetration for the enemy, who rushed into the breach. Contact was broken between the V and VIII US Corps. More seriously, the flanks of the 106th ID were left completely unprotected, which had serious consequences for the unit. It should be noted that instead of being at his command post, Devine spent most of the night at Jones' command post in Saint-Vith, without receiving precise orders.

## A Fatal Imbroglio

Let us take a step back at this stage and describe how events unfolded at an operational level. In the late afternoon of 16 December, Eisenhower was hesitant. He did not yet know what he was dealing with and it was still too early to determine whether it was a feint to delay his planned offensive, or whether he was dealing with a full-scale attack. He nevertheless took the necessary measures to counter the developing situation and decided to bring General Robert W. Hasbrouck's 7th AD up to the line.[25] This unit was held in reserve by the XIII Corps of the Ninth Army to the east of Maastricht. It was Omar Bradley, in a meeting with Eisenhower in Versailles, who transmitted the order to transfer from one sector to another.[26] It was given the task of reinforcing VIII Corps and making for Bastogne. As the situation developed, his orders changed, and it was not until 20:15 that Hasbrouck learned his unit had to move urgently towards Saint-Vith. Middleton HQ informed Major General Jones at 19:00 that he would be reinforced by a full armoured division and that he must not give up any ground. The arrival of the 7th AD was announced in the threatened sector for 07:00 on the morning of 17 December. This time information was false, however: it was impossible for the armoured unit to

Jones' commanding line was partly responsible for the tragedy that his 106th ID was about to undergo. This view shows the main protagonists, from left to right, Major General John Leonard commanding the 9th AD; Middleton, leader of the VIII Corps; Bradley, at the head of the 12th Army Group; and Eisenhower. (*Nara*)

The 7th Armoured Division was ordered to place itself at the disposal of VIII Corps. Its departure was not immediate as it was already engaged in Holland. (*Nara*)

cover this distance in such a short time, having to cut across the supply routes of the First US Army in the middle of the confusion east of Liège. The access roads would not be cleared until much later. In addition, the distance separating the two points of the front was enormous. There was no set speed in the manuals for moving an armoured division. However, from experience, the generals know that the distance covered in one hour was 15 kilometres, or at least eight hours' journey in this particular case.

On receiving this false information from Colonel Slayden, the VIII Corps' liaison officer, Jones had every right to feel relieved at the imminent arrival of this important reinforcement. After consulting Middleton, the leader of the 106th ID ordered his three regiments to hold their positions despite the threat of encirclement. As Hasbrouck's division would be arriving from the north, he decided to review his counterattack plans and therefore ordered Hoge to move on his southern flank with his CC B towards Winterspelt. Hoge tells us what happened:

*During the night, I returned to my command post at Faymonville, about 20 kilometres north of Saint-Vith. The VIII Corps had promised the arrival of the 7th AD at 07:00. The counter-order (ordering us to attack not towards Schönberg, but towards Winterspelt) was logical. My men, who were about to receive their baptism of fire, were rather euphoric:*

The US artillerymen tried to bring all their weight to bear in the battle. (*Nara*)

The lines of 106th ID were about to be pierced. (*Nara*)

*they knew the terrain well, as the mission of CC B, 9th AD had previously been to help the 2d ID in the event of a German counterattack. Unbeknown to us, on another road, but in the opposite direction, a Teutonic column was heading towards Vielsalm. Planes were flying low over it, dropping flares to mark its progress. At a point I can't pinpoint, the two roads were no more than 500 metres apart. At this point, the head of this unit arrived while the tail of my CC B was marching past. A violent skirmish ensued: a panzer was destroyed, while some Maintenance Company vehicles were captured. I was to learn that the prisoners had been brutally shot. We came across some defectors (particularly from the 14th CG); some of these men joined my Combat Command. For the most part they fought very bravely. As we passed through St. Vith the reconnaissance unit came under heavy fire from the first floor of a house. While machine guns from a half-track returned fire, infantrymen broke down the door and climbed four by four to the first floor. There were three civilians armed with German rifles, shell casings littering the floor. They were not captured... you can guess what I mean...*[27]

Hoge's account is interesting because he, too, recognised that Jones was acting in a totally rational manner. He countered the dangerous action of the 62. VGD to the south by estimating that the threat to the north would be quelled the next day by the imposing firepower of General Hasbrouck's 7th AD. In addition, by assigning CC B of the 9th AD an objective south of Saint-Vith, he cleared the roads around the crossroads for Hasbrouck's innumerable vehicles that were about to arrive. He thus avoided the possibility of a huge traffic jam that would have hampered the movement of the armoured division coming down from the north.

# Chapter 4

# The Lucky Seventh Goes Online

## A Veteran's Unit Convalesces

On 16 December 1944, the 7th Armored Division (AD) received the order to rush into the Saint-Vith sector to save a situation that already seemed highly compromised. Nicknamed the 'Lucky Seventh', this large unit could already be described as highly seasoned. It was officially set up on 1 March 1942 at Camp Polk

The 7th Armoured Division was fully combat-ready when it went on alert on 16 December 1944. (*Nara*)

The 7th AD was placed under the command of Major General Lindsay McDonald Sylvester at the start of the campaign in the West. (*Nara*)

The 7th AD had its baptism of fire in Normandy. By December 1944, it was a highly experienced unit. (*Nara*)

The Lucky Seventh also took part in the continuation of the campaign as far as Moselle. (*Nara*)

in Louisiana and was initially placed under the command of Major General Lindsay McDonald Sylvester.[1] It arrived in England on 13 June 1944 and landed in Normandy on 10 August. Three days later, its Shermans received their baptism of fire. After going as far as Moselle in the ranks of Patton's Third Army, on 25 September 1944 it found itself on the left wing of the 12th Army Group, before taking part in securing the right flank of the troops engaged in Operation Market-Garden. On 1 November 1944, it was placed under the command of Brigadier General Robert W. Hasbrouck and ordered to rest on 8 November. It then received a large number of recruits to make up for the losses it had suffered in its ranks during the first phase of the Western European campaign.

The Lucky Seventh was traditionally made up of three tank battalions (TB), the 17th, 31st and 40th, and three armoured infantry battalions (AIB), the 23rd, 38th and 48th. The 87th Cavalry Recon Squadron mechanized (CRS), the 33rd Armored Engineer Battalion (AEB) and the 147th Signal Company completed its combat echelon. This group was supported by the 434th, 440th and 489th Armored Field Artillery Battalion (AFAB). Finally, the 129th Ordnance Maintenance Battalion and 77th Armored Medical Battalion supported the whole. It was organised into three armoured brigades named CC A, B and R, in perfect accordance with American combat doctrine, and went into action without being reinforced by any independent unit.[2]

The fighting had taken its toll. (*Nara*)

At the time of going into action, the 7th AD was in Holland (*Nara*)

The Lucky Seventh was about to go on the offensive on 16 December 1944. (*Nara*)

Brigadier General Robert W. Hasbrouck had been in charge of the division's CC B since 1 November, after a spell on the staff of the 12th Army Group. He was an experienced officer who knew the tactical workings of the arm in which he served. He and Brigadier General Bruce C. Clarke worked hard to get the heavily tested armoured division back into fighting condition, and apparently commanded with some shortcomings until their arrival. Clarke and Hasbrouck did not beat about the bush when they took up their new duties. Lieutenant William Knowlton of the 87th CRS recalled their arrival in these terms: '*Goodness gracious, day after day in the mud of Holland they took up training again! We were furious. We thought we were veterans and didn't need these painful exercises. And yet, it was the wisdom of these two men that enabled the 7th AD to achieve its incredible performance when subjected to this terrible test.*' Hasbrouck fully supported and encouraged Clarke, whom he had put in charge of the CC B, in his strong takeover of the division.[3]

The unit's after-action report provides an update on its status prior to the battle:

*After nearly a month of rest, training and maintenance, the 7th AD was in position straddling the German–Dutch border in the vicinity of Heerlen (Netherlands) to Geilenkirchen (Germany), in preparation for its participation in the US Army's push deeper into Germany. The division itself remained in XIII Corps' reserve, although constituent units were committed attached to other divisions.*

Hasbrouck took charge of a unit in a bad way but turned it into a formidable fighting tool. He is pictured here near his command Halftrack in Germany. (*Nara*)

*During the first half of the month the division moved east of the River Wurm and prepared to attack to the east, north-east or north. Detailed plans were made for the seizure of Brachelen, Germany, but all operations outside the River Rur depended on the seizure or destruction of the dam south of Düren. In German hands, this dam could be used to flood the entire river valley and eliminate or destroy all forces there. Unsuccessful attempts*

The mood was relaxed before the arrival of Brigadier General Hasbrouck at the helm. (*Nara*)

*to destroy the dam by aerial bombardment were made every day, weather permitting, from 3 December onwards.*

*The division's fighting forces were in Germany awaiting the destruction of the dam when, on 16 December, the entire division was alerted to move into the VIII Corps area of the US First Army. Early in the morning of 17 December 1944, the first elements of the division began moving south.*[4]

As a result, the unit that would be marching south was rested, seasoned and perfectly ready for action. Its excellent condition when it went on alert would be one of the factors that would enable it to perform well in the ordeal.

## The Order to go to Battle

At 18:00 on 16 December, Hasbrouck received the order to prepare to move immediately and place himself at the disposal of VIII Corps, First Army, in the Bastogne area. His instructions quickly filtered down to the lower echelons. Brigadier General Bruce C. Clarke, head of CC B, recalled:

*At 20:00, I received a telephone call from General Robert W. Hasbrouck, commander of the 7th AD, saying that the division had been ordered to move immediately south of Bastogne and report to the commanding general of VIII Corps. What we were to do when we got to Bastogne was unknown to us. He told me that the division would march as soon as the road could be cleared. General Hasbrouck ordered me to go immediately to Bastogne and to get in touch with the general commanding the VIII Corps to inform me of the situation. He said that my CC would lead the division on its march of 100 to 110 kilometres south. At 04:00 on 17 December Major Owen E. Woodruff, my S3 and I, with two pilots, were in Bastogne where we informed General Middleton that the 7th AD was marching south.*[5]

At 18:00 on 16 December, Hasbrouck received the order to prepare to move immediately to place himself at the disposal of VIII Corps. (*Nara*)

The unit sets off for the Saint-Vith sector. (*Nara*)

Clarke's CC B was made up of the 31st Tank Battalion (TB), 23rd Armored Infantry Battalion (AIB) and B Company of the 33rd Armored Engineer Battalion (AEB).[6] CC A was warned at the same time and ordered to move south to an unknown destination by 05:30 the following morning. At 23:00, the departure order was postponed until 07:00.[7]

For Hasbrouck, this sudden departure on a mission was a test of the division he had just put through intensive training, and he struggled to get his armoured formation into action:

*We worked feverishly to prepare for the journey to our destination. Putting an armoured division into action (that is, theoretically, 10,998 men, 93 guns, 269 tanks and 1,141 vehicles) required meticulous preparation, regulated like a ballet: everything had to run like clockwork. Liddell Hart compared an armoured division, sometimes to a tiny rock crystal inside a large slingshot, sometimes to the opposite of a tortoise: a small, armoured beast emerging from a huge soft-skinned body. 'It has', he writes, 'too few teeth and too long a tail. Confined to a single road, its normal range stretches over 200 miles.' We knew our assembly area but were still unaware of the precise reasons for this movement and above all that the division was going to go down in history, having first been through hell!*[8]

This clarification is important because it was to cause many difficulties when the men arrived in the combat zone. The fact that Hasbrouck was unaware of the reasons for his move and that he was starting from Holland, a calm part of the front, in another army's sector, to reach an army corps whose command had difficulty in fully grasping the situation, did not make him aware of the danger. The chosen method of movement was administrative.

To understand this choice, it is important to realise that the seriousness of the situation did not seem to be appreciated at Middleton's VIII Corps HQ. Hasbrouck's account gives a good picture of the atmosphere in Bastogne when he arrived there late on the morning of 17 December:

*Around midday, I was with the Commanding General, VIII Corps, who first invited me to lunch (which proves that the situation did not seem too critical to him). During the briefing, he gave me the latest news (vague, fragmentary, and sometimes contradictory). It was a real waste of time because the headquarters in Bastogne didn't know any more than I did. Dejected, I left for Vielsalm, where my Tactical HQ was supposed to have set up, and then for Saint-Vith, where I didn't arrive until around 16:00.*[9]

## Inappropriate Tactical Deployment

American tactical manuals distinguish between two types of movement: administrative marches, where units move in groups for simplicity; and tactical marches, when an encounter with the enemy is possible. In this case, the advance is made cautiously. You move forward with your weapon drawn and your finger on the trigger, expecting to encounter an enemy around every corner. In this scenario, it was precisely this type of movement that should have been the order of the day. To do this, the armoured division usually marches in multiple columns arranged so that it can easily enter combat according to the commander's plan. It is preceded by the reconnaissance battalion, the reconnaissance companies of the tank battalions and the vanguards of each column. These are formed in such a way that entry into bivouac, assembly or combat areas can be made with the least possible delay and confusion. They have to avoid overtaking units on the road, with the number and composition of columns varying according to the road network, the tactical situation and the battle plan envisaged. Columns are made up of tanks, infantry, artillery, engineers and tank destroyers (TDs). Light tanks are generally in the lead, followed by infantry and TD units.

During the hours of darkness, when the employment plan calls for the infantry to engage before the tanks, or when the use of tanks cannot be reasonably foreseen, the artillery is placed well forward in each column. TD elements are placed to protect the flank

When moving close to the front, tank destroyers protected the flanks. (*Nara*)

and rear. Depending on the state of the roads and the need to clear hostile roadblocks, a detachment of combat engineers is placed at the front of each column, including a contingent of a few specialists in the very first vehicles. Infantry should be attached to the vanguard when it can be foreseen that they will be used to reduce roadblocks.

Control is maintained by designating walking objectives, progression zones or routes, phase lines to be crossed at specific times or according to orders, and by prescribing walking rhythms. Air superiority is a prerequisite for a successful day march. When air attacks are expected, the distance between elements must be increased and, in some cases, the advance is made across the country in small groups. In the presence of hostile aircraft, and when secrecy is vital, night marches are the norm. The infantry, with the tank destroyer unit, usually leads the march to secure assembly areas for the division.

The armoured division can march in regimental columns or be formed into CC groups with tank battalions as the nucleus of each group. Each of these groups can be made up of light tanks, medium tanks, artillery, tank destroyers, sappers and infantry. In each column, the light tanks are generally in the lead, and the artillery is placed well forward, generally following the light battalion.

Trains of units with columns are generally grouped together and follow behind the column. They may, however, be with their units. Divisional trains march on a route

As in all US armoured units, each tank battalion was equipped with six Shermans armed with a 105mm howitzer, who provided artillery support as close as possible to the front line. This 105mm Sherman is being refuelled with ammunition. (*Nara*)

The 7th AD columns stretched over two routes. (*Nara*)

away from the exposed flank or in the central column, where they will benefit from the maximum protection offered by the combat echelons.[10] Clearly, this was not the type of movement that was put in place at this time, and as a result, the elements were very vulnerable as they marched towards the enemy. Naturally, the fighters were not on their guard, even though they were close to the danger. To reduce the length of the division, Hasbrouck defined two different routes: an EAST route and a WEST route.

The eastern route was the most exposed, but also the shortest. The route was 82 kilometres long and was used by the division's tactical command and its CCR,

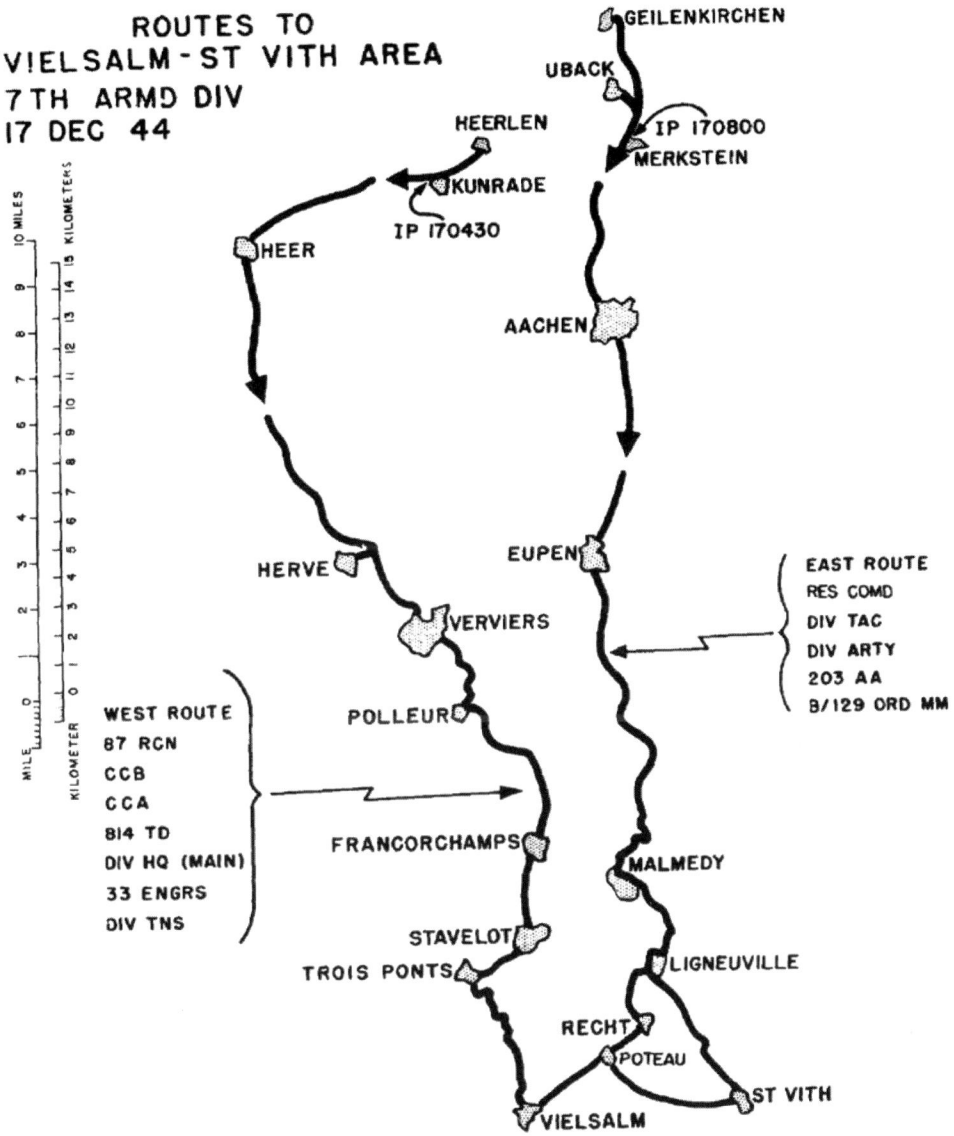

The two columns of the 7th AD marching on parallel routes.

made up of the 17th Tank Battalion (TB) and the 38th Armoured Infantry Battalion (AIB). The artillery followed with the 434th, 440th and 489th Armored Field Artillery Battalions (AFAB).[11]

Meanwhile, the 106-kilometre western route passed through the depths of the US position with the A and B CCs, the 87th Cavalry Reconnaissance Squadron (CRS), the 814th TD,[12] the 33rd Engineer Armored Battalion (AEB), the divisional train and the admiistrative command. The HQ, meanwhile, moved to Vielsalm.

The composition of the columns on the two routes clearly showed that the administrative order of march was used. The artillery was grouped in columns on the most exposed route, which was travelled unprotected by a cavalry screen. The division had 2,800 vehicles, including around 800 tracked vehicles. There were 1,300 vehicles on the western route and 1,500 on the other. The two columns formed queues more than 100 kilometres long, with a six-hour delay between the arrival of the first element and the last.

## Where is the 7th Division?

Although the division was able to move quickly, it was not really able to start until 04:30 due to the difficulty of clearing the chosen routes of advancement. In the confusion of the moment, Middleton HQ failed to warn Jones that the 7th AD's advance party was very late and would not arrive until the afternoon of 17 December. This oversight compounded the impact of the previous day's erroneous information and had catastrophic consequences for the fate of the two infantry regiments of the 106th ID. There were several reasons for this huge delay in the announced timetable.

The western column formed by CC B, under the orders of General Bruce C. Clarke, had to cover around 100 kilometres to reach Saint-Vith via Heerlen, Heer, Herve, Verviers, Francorchamps, Stavelot, Trois-Ponts and Vielsalm. In his grouping, Clarke led the 23rd AIB and the 31st TB. The way was opened by the 87th CRS. The unit's CC B crossed the Dutch–Belgian border at 05:40 and arrived in Vielsalm, a village a few kilometres west of Saint-Vith at the rear of the front line, at around 11:00.[13] The route passed through Geilenkirchen, Merkstein, Aachen, Eupen, Malmedy, Ligneuville, Recht, Poteau and Vielsalm and was under constant threat from the tip of the I. SS-Panzer-Korps. The end of the column was cut off in the early afternoon by Obersturmbannfuhrer Peiper's Kampfgruppe in the vicinity of Malmedy. Battery B of the 285th Field Artillery Observation Battalion, which had joined the advance without authorisation, was intercepted. Eighty-four artillerymen were taken prisoner and brutally shot by the SS at Baugnez, in total disregard for the rules of war.

After having gone as far as Bastogne to take his orders orally, it was not until mid-morning that General Bruce C. Clarke arrived in Saint-Vith to prepare the installation of his unit. He tells us about his arrival at Jones' HQ:

Moving up the line was done in administrative order. (*Nara*)

The carcasses of the vehicles of Battery B of the 285th Field Artillery Observation Battalion were found at Baugnez near the bodies massacred by the SS of the 1. SS-Panzer-Division. (*Nara*)

*On 17 December, at about 10:30, I arrived at the headquarters of the 106th Infantry Division. General Alan W. Jones immediately explained to me what he expected of me:*

*'Clarke, I wish you to launch your CC B towards Schönberg to break the straitjacket which imprisons two of my regiments in the Schnee Eifel.'*

*'General, I have no idea when my unit will arrive,' I replied.*

*The blood ran cold through poor General Jones' veins.*[14]

Following this interview, CC B was ordered to move to take up a position only 20 kilometres west of Saint-Vith. In his After Action Report, Clarke sums up the situation very well:

*At noon the situation in the St Vith area was critical. The 14th CG north of the 106th ID had been pushed back on a north-south line through St Vith. Their situation was confused and extremely unclear. East of St Vith, the 422nd and 423rd Infantry Regiments (106th ID) were cut off south-east of Schönberg. Communications with them were sporadic by radio. South of St Vith, CC B of the 9th AD was attacking to retake Winterspelt. To the south, the 424th Infantry Regiment (106th ID) held a line. The situation in this sector was unclear. There was virtually no link between the units mentioned and the units on their flanks. The commanding general of the 106th ID called for an immediate attack east of St Vith to take and hold Schönberg, then move south to provide escape routes for the two encircled regiments. This was prepared and plans were drawn up which were approved by telephone at around 13:00 by Brigadier General Robert W. Hasbrouck commanding the 7th AD. However, due to congestion on the roads caused by units and vehicles moving to the rear, including artillery, it was impossible to get the 7th AD CC B troops from near Vielsalm to St Vith in time to launch the attack that afternoon. In the meantime, the enemy had approached St Vith from the east and was only 3,000–4,000 metres from the town. At around 15:30, the 106th ID sent elements of the 81st Engineer Battalion from its staff company, the 168th Engineer Battalion, minus a company and an infantry platoon that had previously been used to guard the HQ, to block the road east of St Vith. The Division made available to CC B of the 7th AD, the 275th Field Artillery Battalion (AFAB) stationed at Ober Emmels, and some artillery was still in support.*[15]

Hasbrouck's decision was a logical one; aware of the immense traffic jam, he knew that his CC B would not be in the area in time to take part in the battle, and so he reluctantly decided against implementing this plan.[16] One can only imagine Major General Jones' dismay at seeing two-thirds of his division on the verge of being surrounded as a result of the disastrous consequence of a judgement error by the higher echelons. With the route to the front heavily obstructed by the fleeing troops, it took more than five hours to reach the town threatened by von Manteuffel's troops.

A world of mayhem stood in the way of the 'Lucky Seventh'. (*Nara*)

## Too Little Too Late?

There had clearly been an error of assessment, with the facts showing that the 7th AD could not have arrived on the morning of 17 December to reinforce the 106th ID. General Hasbrouck explains the reason for this:

*Shortly after midnight, the Ninth Army estimated, according to Leavenworth's standards, that the assembly of the Division in the quadrilateral of Saint-Vith, Recht, Vielsalm, Beho would begin at 14:00 on the 17th, and would be completed by 02:00 on the night of the 18th. As for the First Army, two hours earlier it had already told the VIII Corps that it would do so from 7:00 for units taking the western route, and from 11:00 for the others, who were due to arrive by the eastern route. General Jones, with the agreement of General Middleton, had based his entire tactics on these over-optimistic assurances. He is in no way to blame.*[17]

So, Jones did not in any way lose out, but the burden of the mistake would fall on him. From Hasbrouck's testimony, the problem lay in the exchange of information between Hodges' HQ in Spa and Lieutenant General William Hood Simpson's Ninth Army HQ. Decisions taken in Spa were communicated to VIII Corps HQ in Bastogne, which drew up the consequences and gave orders on the ground. They reached Jones' HQ in Saint-Vith, where Colonel Slayden, the VIII Corps liaison officer, was supposed to avoid coordination problems. Although direct links existed between neighbouring armies through liaison officers, decisions on the coordination of operations affecting them were taken at a higher level, i.e. Bradley's 12th Army Group. But on 16 December, Bradley was not at his tactical HQ 'Eagle Tac' in Luxembourg, but in Nancy to confer with Eisenhower, meaning he did not hear about the offensive until the afternoon of 16 December. He found it difficult to gauge the scale of the German assault, at first thinking it was a diversionary manoeuvre to force him to delay his winter offensive, which was due to start imminently. In the north, the orders given to the Ninth Army

The sides of this Sherman are covered with a trellis laid by the field workshops. The aim was to imitate the German practice of using netting to fix natural camouflage. This is more effective than camouflage netting and, above all, did not catch fire. (*Nara*)

From Eisenhower (right) to Middleton (left), the US hierarchy did not immediately realise the scale of the German attack. (*Nara*)

were to take the Roer dams and in the south, Patton's Third Army was to attack towards the Saar. Bradley stuck to what he thought he knew about the German position and only gave orders to counter what he thought was a minor attack. Not being in Luxembourg, he gave his instructions by telephone to his chief of staff, Major General Leven Cooper Allen. Two armoured divisions were detached from the two armies that were to go on the offensive, with Bradley's aim being to stem the German assault by reinforcing the wings of the First Army to flank the enemy's leading units. The Ninth Army in the north dropped the 7th AD, and the Third Army in the south allowed the 10th AD to move up towards Luxembourg. These movements should therefore not be seen as a crisis reaction, but rather as a limited countermeasure to curb a diversionary attack to maintain the initial American plans.

Having given his orders, Bradley spent the evening in Nancy and did not return to Luxembourg until the afternoon of the 17th, when he finally realised the maelstrom in which his First Army was caught. On discovering the number of German divisions attacking his thin curtain of troops in the Ardennes, he exclaimed: '*Where in God's name did the bloody bastards get all that?!*'[18]

It is easy to understand why the various levels of US command were so confident; the staffs in Bradley's chain of command had just lost the initiative but did not know it yet. Only the generals on the front line understood what was happening, albeit within the limits of their field of action. It was already very late, and the US front was cracking under the German armoured spikes to the north and south.

# Chapter 5

# Crisis in Saint-Vith

## Two Regiments of the 106th Infantry Division in the Cauldron

As the 7th AD struggled to reach the 106th ID's sector, things continued to go wrong. Precious time had been lost in orders and counter-orders. The staff of CC B of the 9th AD had to reorient all its units to take account of the imminent arrival of the 7th AD in the sector. Apart from the fact that the decision was based on inaccurate information, which was already going to prove catastrophic for the US, this providential delay was put to good use by the enemy, who was working feverishly to reinforce its two claws enveloping the Schnee Eifel.

When the 7th AD arrived in the sector, it realised that it had to redeploy completely. (*Nara*)

The men of the 106th ID were gradually surrounded. This infantry squad is under fire. (*Nara*)

Gradually, two deadly jaws closed in on the 422nd and 423rd Infantry Regiment (IR) of the 106th ID. An officer of the German division explained how the day of 17 December had unfolded:

*That day brought the success we had hoped for. The vigour of the divisional commander, who had been with part of the regiment (about a battalion) above Wischeid in the Our valley during the morning, succeeded in reaching Andler by a considerable effort of the troops and their command. At daybreak, crossing the main line of resistance, the schnelle Abteilung,[1] which came under Grenadier-Regiment 294, reached the Our valley without difficulty, and broke through further. The rest of the regiment (about one battalion) attacked from Auw in a southerly direction. However, it remained blocked with its most advanced*

The Volksgrenadiers make a determined advance towards Saint-Vith. (*Nara*)

*point at the bend in the road 1 kilometre north of hill 612. Grenadier-Regiment 295 succeeded in taking Rodt and attacked Kobscheif, where enemy resistance was considerably stronger. Grenadier-Regiment 293 took Bleialf during the day in a powerful attack and remained in action above Schönberg. This action continued to be halted by multiple failed attempts to the west by enemy elements threatened with encirclement in the Schnee Eifel. Before noon, led by the division commander, it managed to take the undestroyed Schönberg bridge along the River Our. During the afternoon, it approached Heuen-Atzerath and its advanced element reached Walleroder-Mhüle (4 kilometres west of Saint-Vith) at dusk.*

*Renewed assaults by the Division-Kampfschule in the direction of Schneifel-Kamm were again unsuccessful. The exploitation of Prüm–Sellerich by the road leading to Bleialf was not possible due to the actions of the enemy coming out of Schneifel.*

*That day, the division managed to completely break through the enemy positions. From then on, the enemy elements in the Schnee Eifel were surrounded. It was only possible for these enemy formations to move away from the roads and strike across the countryside because there the roads were in German hands. Isolated troops of varying strength could still be seen that day and the next day breaking through to the west under cover of darkness. The enemy's behaviour was completely incomprehensible. He really did almost nothing.*[2]

Little by little, the German infantry infiltrated behind the lines of the two American regiments. (*Nara*)

When the two wings of the 18. VGD were about to join up at Schönberg and then attempt to drive towards Saint-Vith, Major General Jones, who had been expecting Hasbrouck's tanks at around 07:00, watched in anguish as his two regiments were gradually surrounded. His anxiety grew by the hour, especially as he was alone to deal with the situation. If this line of defence broke down, he had nothing left to prevent the capture of Saint-Vith, with the only solution being to scrape together some of his combat engineers. The crisis in front of Saint-Vith was in danger of becoming unmanageable.

## Two Regiments Surrounded

In the sector of the 422nd and 423rd Regimental Combat Team (RCT), German shells began falling at 03:00 on the night of 17 December. One of the battalions of the 423rd positioned to the south of the pocket in formation reported that armoured vehicles followed by infantry were approaching its positions. Communications with the 590th Field Artillery Battalion were again cut, as were the lines to the Command Post of the neighbouring 422nd Infantry Regiment to the north.

Before daybreak, the Volksgrenadier broke through the first line and penetrated the position between the anti-tank company and B Company of the 81st Engineers Battalion. At 06:30, Bleialf was taken and a powerful pincer developed northwards towards Schönberg. In less than two hours, the Germans joined up with the elements

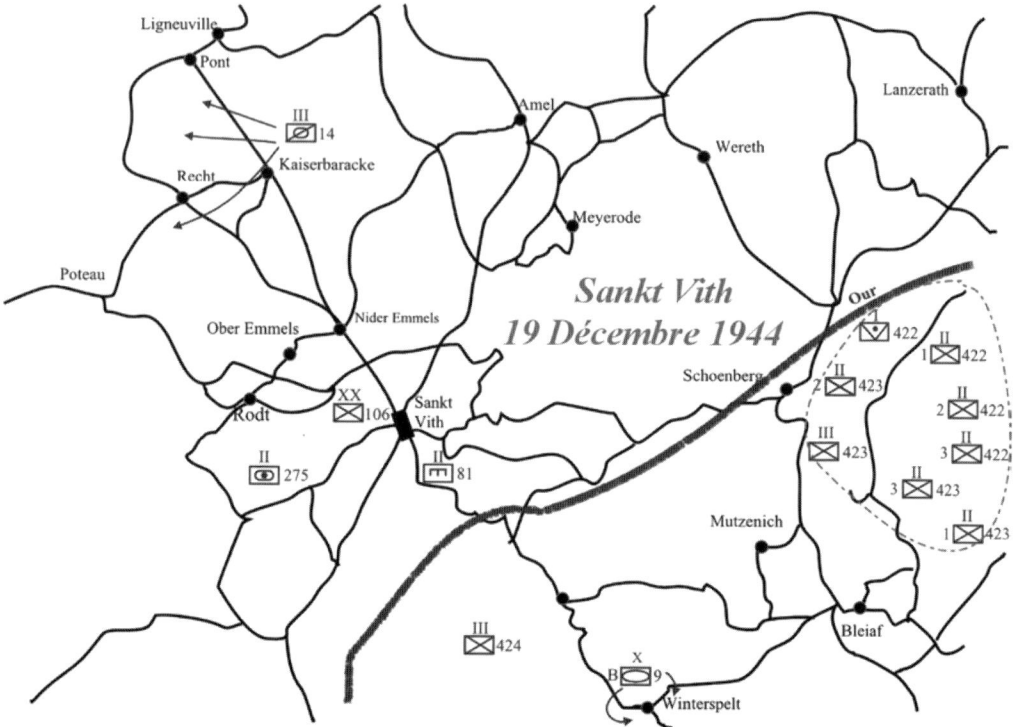

The refluence of the 14th CG exposed the flanks of the RCT of the 106th ID. (*Nara*)

The commander of the 423rd Infantry Regiment reorganised his position on his southern flank by taking C Company from his first battalion and directing it towards the threatened point. (*Nara*)

coming from the north, whose movement had been facilitated by the withdrawal of the 14th Combat Group. The first act of the tragedy was consummated: two regiments of the 106th ID now found themselves surrounded in a pocket.

The commander of the 423rd RCT had to reorganise his position on his southern flank, so he took C Company from his first battalion and directed it towards the threatened point. The contingency battalion that had been allocated to it was disbanded and its soldiers were placed in line wherever necessary. The hole created by the movement of C Company was filled by the engineer and supply platoons, cooks, drivers and administrative staff of the first battalion's headquarters, forming a provisional company.

Meanwhile, the rear of the Second Battalion, 422nd Infantry Regiment (IR), was heavily engaged, having been protecting the withdrawal of the 589th Field Artillery Battalion from the German thrust through Schönberg since dawn. At 07:00, its radio command post was destroyed by an artillery shell, but during the fighting the regiment showed great pugnacity, claiming the destruction of seven German tanks. However, the enemy's continued push forced the battalion to retreat. At dawn, the entire battalion fell back under the protection of the guns of the 590th Field Artillery Battalion. Early in the morning, the divisional artillery commander ordered the battalion to move to the vicinity of Schönberg. As the village was occupied by the enemy, it also withdrew. The two formations then joined the defensive perimeter of the 423rd IR, bringing three howitzers with them. The regimental commander placed the second battalion in the

The encircled regiments announced that they would hold the perimeter as long as they were supplied with ammunition, food and medical supplies until the road was reopened. (*Nara*)

north-eastern sector of his position, while the artillerymen took up positions inside the perimeter and the gunners who could be recovered held the front line as riflemen. The divisional command was informed of the arrival of these units, adding in his message: '*Hold the perimeter, drop ammunition, food and medical supplies until the road is reopened.*'

Shortly before 15:00, a message from the division was received: '*We plan to clear the area west of your positions this afternoon with reinforcements. Withdraw from your current positions if they seem untenable. Save all possible means of transport.*'[3]

The messages sent by Major General Jones to these two regiments were dictated by the arrival of the 7th AD in his sector, who he was counting on to open his encircled units.

## The 9th Armored Division Saves the 424th Infantry Regiment

To the south of the 106th ID's position, the 424th IR was also in a precarious situation. Both its flanks were exposed and contact was lost with the other units. The thrusts of the 18. VGD to the north and the 62. VGD to the south also cut it off from the rest of the division. The hinge with the 28th Infantry Division to the south was also broken. In addition, the bridge over the Our at Steinebrück was in German hands, making it very difficult, if not impossible, for the infantry regiment to withdraw. The intervention of CC B of the 9th AD pushed the Germans back to the east of this village, which was of crucial importance to both sides. Hoge describes the events:

*At 9:30, Company B of the 27th Armored Infantry Battalion crossed the Our at Steinebrück. Shortly afterwards, an infernal crackling sound broke out: the Germans were firing at my men as if they had been ordinary targets on a shooting range. In a few moments, we lost forty infantrymen. Then, supported by a platoon of tanks, the two companies Colonel George W. Seely had ordered to clear the hills around Elcherath set about dislodging the Grenadiers. Ninety of them arrived with their hands in the air! As we were completely unaware of the enemy's strength in Elcherath, we prepared a well-*

At midday, the Priest M7s from the 16th AFAB were in place to support the clearance attack. (*Nara*)

The 9th AD storms Winterspelt. (*Nara*)

*coordinated attack: by noon, the 16th AFAB was in place, west of the Our, and the 14th TB was ready to support the three companies of the 27th AIB. Having decided to push on to the Winterspelt heights, I ordered the infantry to dig in while the tanks advanced. Just then, General Herbert T. Perrin, second in command of the 106th ID, arrived. He told me that I could continue my advance but that, for the night, I would have to re-cross the river and establish a defensive position. It was an ambiguous order. I assume – for I received no explanation – that General Alan W. Jones was aware of the scale of the offensive and that the forces at his disposal were forced onto the defensive because of their excessive numerical inferiority, that as the hours passed the situation could only get worse and that his problems would become more and more insoluble. With General Perrin's approval, I decided that there could be no further question of recapturing Winterspelt.*[4]

Indeed, Jones remained very worried about his regiments in the north of his position and preferred to prevent Hoge's CC B from being stretched too thin. He decided to make a tactical withdrawal to more solid positions on the other side of the River Our, while maintaining a bridgehead at Steinebrück. Knowing that the wet cut-off would make it very difficult to pull out later, Hoge ordered his infantrymen to bury themselves in the positions they had reached and sent his tanks back to the rear. The GIs, meanwhile, joined them during the night without being harassed. These assertions were confirmed on the German side, with von Manteuffel giving more details on the real impact of the opening-up operation:

*The Kommandeur of the 62. VGD intended, by 17 December, to fix only the enemy parts at Gross Langenfeld and Hockhuscheid, in order to break through with the mass of forces and resources via Winterspelt and Wallmerath to Bruesssel Berg. The valiant GR 190*

Three photographs of the Steinebruck sector taken after the battle. The first shows the American bank giving access to Saint-Vith. The second shows the railway station completely flattened. The military vehicles belong to the Belgian army's mine clearance services. The third photograph shows the German bank with the bridge rebuilt by American engineers. (*Rights reserved via Bastogne War Museum*)

*also took the high ground to the north, at Winterspelt and to the north-east-west. Its Mobile Battalion broke through Wallmerath and drove the enemy back in the western part of Winterspelt. Parts of this battalion attacking south of the advance road succeeded in driving the enemy out of the forest at Heckhalenfeld. However, GR 183, which had twice penetrated the locality, was unable to hold on. The division's losses from the fighting in the forest were once again higher than expected. The enemy defended, taking advantage of particularly favourable terrain. Their artillery fire showed, judging by the quantity of ammunition used, that the artillery was very well supplied. The fighting of the first two days had enabled these formations to break through the most advanced enemy position. Indeed, on that day and in the days that followed, enemy groups of various strengths took advantage of the darkness to penetrate the parts of the GR 293 that followed them and cross them from east to west.*[5]

Thus, as confirmed by the assertions of both sides, it has to be said that the first intervention by Hoge's CC B was not a complete success, as Winterspelt was not recaptured. However, it did allow the 424th RCT to withdraw, temporarily stabilising the situation in the sector and ensuring that the Steinebrück bridge, which opened the road to Saint-Vith, remained in American hands. It should be noted, however, that the rapid withdrawal of the American infantry unit meant that a large quantity of equipment was abandoned. The US armoured attack disconcerted the general in command of the 62. VGD, causing a major delay in the development of his offensive plan and very heavy losses. Von Manteuffel did not yet have his supply line for the drive westwards, let alone the railway station he would need most.

## The Cavalry Fails to Arrive

With his two regiments surrounded, Jones and his 106th ID were no longer in control of events. All he had left to defend the town was a platoon of infantry and a detachment of combat engineers. He urged an immediate attack by CC B east of Saint-Vith to take and hold Schönberg in order to provide an escape route for his two regimental combat teams, and so a clearing operation was prepared, with plans being drawn up and approved by the divisional commander. However, because of road congestion, the troops of CC B were unable to get from near Vielsalm to Saint-Vith quickly enough to launch the clearing attack on the afternoon of the 17th.

At HQ near Jones, Clarke anxiously awaited the arrival of the first elements of his division. A veritable race against time was under way, with the faster of the two belligerents gaining the benefit of the roads serving the town and thus gaining the advantage of being able to take the initiative and impose his law on his adversary. At 13:00, von Manteuffel's most advanced elements were no more than 5 kilometres from the town. Jones insisted that the armoured tanks should hurry up and around 15:30, he sent elements of the command company, the 168th Engineer Battalion, to set up a roadblock on the road leading from Setz to Saint-Vith. At around 13:30, three tanks and

Reconnaissance elements from the 7th AD arrive on the scene. (*Nara*)

Volksgrenadier appeared in front of their position. The crew of the lead tank climbed down without taking any precautions, and the US combat pioneers opened fire, sweeping away the reckless crew and destroying the second tank with a bazooka. Meanwhile, the infantry and the third tank retreated. The Germans made a second attempt an hour later but, faced with resistance from the engineers and the unexpected appearance of a fighter-bomber, soon withdrew. The Germans' hesitation gave the defenders precious time, but General von Manteuffel explained the reasons for his units' lack of bite:

> *In the sector between Schönberg and Saint-Vith, the inexperience of the junior commanders explains our failure. Although the town was in sight and the heavy armament was able to provide the necessary cover, they continued along the road (or at a short distance from it) without trying to outflank their opponents laterally by advancing through cover. Far be it from me to diminish the merit of the American troops, who, split up into very small and scattered units, did not retreat when they were unaware of what was happening on their flanks and in their rear and who, nevertheless, held out with determination and bravery until General Clarke had organised a coherent defence.*[6]

The German points approached Saint-Vith from the east and were now only 3 or 4 kilometres from the town. At around 15:30, the 106th ID sent elements of the headquarters company, the 81st Engineer battalion, 168th Engineer Battalion minus a company, and an infantry platoon, formerly used as HQ guard, to block the road east of Saint-Vith.[7] Jones had just brought his final reserves online.

Little by little, an insurmountable barrier was established in the sector. The tank destroyers took up positions and dug in to protect their lightly armoured tanks. (*Nara*)

Around 17:00, the first units of the 7th AD finally reached the town and were immediately sent to reinforce the 168th Engineer Battalion's thin defensive curtain. General Clarke describes the course of events during this crucial afternoon:

*I had sent Major Owen Woodruff to the crossroads west of the town with the task of directing the first troops towards the Prümerberg as soon as they arrived. When, shortly afterwards, I went to rejoin my S3, a lieutenant colonel of artillery threatened to shoot Woody if he persisted in blocking the way to his convoy. My blood ran cold: 'Withdraw all your damned vehicles immediately... If one of us has to shoot, know that it will be me. Back up and hurry!' So that's how I started the memorable battle of Saint-Vith... What I didn't know was that I had to end it in the same way! For me, it was the longest day of my life, or more accurately, the first day of the longest week!*

*The first unit to enter Saint-Vith was Troop B of the 87th CRS. It had six officers and 136 men... On the 23rd, it was down to forty-three men and not a single officer. I told the horsemen to go down until they met the engineers, dig their individual holes and hold on!*

*Then my CC B arrived, drop by drop, company by company. These small units were scattered to flesh out the existing system, create strong points or barrages and extend the cover. After struggling to make their machines devour the kilometres on the rough ground, from Vielsalm onwards the drivers had to painstakingly make their way against the current, sometimes brutally.*[8]

The Priest M7 was a 105mm self-propelled gun. These guns equipped the 275th Armored Field Artillery Battalion, which was the only support unit available to the 7th AD when it arrived in the Saint-Vith sector. (*Nara*)

The CC B report gave more precise information on the course of events that afternoon around Saint-Vith. The 106th ID made available to CC B the 275th AFAB in position at Obremmels. On the afternoon of the 17th, the 38th AIB was the first CC R unit to arrive south-east of Recht by the eastern route. The 87th CRS was the first unit to arrive by the western route. The troops of CC B were rushed east of Saint-Vith, arriving in dribs and drabs, and were placed on the defensive by the CC B commander. When the defensive screen was in place at 15:30, Major General Jones handed over responsibility for the defence to the 7th AD. At 20:30, the situation began to stabilise. Despite alarmist reports of up to sixty enemy tanks in their sector, the men of CC B came under relatively little fire; hardly any small arms or mortar fire hit their positions, causing very few casualties. CC B's reserve consisted of the 38th AIB minus one company, but Clarke felt he could handle the situation. It should be noted, however, that at 16:40, the 87th CRS and the 38th AIB were attached to CC B.[9]

The sun set around 16:00 and Hasbrouck's division continued to arrive in darkness. Given the circumstances, the attempt to clear the two regiments of the 106th ID was postponed until the following day. The US armoured division was stretched very thin, and its artillery did not arrive until late in the evening of the following day. The only support available was provided by the 275th AFAB belonging to VIII Corps, which had been there before the German attack began.

A 105mm Sherman of the 7th AD, which provided immediate support for the Tank Battalion. (*Nara*)

The artillery of the 7th AD was still on the road. (*Nara*)

At 20:30 on the 17th, CC B sent a message outlining the measures taken:

*Request that CC B Liaison Officer at Divisional HQ be released and return to CC B HQ to obtain an overview of the situation. We have established a defensive line east of St. Vith which is linked in all but two areas. These are being corrected at the moment.*[10]

## The 17th Tank Battalion Leaves the Poteau Road Open

The problems had begun even before the 7th AD reached its prescribed assembly area. The road was cut off by the enemy south of Malmedy by the advance of the 1. SS-Panzer-Division Leibstandarte Adolf Hitler between the division's tactical headquarters and the artillery, forcing the latter and all the elements following it to turn around and move to the west road to the rear of the troops already moving there. This transfer was successfully completed, but caused a considerable delay in the arrival of the artillery at its firing positions. On the western route, traffic continued to flow fairly well until

On arriving at Recht, the 17th TB discovered that German columns were nearby and so prepared to resist on the spot. (*Nara*)

midday on the 17th, when it slowed due to congestion resulting from the ever-increasing flow of American troops withdrawing as they moved west and north-west from the threatened area between Poteau – Vielsalm – Beho – Saint-Vith. Towards nightfall, the traffic jams increased and the 7th AD column stretching northwards from Poteau to Vielsalm and from Trois-Ponts to Stavelot came to a complete standstill. On the evening of 17 December, the only troops to arrive in the Vielsalm – Saint-Vith area were from the 87th CRS. The rest were still on the road, unable to move quickly. At daybreak, the column set off, but was again intercepted by the enemy, this time near Stavelot at 08:00 on 18 December. Battery D of the 203rd Battalion AAA AW (SP) came under fire from south-east of Stavelot, but managed to disengage and with the artillery company to its rear, withdrew northwards. These elements finally rejoined the division via a circuitous route through Spa and Aywaille.

For the troops sent as reinforcements, the situation quickly became worrying. This was particularly the case for the 17th TB, which received orders to leave its bivouac area at Bauschelan in Germany on the morning of 17 December and head south to an assembly area near Recht in Belgium to help protect the north of Saint-Vith. The officers were given no information about the purpose of the move. Worse still, they were given no information about enemy or friendly forces. The march south was uneventful and there was no indication that the situation was potentially dangerous until the head of the column reached the junction of a side road leading from the Malmedy – Saint-Vith road at Recht at 14:44. At this point, a battery of field artillery from the 106th ID was encountered, feverishly preparing a hedgehog defence of its position near the road junction. Information gleaned on the spot revealed that German armoured formations advancing from the east had broken through the 106th ID's defences and were rapidly approaching the position. For the commander of the 17th TB, it was a cold shower. His troops in columns were in no position to face an encounter battle, but to be on the safe side, he ordered one tank company (B Company) to move into position and cover the crossroads, as well as another crossroads about 800 metres to the north, using one tank platoon in each position, with the third platoon in reserve. The remainder of the battalion gradually approached the assembly area on the heights just west of the town of Recht at 13:46 and deployed there in a defensive position.

The assembly area was far from ideal but had the advantage of providing good defences in an easterly and north-easterly direction towards the town of Recht. However, it had the disadvantage of being heavily wooded in all other directions, exposing its flanks and rear to infantry attacks on foot. The only communication route to the east was a narrow, road in poor condition leading through the forest to the Malmedy – Saint-Vith road.

At 14:36, elements of the 106th ID reported that an enemy armoured column had seized the town of Ligneuville on the Malmedy – Saint-Vith road, about 6 kilometres north of the battalion's position, and that the enemy had seized the town of Born to the west. It was in fact the Kampfgruppe Peiper that was charging towards Stavelot. The battalion commander and the CC executive officer headed to Saint-Vith and contacted G-3 of the 7th AD, who ordered the battalion to hold its present position. The battalion

The 17th TB was deployed to cut off access to Saint-Vith from the Kaiserbarracke crossroads. (*Nara*)

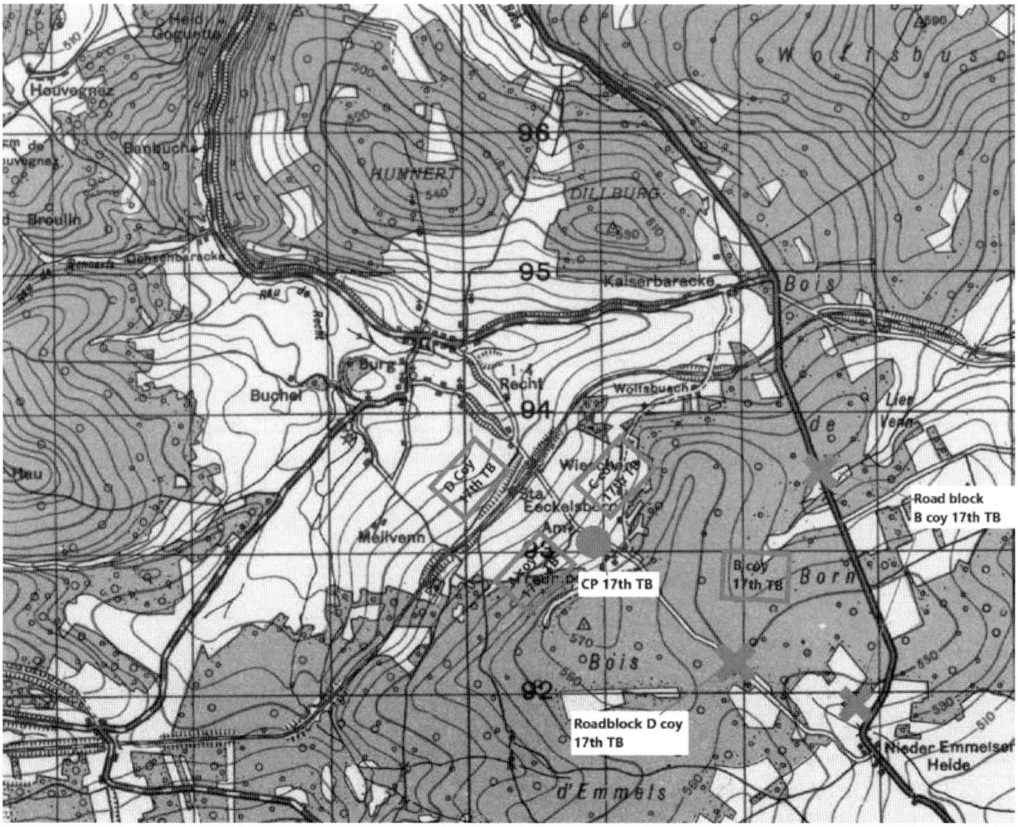

commander returned to the assembly area and shortly afterwards received information that the enemy had seized the town of Neider Emmels on the main road between his battalion's position and Saint-Vith. The clash was therefore imminent, and a strict alert was given to all his companies.

At around 18:00 reports came in that an enemy force was approaching the town of Recht from the north. As the commander of the 17th TB did not know the disposition of the friendly troops and had very little information on the enemy situation, he decided to deploy his troops as best he could to defend and hold his current position. The battalion HQ was set up 1 kilometre south-east of Recht in Am, where it had a clear view of Recht. A Company was deployed along a line parallel to the railway line to the south of Recht, while C Company extended its position to the north-east. The service company was just to the rear of A Company and D Company was assembled just south of Recht to protect the rear and act as a reserve to fill in any threatened points in the position. B Company was moved, protecting the right flank and setting up two roadblocks, each

SS-Obersturführer Heirich Golz commanded the staff company of Panzer-Aufklärungs Abteilung 1, which was integrated into KG Knittel. He was one of the first to arrive at the crossroads. The direction sign here is tilted, but in the following photographs it will be straightened. (*Nara*)

consisting of a platoon of tanks, along the road from the Kaiserbaracke crossroads to Saint-Vith. A section of tanks from D Company was positioned 1 kilometre south-east of the HQ to block the forest road coming from the east.

The ground on which the 17th TB was set up overlooked Recht and was a fairly good defensive position against an attack from the north and north-west, but the flanks and rear were very vulnerable to an infantry attack on foot through the forest, which extended in an arc behind the position. The railway line provided an ideal anti-tank barrier, as it was on a slope, and the road to Recht passed under the railway line in front of the Shermans of A and C companies, providing the logical access route to the positions of the 17th TB from Recht. The deployment was designed to block access to Saint-Vith and, in theory, to block the east-west axis by flanking fire from the south. The AAR of the 17th TB stated: '*At 01:00 we received reports that the enemy was approaching the town of Recht from the east.*' C Company was ordered to enter the town and block the road from the east by taking up position on the road leading to Poteau. A section of tanks from A Company was moved to a position at Wolfsbuch behind the railway ditch east of Recht to block the road from the Kaiserbaracke junction. D Company, meanwhile, was moved closer to the railway line to stop any infiltration attempts from the town of Recht. The battalion's service company and maintenance platoon were ordered to return to Sart-Lez-Saint-Vith and try to catch up with other divisional trains. They finally met

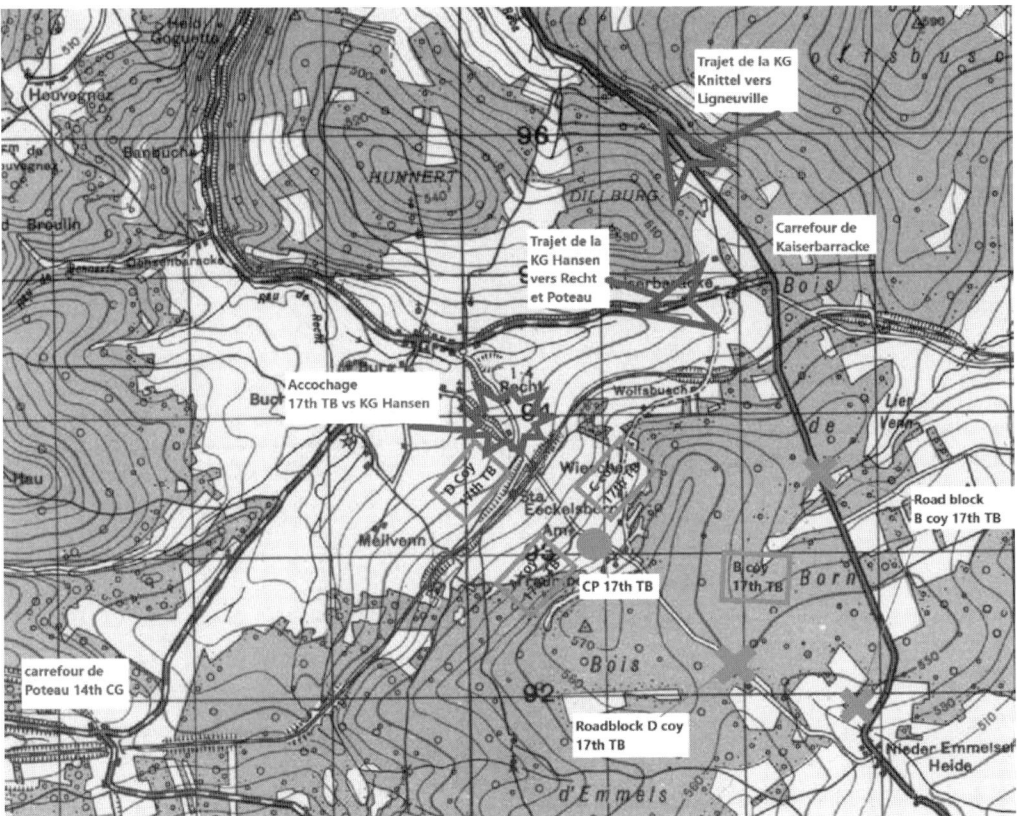

up during the night near Crombach with elements of CC B of the 7th AD and later moved west to the vicinity of Laroche. The mortar section and the assault gun section were moved into position near Am so that they could fire on the subway or any other area in front of the battalion HQ.[11]

As C Company of the 17th TB moved into position east of Recht, it came into contact with KG Hansen. The SS-Panzergrenadier of III. Panzer-Grenadier Regiment 1 were supported by Panzerjäger IV, equipped with automatic weapons and Panzerfaust. While C Company engaged the enemy force, CC R Headquarters moved south-west near Poteau. As the attack progressed, CC R command headquarters and 14th CG reconnaissance troops withdrew south towards the town of Poteau. The American barrage blocked the southern direction, but KG Hansen moved west without being troubled.

## A Game of Dominoes at the Head of the 14th Cavalry Group

The inability to block KG Hansen at Recht would have unfortunate consequences for the 14th CG.

On the afternoon of 17 December, Devine ordered a further withdrawal, with the remnants of his two squadrons taking up positions precisely at Recht, while the command post was to be established at Poteau. However, due to a mix-up in the orders given, the cavalrymen all found themselves on the same road heading west, causing another nightmarish traffic jam. It was at this point that almost the entire staff of the cavalry group set off to reconnoitre the road leading from Recht to Poteau. On leaving, Devine handed over command to Damon. An M8 and three jeeps set off with Devine, Dugan, the group's second-in-command; Major Smith, the operations officer; Major Lee, the logistics officer and Major Jim Worthington, the intelligence officer. It was a terrible risk to venture all the group's senior officers on this route so close to the enemy lines without worrying too much about coordinating operations.

To avoid the traffic jams and to try to save time, the column chose a circuitous route through the Kaiserbaracke crossroads. At 19:00, as they approached the crossroads in the half-light, they saw German semi-tracks in the distance. The staff of the 14th CG had just been thrown into the jaws of a terrible wolf: the Panzergrenadier of KG Hansen. A German sentry called out a thunderous 'Halt!' Worthington, in the lead M8, shouted: 'Hey, that's a Jerry!' and shot him with his Colt. The .50 machine gun on the turret of the armoured car swept through fifteen or so light vehicles and sped backwards, pushing the jeep behind it, carrying Devine, Smith and their driver into the ditch. Smith climbed into the M8 and managed to escape with the other two jeeps, leaving the two senior officers to their fate. Taking advantage of the confusion, they disappeared into the thicket and crawled through the first flakes of snow to the railway line leading to Poteau.[12]

Lieutenant Jack Shea, who had been asked to write an enquiry report, confirmed the facts:

Reconnaissance elements of the 1. SS-Panzer-Division cross the Kaiserbarracke junction in the direction of Recht. The point of tactical importance was not defended. The road from Recht to Poteau came under fire from the Shermans of the 17th TB, but the visibility was such that they could not stop anything. For a long time, it was thought that one of the protagonists photographed was Peiper. The man in the cap is SS-Unterscharführer Oschner, the driver of the Schwimmwagen is SS-Oberscharfürher Persin. (*Nara*)

*At 15:30, Colonel Mark Devine had ordered a retreat to new positions between Recht, Poteau and Sart-Lez-Saint-Vith. The command post was to be set up in Poteau, from where, shortly afterwards, preceded by an Armored-Car, three jeeps took off with the colonel, his second in command, Lieutenant Colonel Augustine D. Dugan, his S2 officer Major James Worthington and his S3 officer Major Lawrence Smith, along with a few soldiers. The colonel intended to meet General Alan W. Jones. After several attempts by different routes, during which MPs had warned them of the nearby presence of the Germans, the colonel and his party returned to Poteau and attempted to reach Saint-Vith via Recht. Despite the darkness, the vehicles were driving without headlights, 25 metres apart. They were about 2 kilometres from Recht. An imperative 'Halt!' The Armored-Car stopped as the jeeps drew closer. A shadow stepped forward. Colonel Dugan drew his gun and whispered: 'I don't like this.' The German sentry, after staring incredulously at the white star for a few moments, backed off slowly. Colonel Dugan's revolver clicked. Then, either the Heinies threw up a flare or the drivers put on their big headlights, but it was as if it was daylight: there were several halftracks and a swarming mob around. Individual weapons began to cackle like a hen about to lay. Turning back, the Armored-Car hit a jeep, whose occupants were thrown into the ditch. Late in the evening, in small groups, the cavalrymen returned to Poteau. The colonel, very concussed, relinquished his command and went to bed.*[13]

Devine comes face to face with KG Hansen at the Kaiserbarracke crossroads. (*Nara*)

Major Lawrence J. Smith said of Devine:

*Colonel Devine was not much liked. He was a 'spit and polish officer' who went into a rage when his instructions were not obeyed. After the ambush, he and I, his S3, returned to Poteau along the old railway line. During this 5-6 mile walk, I noticed that his words were incoherent. Captain Benson, one of our dentists, was ordered to evacuate him. He was as docile as a little child. I understand that he frequently asked General Middleton to be relieved of his command.*[14]

Meanwhile, another unexpected event occurred when an instruction from Middleton arrived in Poteau: the commander of the 14th Cavalry Group was to go to Bastogne to make his report. This instruction was clearly the result of the unfortunate meeting between Devine, Clarke, and Jones earlier that afternoon. It was, of course, Devine who should have gone to Bastogne, but in his absence, Damon set off, handing over command to Ridge on his return from Vielsalm. Half an hour later, Dugan returned from the disastrous reconnaissance. He was the senior officer and consequently took over command, while Ridge slipped away again for Vielsalm.

After covering around 10 kilometres through the woods, Devine and Smith finally arrived back at the HQ. It was late at night and the five hours of arduous marching had

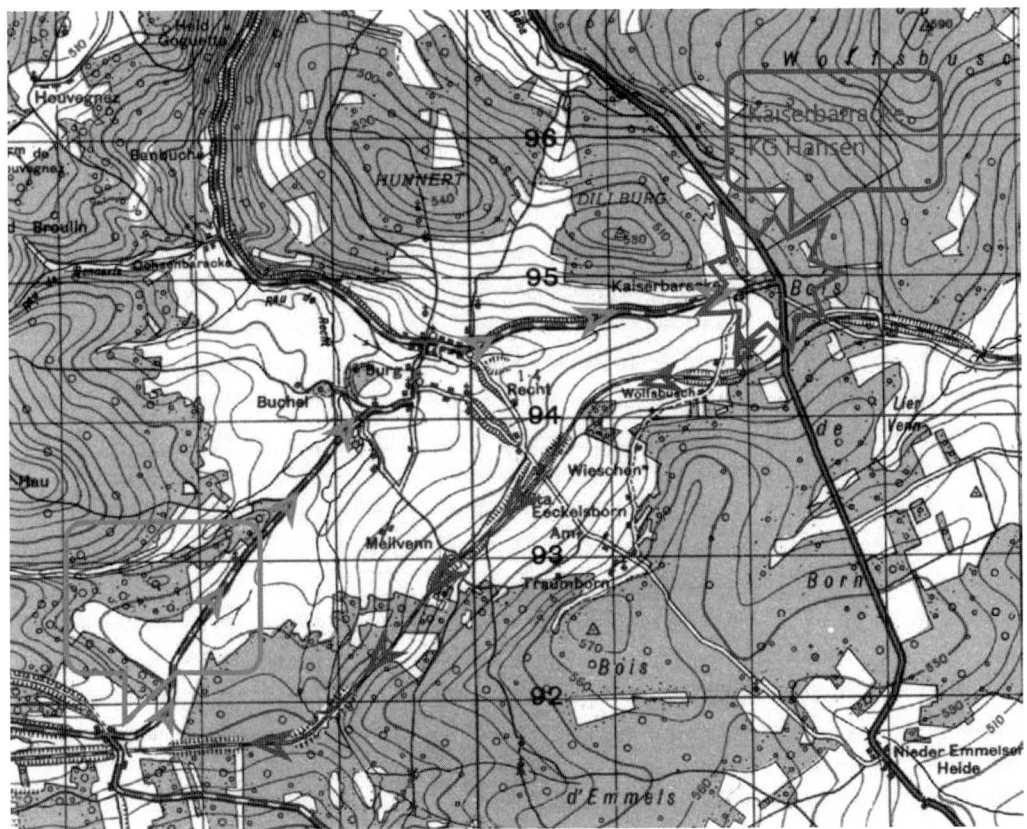

Civilians leave Recht, which has been devastated by fighting (*Nara*)

clearly taken its toll on the colonel. He had had enough, and broke down nervously, handed over his command to Dugan, and went to bed! He was finally medically evacuated, as was Lieutenant Colonel Ridge for 'loss not incurred in action'. The Executive Officer (XO), Major Kracke, took over command of the 32nd CRS and was replaced by the S3, Major Mayes, who in turn handed over his duties to his deputy, Captain Oline.[15] As you can see, the two nervous breakdowns of the unit's main leaders were no trifling matter, initiating a game of musical chairs in the midst of battle. Sometimes, this kind of rotation poses no problem and even uncovers real talent. The most famous case during the Battle of the Bulge was that of General McAuliffe, who temporarily moved from being commander of the artillery to the head of his division in the absence of General Taylor, with great success. In any case, such changes meant that men under the already intense pressure of combat had to take on a task for which they were not always experienced. This case study shows that during a crisis, it is not just the number of personnel that shrinks, but also the average skill level of the unit.

The retreat of the 14th CG on 17 December further exacerbated the problems of Major General Jones' 106th ID, as its entire northern flank was now completely exposed, and its two regiments in the front line were soon no more than an unfortunate island of resistance facing the right wing of the powerful 5. Panzer-Armee.

## Hasbrouck Beats von Manteuffel to the Punch

The other troops of the 7th AD gradually arrived in the area. CC A, which had transited via the western route following CC B, assembled near Beho. CC A's HQ arrived at 17:55 and the rest arrived in the area at 19:05. Because of the seriousness of the situation east of Saint-Vith and at Recht, and in view of the enemy's approach to the Poteau area from the north-east, which was threatening to overrun CC B to the north, the commander of CC A was instructed at midnight on the 17th to report to Division HQ the following day at 07:00 and to put his armoured brigade on alert so that it would be ready to go into action with thirty minutes' notice from then on. That night, Hasbrouck worked hard to deploy his division. Major Owen E. Woodruff Jr., S3 of CC B, witnessed the scene:

*On 18 December, from 02:00 onwards, I had the privilege of witnessing the colossal work that General Bruce C. Clarke did in a small bistro in Saint-Vith, by the light of a Coleman lamp, with a vague 1/50,000 map and his operations officer, who, incidentally, would have offered an empire for a good bath. Imperturbably, he transformed the chaos into a coherent system, giving precise instructions. There's no doubt that this was the mark of a leader and, in hindsight, it's easy to understand why some officers managed to collect stars.*[16]

KG Hansen advances westwards north of Saint-Vith. (*Nara*)

As soon as the 814th TD arrived in the Vielsalm assembly area at 23:00, a destroyer platoon with reconnaissance elements was assigned to support Recht.[17] The TD platoon sent as support nevertheless reached the road junction in the centre of the village without incident and stayed there. The TDs were also ordered to send a company to CC B via Beho first thing on 18 December.

At midnight on 17 December, the division's artillery was still stuck in the traffic jam north of Vielsalm. For them, too, moving was problematic, and Hasbrouck was only just beginning to get a clear picture of the situation into which his division had just been plunged. At 03:00, a fragmentary field order was issued, assigning troops and missions to each of the division's main subordinate commands and reorganising its position.

CC R was given responsibility for defending the division's northern sector, which included the stopping point at Grand Halleux. The division was reorganised so that C Company of the 38th AIB, an engineer company from the 33rd AEB, a company from the 814th TD with one platoon cut off, a platoon from the 203rd AAAW Battalion and a company from the 87th CRS could carry out this mission. All of this had to be in place by 08:00 on the 18th. CC R had to maintain contact with CC B at Nieder Emmels.

CC B was given responsibility for the sector to the east of the division. It was also reinforced by a platoon from the 203rd AAAW Battalion, a company from the 87th CRS and A Company from the 814th TD. All these changes had to be effective by 08:00 the

The Shermans of the 7th AD went into action immediately. (*Nara*)

next morning. CC B's limit of responsibility on the line of contact with CC R included the Nieder Emmels stopping point.

CC A was placed in divisional reserve. The 7th AD's After Action report states:

*At this time, information on the enemy was extremely sketchy, the only source being the divisional units that had just arrived in the area. Divisional artillery observation aircraft had not yet arrived. With the enemy strong to the east and approaching Poteau from the north-east, and with CC B of the 9th AD and the 424th RCT to the south protecting this flank, the divisional commander decided to ask CC A to attack the enemy at Poteau. CC A's mission was to take Poteau and secure the Saint-Vith – Poteau area. The plan was for CC B to push east of Saint-Vith sufficiently to allow CC A to move from Beho via Maldingen, Saint-Vith and Rodt against the enemy at Poteau. At the same time, CC R, minus 17th TB still in position south-east of Recht, was to establish patrols on the division's northern flank from the River Salm along the heights north of Petit-Thier to Poteau and establish contact with CC A on its right.*[18]

The MPs lead the columns at the entrance to Saint-Vith. Deployment for an encounter battle was straightforward, given the difficulties involved. (*Nara*)

It should be noted that no mention was made in these orders of the movements of the 14th CG, with which contact had been cut off. In addition, it took the whole night of 17 to 18 December to set up the system and reorganise the division so that it was ready for battle. The division could have been organised in battle order as soon as it got under way and could have been determined on the night of the 16th to the 17th in Holland if the American command had been aware of the situation and had warned Hasbrouck of the possibility of an encounter.

As for the Germans, after taking Schönberg and the intact bridge over the Our, they continued to advance towards Saint-Vith, arriving 4 kilometres east of the town at the Wallerode mill on the road to Manderfeld. There was only one high point left for them to take in order to enter the town: the Prümerberg. The commander of the 18. VGD did not understand the Americans' intentions:

> *The complete breakthrough of the enemy positions has now affected the hostile forces still resisting in the Schnee Eifel. They can only move across the fields since the roads have fallen into German hands. Over the next few days, a few enemy groups of varying strength managed to get through under cover of darkness. The enemy's behaviour on the second day of the attack was totally incomprehensible. In general, they did not react. Nevertheless, local resistance was fierce and could only be eliminated with difficulty. This is to say that the Americans fought bravely when the fighting came, but their tactics were not systematic.*[19]

The next challenge for the 18. VGD was to move its artillery into new positions to support its assault on Saint-Vith. The German comment says a lot about their assessment of the situation. They had not yet realised that an entire American armoured division was rushing towards Saint-Vith and that Jones had not moved in the hope that it would arrive in time to relieve his regiments in the front line. The commentary is also complimentary about the determination of the American troops: the 14th CG and the 106th ID having fought very well for the first two days of the battle.

## Hope Lives On

Enemy pressure on the entrenched core eased in the late afternoon and at nightfall, the lull being the logical consequence of von Manteuffel's desire to press his troops towards the town. Although they posed a threat to his rear, the two enclaves of the 106th ID were not the focus of his attention. What mattered to him was capturing the road junction so that he could develop his push westwards as quickly as possible.

In the pocket, the situation was still not too bad. Although both units were exposed, a defensive perimeter had been set up and artillery support was available due to the presence of the 590th FAB, although it only had 100 rounds in reserve. Links between the two regiments were maintained by patrols. The 422nd RCT had not yet suffered too many casualties: 250 men were out of action, but 60% were accounted for by

In the encircled perimeter, hope still remained. This artilleryman is preparing his remaining 105mm rounds. (*Nara*)

A .50 from the 7th AD in position in a field covered in snow. (*Nara*)

the contingency battalion that had returned to its positions. Although supplies were dwindling, the promise of aerial refuelling the following day kept the men's hopes of a happy ending alive.[20]

Further west, on the evening of the second day of the battle, Saint-Vith had not yet fallen into German hands, with the heights to the east of the town still under the control of the American forces. The surprise effect was in full effect until the middle of the second day. The two Volksgrenadier divisions of the LXVI. Korps managed to push the 14th CG through the Losheim Gap and surround two battalions of the 106th ID. Nevertheless, the American reaction could be described as effective and very rapid. On the morning of 17 December, CC B of the 9th AD counterattacked and disrupted the southern pincer, thereby thwarting the first attempt to encircle the town. By late evening, a second armoured division was in action, having presumably covered almost 100 kilometres. It is worth highlighting the excellent organisation and admirable coordination of the staff's work here, who succeeded in transferring a complete armoured division, held in reserve in the Ninth Army, to the southernmost corps of the First US Army. The thousands of vehicles of the 7th AD and its attached units had to cut perpendicularly across the supply lines of two army corps attacked in force by the enemy. The next day, two airborne divisions did the same, arriving from the Reims region. It was this flexibility in the articulation of US units that really made the miracle of Saint-Vith possible.

On the evening of 17 December, von Manteuffel's assessment of the situation was still very positive:

Behind Saint-Vith, in front of Vielsalm, a second line of defence was erected. (*Nara*)

The resistance in front of Saint-Vith was to cost the Wehrmacht dearly. These destroyed Stug IIIs were found when the 7th AD recaptured the town in January 1945. (*Nara*)

*The engagements of the first two days had resulted in the corps breaking through the defensive lines of the enemy front; the enemy positions in the Schnee Eifel were surrounded. The enemy troops could only fight their way through the terrain, away from the roads, which were in German hands. Moreover, during that day and the next, enemy units of various strengths tried to infiltrate through Regiment 293 from east to west, under cover of darkness. However, the vigorous defence against the attacking units of our two divisions indicated that only small forces of the 106th ID were surrounded. Although the corps' success during the morning suggested that the delay in the timetable could still be made up, the course of events during the day proved otherwise. Despite exemplary tactics on the part of the troops and their leaders, we were unable to pursue the attack with the necessary vigour by capturing Saint-Vith, which would also have had a decisive influence on the commitments of the left wing of the 6. Panzer-Armee. For the latter, breaking the resistance in the Saint-Vith sector was of great importance, as these Army units had made little progress beyond the initial front lines.*[21]

A battle for the town now began. To overcome the defenders, von Manteuffel was going to have to expend considerable offensive resources, but he had no idea of this at the time. The time lost to the Germans and gained by the Americans would allow the balance of forces in the sector to be balanced. Monday, 18 December was to be a crucial day, as the American commanders realised that they were facing a major attack and were forced to call up their last immediately available reserves.

# Chapter 6

# The Priceless Postponement of the Attack

## Von Manteuffel Pushes Forward

Hasbrouck revised his position just in time. At dawn on 18 December, the Germans attacked again, this time determined to finally capture the logistical hub of Saint-Vith. However, the roads were clogged and the 18. VGD was unable to bring up essential parts of its artillery or heavy weapons on the night of 17 to 18 December, meaning it was only able to make very slow progress towards Saint-Vith. German losses were described as light and prisoners few. The difficulties of movement were caused by the American mines and the poor quality of the roads, which were torn

Resistance from the 106th ID on Skyline Drive significantly slowed the advance of the 66. Armee-Korps. (*Nara*)

up by shells and the passage of tracked assault guns. The effects of the torrential rains in November were still being felt, as the few small roads in the region became veritable quagmires.[1] As a result, von Manteuffel was simply unable to oppose the reinforcement of Saint-Vith. His chances of making a breakthrough quickly were diminishing. One of the reasons for this failure is partly operational: the 18. VGD suffered from the traffic jams created by elements of the 1. SS-Panzer-Division, which encroached on the LXVI. Korps' sector, particularly between Auw and Schönberg.[2]

However, von Manteuffel's plans remained unchanged. There was no alternative; the town had to fall. The presence of American armoured vehicles in the sector meant that Panzer units had to move up to the front of the line, but the three Panzer divisions available were at the forefront of the fighting further south. The 5. Panzer-Armee therefore decided to commit part of its reserves to the precious Führer Begleit Brigade. Von Manteuffel explained his reasons for giving this order:

> *Field Marshal Model's suggestion that the Führer Begleit Brigade be used as an army reserve for the attack on St. Vith corresponded to my plans for the use of this brigade. The original intention of the army command was not to employ this brigade in the corps sector, but in the army's centre of gravity, i.e. in the sector of either of the two armoured corps after the breakthrough in order to exploit this penetration. The commitment of this brigade in the LXVI AOK sector therefore meant nothing less than abandoning the idea of using this mobile armoured unit, which could potentially have a very unfavourable effect on the <u>rapid</u> development[3] of the main attack. On the other hand, the capture and therefore the elimination of St. Vith was of the utmost importance for our own army and especially for the 6. Panzer-Armee. This is why Field Marshal Model enthusiastically welcomed the use of the brigade there, as he expected it to have a favourable impact on the continuation of the battle on the left wing of the neighbouring army on the right.*
>
> *In the event of the rapid capture of St. Vith, we planned to employ parts of the 6. Panzer-Armee or the Führer Begleit Brigade itself from the St. Vith area. In addition, the capture of the town made it increasingly difficult to reorganise the enemy's forces. I agreed to the employment of the Brigade within the LXVI AOK, in the hope that this well-trained and equipped force could bring about a rapid decision in the St. Vith sector. Within a few days it would have been ready for further action by the army.*
>
> *The brigade that my chief of staff had finally assembled early in the morning of 17 December was put on the move in anticipation of further action. On the night of 17 December, the order was given to advance through Prüm–Bleialf to Schönberg for operations with the LXVI AOK. The weather was good enough for the brigade to arrive by midday on 28 December. The brigade was ordered to use this route of advance because of its light traffic, offering far fewer difficulties than the Roth – Auw and Auw – Andler routes, which delayed supplies because of traffic jams, steep gradients and mud holes.[4]*

So, the resistance at Saint-Vith, even before the 7th AD went into action, was already disrupting German plans for the rest of the Ardennes offensive.

The pastures were surrounded by barbed wire, which helped the defenders. (*Nara*)

Pressure from the VGDs and SS Panzergrenadiers north of Saint-Vith increased during 18 December. (*Nara*)

The losses of the first few days were significant on both sides. This Volksgrenadier died alone in the snow. A poignant detail: he died holding a photograph of his wife. (*Nara*)

## The Führer Begleit Brigade

To appreciate the significance of this decision, we need to understand what this famous Führer Begleit Brigade represented. It was placed under the command of Oberst Otto Remer, a convinced Nazi and one of the regime's most loyal followers, although he did not belong to the Waffen-SS. In April 1933, Remer had joined a Prussian infantry regiment of the Reichswehr in Kolberg as a Fahnenjunker. On 1 September 1939, he became Oberleutnant and commanded an Infanteriegeschützkompanie during the Polish campaign, a post he held again during the Weldfelszug, this time with the 9. Panzer-Division. He remained with this division until April 1942, when he was transferred, with the rank of Hauptmann, to the newly created Infanterie-Division (mot.) Grossdeutschland. Appointed Major, Remer was awarded the Knight's Cross of the Iron Cross in May 1943 for his involvement in the Battle of Kharkov. In November of the same year, he was awarded the oak leaves of the Knight's Cross. After recovering from a serious wound, he was transferred to Berlin at the beginning of 1944 as commander of the 'Grossdeutschland' guard battalion. It was here that his career took a new turn, his action being decisive in the failure of the aftermath of the attack of 20 July 1944. Asking to return to combat, he was seen by Hitler himself as one of his most loyal Praetorians. From September 1944, Remer headed a brigade that bore his name. The dictator feared that the Allies would attempt an airborne assault on his headquarters, and so Remer's mission was to ward off this possibility. His brigade was made up of his Führer Begleit Battalion,[5] the Flak Regiment Hermann Göring, with its assortment of fourteen anti-aircraft batteries, a Schwere Artillerie Kompagnie with 150mm guns, a Pionnier-Kompagnie and a Pak Kompagnie equipped with Pak 40s. He also had under his command the z. b. v. battalions 828 and 829, which were special-purpose units acting as guards at headquarters. Remer's Führer Begleit Battalion replaced them when Hitler was at the Wolfsschanze in Görlitz. At the end of November, the advance of the Red Army forced Hitler to leave East Prussia for Berlin, and Remer's unit found itself without

Otto Remer defeated the coup plotters in the attempt on 20 July 1944. (*Bundes Archiv* (*Bild 183-2004-0330-500*))

any real use. It was transformed into a combat brigade and the resulting unit bore a striking resemblance to a Panzer Brigade in principle, but retained traces of its origins in its DNA. It was made up of :

1. Führer Begleit Regiment comprising:
    a. An armoured car battalion with five companies, equipped mainly with anti-aircraft weapons
    b. A four-company motorised battalion
    c. A four-company cycle battalion
    d. A schwere Infanterie Geshutz Kompagnie with 150mm guns
    e. A pioneer company and an anti-tank company.
2. Panzer-Regiment comprising:
    a. An Abteilung of forty-five Panzer IVs
    b. A Sturmgeschutz Abteilung with thirty-five StuG IIIs or IVs.[6]
3. Flak Regiment Hermann Göring including:
    a. An artillery battalion with four batteries of six 88mm Flak
    b. A self-propelled anti-aircraft battalion with three batteries of four guns, the first equipped with 20mm Flakvierling, the second with 20mm and the third with 37mm guns.

The Remer Brigade had a Panzer Regiment equipped with Panzer IVs similar to the one formed a few months earlier. (*NAC*)

4. A field artillery battalion with two batteries of six 105mm guns, the third having only four.
5. The usual support services: a medical company, a logistics company and a maintenance company.

This reserve was certainly a motley crew, but it had a great deal of firepower, served by soldiers who were as well trained as they were motivated. It was commanded by a highly experienced officer, a fanatical Nazi who was well aware of what was at stake in the offensive. In practice, it was the equivalent of half an armoured division. Remer's testimony confirms von Manteuffel's assertions about the original purpose of his unit. However, he points out that he himself was on the staff of the 5. Panzer-Armee. His units were unloaded from the train between 10 and 12 December in the Daun region, in reserve for Heeresgruppe B, and were ordered to move on the morning of the 18th

This Stug IV was destroyed at Crombach. It seems that it was incorporated into the Remer FBB for logistical reasons. The parts of the self-propelled gun are interchangeable with those of the Panzer IV. (*Rights reserved via Bastogne War Museum*)

towards Prüm and Bleialf.[7] An engagement by the Panzer units of the Führer Begleit Brigade, theoretically attached to the LXVI. Korps, could, without great difficulty, have taken the crossroads town at the start of the operation or at least on the morning of the 17th, in the wake of the capture of Schönberg. However, the order to line up came much too late. A basic rule of Blitzkrieg theory is to reinforce the sectors that are making the most progress and, above all, to strike hard from the outset to achieve a rapid breakthrough with a tetanising effect. This axiom was not respected and von Manteuffel was powerless. Yet it should be noted that the decision to employ the Führer Begleit Brigade was not his. Daun was around 40 kilometres from the front and it would have taken the brigade three days to reach the lines.[8]

## The Clashes of 18 December

At 08:00 the German attack resumed against the 7th AD CC B sector from the north-east and east. Hasbrouck requested reinforcements from CC B of the 9th AD: two companies of medium tanks from the 14th TB and A Company of the 811th TD. These elements were sent north to reinforce the line of the 87th CRS. At 11:00, the attack was halted, and the line was restored to its initial position. At noon, the situation improved as a tank destroyer company from the 814th TD, which had been ordered forward the previous night, finally arrived in the CC B sector and moved into position. D Troop of the 87th CRS was finally transferred from CC B to CC A in accordance with the orders given during the night. However, it had never been possible to send a reconnaissance troop to CC R. A serious danger had been averted. The 18. VGD sent its mobile battalion towards Saint-Vith, advancing along the road and beginning to descend the western slope of the Prümerberg. It was at this precise point, 2 kilometres from the town, that its progress was halted by US tanks.[9]

In fact, the German assault was almost successful when the 14th TB of the 9th AD was called in as reinforcements to re-establish the situation, and two Sherman companies were sent in. The order to move came at 09:30 with the tanks encountering the German assault battalion just 900 metres from the edge of the town. Clashes lasted until 14:00. C Company was in the lead, with A Company in the second echelon. The units took turns on the front line only to replenish their ammunition.[10] Von Manteuffel himself witnessed the attack, but what he saw with his own eyes did not reassure him for the rest of the operation:

*I met the divisional headquarters at the Wallerode mill and the Kampfgruppe at Schönberg, where the division's left wing had joined it in the afternoon after fighting to clear the roads from Bleialf to Schönberg. The enemy portions in the Schnee Eifel surrendered one after the other; small detachments were still advancing westwards in the dark. At around 16:00, the commander of the 18. VGD division reported stiffening resistance east of St. Vith, near Prümerberg. The enemy appeared with tanks which were clearly trying to break through the town's defence line to the east. I also witnessed a small tank-supported push along the road, which was, however, stopped by our assault guns.[11]*

The CCB of the 9th AD came to the rescue at a critical time (*Nara*)

The Americans fought like lions to prevent the Germans from reaching the eastern edge of Saint-Vith. Major Donald P. Boyer, S3 of the 38th AIB, remembers the Dantesque conditions of the fighting:

> We gave them a good thrashing in fierce fighting (as soon as one assault was repulsed, another started). Our lines were still holding, but Engineers had to be sent in to fill a gap (a paltry result from these desperados). It should be noted, however, that throughout this action, the 275th AFAB fired concentration after concentration on the road from Schönberg (some 900 shells) and that the A/31 and C/31 had explained themselves, in direct fire, with the tanks and assault guns at Wallerode. The night would have been calm... if patrols hadn't been constantly searching our lines for a weak point for the next morning's assault... if we hadn't been constantly hearing heavy traffic, especially towards Wallerode... if the big artillery pieces (which up until then had been like huge hunting dogs on a leash) had not been unleashed on Saint-Vith and all the road junctions, in the middle of apocalyptic lightning, to prevent our men from reinforcing our positions during the night. It was very cold. Snowstorms had been followed by rain. The roads were covered in mud.[12]

At 15:30, a second attack, estimated to be the strength of one infantry battalion, was launched against the positions to the east of Saint-Vith. This attack was again repulsed.

These two photographs were taken at Wallerode. A Hetze from the 62. VGD had taken up position at the corner of a farmhouse but was destroyed. Given the state of the carcass, it is highly likely that the vehicle was blown up by American engineers after the village had been retaken. This could explain why the remains of the vehicle are still smoking. (*Nara*)

The two CCBs of the 7th and 9th AD resisted tooth and nail on the heights of Saint-Vith. The Shermans supported the infantry. (*Nara*)

Troops were readjusted around 16:00 and elements of CC B, 9th AD, were withdrawn and sent back to their original headquarters at 21:30. An hour later, the German tank attacks were repulsed, but continuous noise and troop movements could be heard throughout the night.[13]

## The Forced Procrastination of the 18. VGD

On the morning of 18 December, the 62. VGD reported that early in the morning, American resistance at Gross Langenfeld had eased, but that the enemy had still defended Heckuscheid and Winterspelt in the afternoon. GR 190 captured Ihren in the morning, as well as the dominant height to the east, while GR 164 cleared Winterspelt during the morning and advanced as far as the Our level crossing near Steinebrück. The Grenadiers were in for a pleasant surprise: the bridge had not been damaged, and so the division's left flank advanced through the river valley west of Heckuscheid to Heckhalenfeld. Reconnaissance employed by the division reached the Auel-Steffeshausen area, where the enemy was reported near Bracht and Burg Reuland. Local counterattacks from

A counterattack allowed space to be gained to pick up the wounded, who needed to be taken care of as quickly as possible to increase their chances of survival. (*Nara*)

Elcherath and the Our valley were detrimental to the success of the attack: the crossing point near Steinebrück was once again lost to the Germans during the afternoon, before the bridge was destroyed by American engineers. The US manoeuvre once again defeated von Manteuffel, who was forced to postpone his assault on Saint-Vith. He explained:

> *At the 18. VGD, I discussed with the commanding general the conduct of the battle for the attack on St. Vith. Based on reports from the troops and the Corps, I expected the battle to start on 19 December. I had the impression, and developments during 18 December confirmed my observation, that even the most important parts of the division were fighting only along the Muehle-Prümersberg road. I therefore ordered the immediate use of reconnaissance on a broad front in the direction of St. Vith, engaging the elements arriving from the Führer Begleit Brigade (FBB) through Wallerode and Meyerode towards the Büllingen – St. Vith road, and through the 18. VGD from Wallerode to Vollmersberg, activating the portions of all the regiments of the division with the necessary combat strength. To this end, the regiment of the division, fighting on the left, was to be quickly brought up to Schönberg where it would assemble. This regiment, having cleared the road to Bleialf, wasted too much time in reorganising these units.*

In addition, all the division's combat formations, and all the artillery, had to be brought up from Auw – Andler very quickly. The Führer Begleit Brigade had to be moved forward

The artillery was immobilised having been the target of American guns. The lorries (here a Maultier) were not armoured and were very vulnerable to machine gun fire. (*Nara*)

quickly and unhindered through Schönberg and Heuem, into the Medell – Wallerode area, to prepare it for action in preparation for the attack through Emmels towards Sart-Lez-Saint-Vith. The 18. VGD was tasked with carrying out the attack based on the results of the reconnaissance and preparatory bombardment, in which all the available guns, well supplied with ammunition beforehand, took part. It also had to leave behind a strong contingent to secure its route of advance with two combat groups of equal strength towards the northern and southern parts of Saint-Vith, which was to include Vollmersberg and Mailust. The attack was to be supported by the 62. VGD so that the attack through Lommersweiler – Neidingen – Gahlhausen against Neundorf could be carried out.

Von Manteuffel added:

> *My journey back to army headquarters via Schönberg – Auw convinced me of the seriousness of the traffic situation.*
>
> *I therefore agreed that evening to postpone the attack until 19 December, stressing the need to continue intensive reconnaissance in the indicated attack sector. The Führer Begleit Brigade (FBB), whose spearhead had already arrived twelve hours late at Schönberg, reported further delays.*[14]

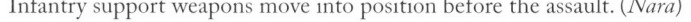

The American fire was very intense and progress could not be made without substantial support. (*Nara*)

Infantry support weapons move into position before the assault. (*Nara*)

Oberst Remer, commander of the FBB, was unable to get his brigade into line because of traffic problems. The road between Schönberg and Saint-Vith was completely jammed, meaning it was impossible for him to take part in the attack. He sent his self-propelled reconnaissance guns forward to find a practicable route and abandoned the option of forcing a passage through the south of the town. Instead, he proposed changing wings and going north to attack the American lines of communication. This adaptation of the plan began on the afternoon of the 19th.

Remer's problems did not end there, however. The traffic jam during which his vehicles had been idling without making any headway was the cause of heavy fuel consumption and now the tanks of the FBB's Panzers were empty. In reality, Remer was subject to the same problems as other armoured units, in that its initial fuel supplies were totally inadequate. He had only received 1.4 units of fuel instead of the 3 he had been promised. He also pointed out that, in his opinion, his unit had been committed too early, before the breakthrough had been achieved and before it had been able to get moving on clear roads. His unit would consequently not really be able to go into action until the night of 19 to 20 December.[15]

In fact, the German problems were identical to those faced by the Americans. The Saint-Vith sector was of great operational importance and so both sides decided to hold on to it. Of the six roads converging on Saint-Vith, five were the focus of a fierce battle.

On the evening of the 17th, the battle for the northern route began at Recht. The road south was cut off by the advance of the 116. Panzer-Division and for the moment was of no use to the Germans, who were thinking only of rushing westwards with the

18 December was a lost day for the German offensive, and the pause in operations would have serious consequences. (*Nara*)

Meuse in their sights. The north-west road was cut off at Ligneuville by the advance of KG Peiper. The two link roads coming from the east were contested by fighting between the 18. VGD to the east and the 62. VGD to the south-east. Five blocked roads, towards which thousands of men and vehicles were converging, could only turn into gigantic traffic jams.

For the moment, only one major road remained under American control: the one that passed through Vielsalm – Petit-Their – Poteau – Sart-Lez-Saint-Vith – Saint-Vith in a west-east direction. Poteau is a small hamlet of a few houses located at the convergence of three roads: one comes from the Kaiserbaracke crossroads, the second from Saint-Vith and the third from Vielsalm. The fate of the Battle of Saint-Vith now depended on this road being maintained.

# Chapter 7

# Strategic Point Post

## The Famous Ambush

On the morning of 18 December 1944, German intentions began to become clear to the American command. The headquarters of the 14th CG and its two CRS were set up in Poteau, with the 14th CG being ordered to retake Recht and move towards Born to cover the northern flank of the 7th AD defending Saint-Vith.

The Poteau ambush was extensively photographed. Most of the photographs were taken after the engagement and show three elements: the staging, the Waffen SS taking advantage of the opportunity and information on the composition of the US column. (*Nara*)

Task Force Mayes was ordered to go and meet the enemy and was reinforced by disparate elements of the 18th CRS: members of Troop C and four assault guns.

In accordance with its instructions, at around 07:00, Task Force Mayes left Poteau towards Recht in the direction of the River Amblève. On leaving Poteau, the Task Force came across a column of light tanks belonging to the 7th AD. It had arrived in Poteau at around 02:00, and its men explained that they had been driven out of Recht in flames. They were probably elements of D Company, 17th TB. They were stationary, with their rear facing in the direction of the enemy. Captain Martin commanded Troop C of the 32nd CRS and in his eyes, light tanks were an easy target for the enemy. He sent twenty-six men from Troop A to protect the rear of the immobilised column. The Task Force set off again; the sun having not yet risen by this time in early winter meaning it was still pitch dark. You can imagine the stress the cavalrymen were under as they rode east

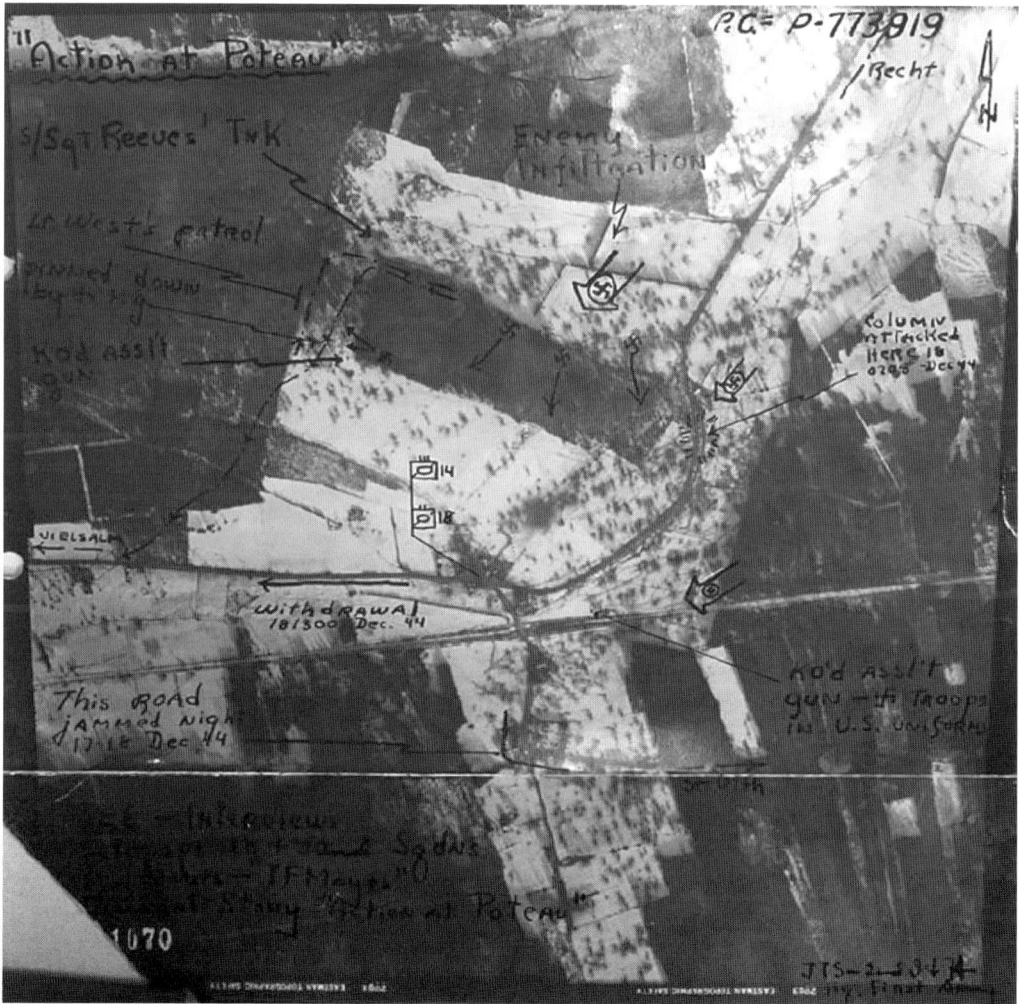

Aerial photograph taken from the investigation into the behaviour of the 14th CG. The ambush was triggered at the precise point where the woods most closely bordered the Poteau–Recht Road. (*Nara*)

along the Recht road. At the head of the column were survivors of the 18th CRS: Troop C followed by four light tanks, then elements of Troop C of the 32nd CRS in order: 1st Platoon, the staff, the 2nd Platoon, a reconnaissance team from 3rd Platoon, four assault guns and two towed anti-tanks. The cavalrymen had no idea that KG Hansen had arrived nearby during the night, and took advantage of the cover provided by the woods to the north of the town to mask their approach and deploy. SS-Obersturmbannführer Max Hansen gave his instructions after Recht had been cleared. The idea was to head straight west to Vielsalm and its bridge over the Salm.[1] To get there, they first had to pass the few houses that made up the village of Poteau.

The road here traces an S shape towards the north at the level of a forest strip. Where it turns north-east again, at precisely 08:05, two German bazookas opened fire,[2] simultaneously

It was probably a Panzerfaust shot that marked the start of the ambush. (*Nara*)

destroying a light tank and an armoured car. This was followed by an inferno of fire on the column, illuminated by the blaze from the first two vehicles that had been destroyed. The fire sent the 7th AD column scurrying towards Vielsalm, while the cavalrymen left the road as best they could to find a suitable firing position to return fire. Meanwhile, two Panzerjäger IVs appeared to the east of the Poteau – Recht road. Bill Barton and his M8 Greyhound were part of the column:

*We drove through Poteau in total darkness. The village at that time was just a hamlet of a few houses on the right-hand side of the road plus a barn on the left. We were in contact by FM radio with the two jeeps in front of us. I was supposed to be in contact with HQ via AM, but it was impossible to establish a link because the radio network was so jammed. The operator of the first jeep said, 'there's something ahead'. Lieutenant Crawford then got out of his M8 and walked forward. Shortly afterwards, Captain Walker's Greyhound pulled up alongside mine. My vehicle was hidden by hedges and the early morning darkness. This is probably what enabled us not to be spotted, which was not the case with the other armoured car on which the first German shot fell, killing La Troop's best radio operator on the spot: Charlie Yost and the driver, while Ray Bacon was cruelly hit in the turret. Sergeant Ford Kyes and Captain Edmund Storms evacuated him to the rear on a jeep.*

*My M8 couldn't manoeuvre without risking being lit. There was a wood on the left, vehicles behind and a steep embankment on our right. The two German tanks were firing at anything that moved. I saw the turret of an M8 75mm howitzer directly behind us being thrown up in the air with the gunner still in it. Captain Walker ordered me to help him clear the vehicles and then return to the column. I was wounded. Lieutenant Crawford joined us at about the same time, having fired a bazooka at the panzer. The enemy fire on the column was beginning to fade as I crawled towards the shelter offered by the houses in front of which many vehicles were still parked. Fortunately, Lieutenant Crawford came along. He was the only officer fighting. He said he was sorry he hadn't given the order to withdraw when the lead jeep gave the alert. When I told him I was glad to see him, he replied that he was glad to see me too. He ordered me to find a gun and take up a position in the barn to take on any Germans coming from the woods who might attack the crossroads. A little later, on the road, I bumped into Captain Storms, who was complaining about not being given a target for his mortar.*

An M8 Greyhound from Troop C of the 18th CRS. It is interesting to note that the barrels are facing east. The column was probably initially engaged from this direction and then engaged from the wood. (*Nara*)

The ambush in no way marked the end of the 14th CG's resistance. (*Nara*)

Captain Martin estimated that at this point in the engagement, there were between 75 and 100 German soldiers supported by armoured vehicles. The cavalrymen quickly set up a defensive arc 130 metres east of the Poteau crossroads. The ground was clear and slightly overhanging the direction from which the Germans were coming. The cavalrymen managed to battery one of the two towed 76mm guns near the corner of a village building, but the view was limited by the woods 400 metres from the village and

Captain North commanded the 14th CG staff company. (*Nara*)

unfortunately, they had no ammunition to spare and no gunner to man it. According to eyewitness accounts, there was no fog at the time. The cavalrymen had plenty of firepower; mortars and .50 machine guns were brought into action to interdict the ground. Colonel Dugan showed incredible composure as he rode among his men, cigar in hand, cheering them on.[3]

Opposite them was KG Hansen, made up of SS men belonging to III/SS-Panzer-Grenadier Regiment 1, reinforced by 1. Kompagnie of SS-Panzer-Jäger Abteilung 1. For them, it was the first real clash since the start of the offensive. Gunther Junker of 3 Kompagnie recalled:

> We wanted to attack the town directly. We didn't know whether the town was free of the enemy because we came under fire from tanks that were very well camouflaged. The company commander, Hauptsturmführer Griese, had his arm blown off. He was picked up by an armoured ambulance, still in a lot of pain, and shouted: 'To Poteau'. Until then we didn't know where we were supposed to go. That's where 3 Kompagnie got its first combat casualties. We took up a position on the slope and dug in. There we were in contact with the enemy. We withdrew in the early hours of the morning.[4]

This account is echoed in the post-combat interviews with Captain North, commander of the 14th CG's headquarters company, who said that long bursts of machine gun fire could be heard in Poteau from 05:00 and that Germans had infiltrated at daybreak. Faced with the attack, the vehicles lined up behind the ridge, which ran from north to east of the village. Fifteen cavalrymen and a machine gun carried out a harassing fire that silenced the German weapons.[5]

These testimonies already give a very different view of the stereotypical image that the historiography of the Battle of the Bulge has often conveyed. The lead vehicles had indeed been ambushed, but there was no panic in the American ranks. On the contrary, the men of the 14th CG quickly drew up a line of defence, judiciously using everything the terrain had to offer. The ambush was therefore only the first act of a battle whose outcome would depend not on the resilience of the defenders, but on the tactical specificities of the weapons systems engaged.

## Five Hours Face-to-Face

At daybreak, a patrol wearing American uniforms appeared south of the Recht road to the east of Poteau, but it kept a respectable distance from the hamlet. From 10:00, the Germans pounded Poteau with artillery and mortars, making the position untenable. The 14th CG's AAR reported high velocity fire, possibly 75mm rounds fired by Panzerjäger IV l/70s. The length of their barrels meant they could be fired at a muzzle velocity of 935 m/s,[6] and the sound of their trajectories could be mistaken for 88mm shells. The 14th CG asked for permission to withdraw, which was granted at 11:30.[7] It would still be necessary, however, to be able to take off safely to reach Petit-Thier, where the cavalrymen were ordered to go next.

The sector's weakness lay in Salmer Venn Wood, the edge of which was 350 metres from the village to the north. Captain North sent a patrol towards the northern corner of the wood, its aim being to enfilade the clearing behind it, which would make it possible to block this route of approach. The patrol was under the command of Lieutenant West

The shelling may have come from the Panzerjäger IVs on site. (*Nara*)

and consisted of the 14th CG's HQ Troop, with four light tanks, an assault gun and two halftracks equipped with .50s. The first light tank, commanded by Staff Sergeant Reeves, arrived at the corner of the wood at 11:40. Lieutenant West dismounted and headed south-west into the wood, along the edge of the forest. He soon came across Panzergrenadier, who pushed him back. At 12:00, a German attack began, and Reeves' tank was destroyed. Fifteen minutes later, the Germans bypassed the horsemen to the north and flanked the patrol. Meanwhile, an MG42 was brought into action and cut off the withdrawal route on the southern flank, but it was silenced by US fire support at 12:30. However, by this time the drama was over and only the assault gun, a light tank and a half-track had managed to escape.[8]

To the south-east of Poteau, the presence of Germans disguised as Americans caused concern. Sergeant Meyer of Troop C, 32nd CRS, was sent to reconnoitre with five men. The suspicious GIs were standing near an abandoned M8 assault gun south of the Recht road. As they approached, Meyer asked if they were Americans. '*Yes we are E Company*', came the strange reply, and the sergeant's suspicion grew, but he nevertheless continued to approach. When he was about 40 metres away, Meyer discovered that they were equipped with German weapons, and slowly backed away from what he now knew was a trap. The fake GIs threw themselves on the ground and started firing. Meyer returned fire, killing one and wounding another. Thanks to covering fire by his companions, the sergeant managed to retreat. He was later recommended for the Silver Star, having volunteered for the reconnaissance mission.

Similar half-tracks were sent to clear the woods in the northern sectors. (*Nara*)

The assault gun was an M8 light tank with a 75mm gun. It supported the attack ordered by Captain North. There are no photographs of the Poteau vehicle, which belonged to the 3rd Army operating further south. (*Nara*)

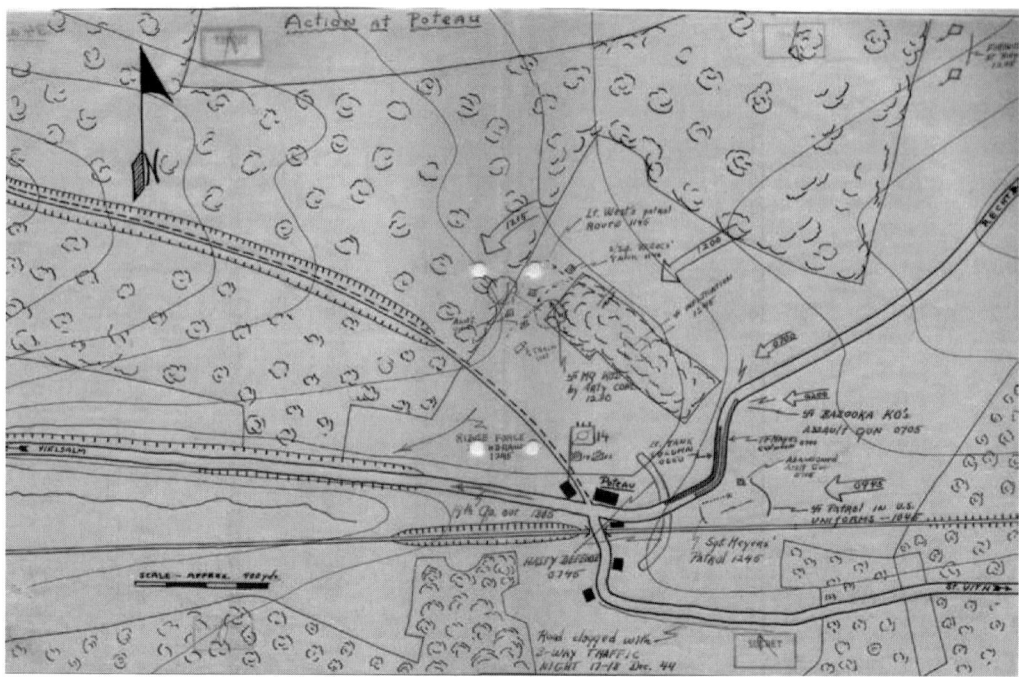

Tactical diagram taken from the report on the Poteau engagement. A second line of defence was established in front of the village. (*Nara*)

It was now 12:45 and first elements of the 14th CG began to withdraw. Bill Barton continues his account:

*Crawford arrived and ordered me to warn the inhabitants that we were leaving the village and that they should seek shelter in their cellars. I checked all the houses, only coming across a small group around a sick old man who wanted to die in his own bed. I returned to the barn to load a Jeep and a GMC with communications equipment and set off for Vielsalm. Shortly afterwards, having found an M1, I took up a position behind the crossroads to try to hinder enemy infiltration from the rear. Tanks were rolling along while two High Speed Tractors were trying to winch out two 8" howitzers. German fire began to fall on them killing seven gunners and forcing them to abandon their other eight guns.*

At 13:05, after a total of six hours of fighting, the rest of the cavalry group withdrew to Petit-Thier as ordered.

It was precisely after this skirmish and the loss of the hamlet of Poteau that the most famous newsreel sequence of the Battle of the Bulge was filmed. In propaganda images seen around the world, US tanks are shown on fire, with the SS sharing out American rations, in particular numerous packets of cigarettes. In the light of this photographic evidence, the disorganisation of the 14th CG seemed complete, despite the energy deployed by its acting commander, Colonel Dugan, to maintain cohesion. This hasty

The withdrawal of the 14th CG allowed the SS-Panzergrenadier to approach the destroyed American column. (*Nara*)

evacuation resulted in many losses of equipment, to the advantage of the enemy. The SS set fire to some of the vehicles to give the scene a more dramatic realism and erase the fact that it was shot after the event.

## Poteau Must Remain in US Hands

As the cavalrymen retreated in disorder, First Lieutenant Joseph 'Navajo' Whiteman of the 23rd AIB of the 7th AD decided to defend the village of Petit-Thier, where he was located, to prevent the divisional artillery from being completely overwhelmed. He rallied and galvanised all the fighters he could recover by setting up a barrage with half-tracks at the entrance to the village. He was soon joined by two M8 light tanks, two Dozer tanks and two Shermans belonging to his division's 31st TB. Eighty men from the 424th Infantry Division joined in. At the end of the day, the 'Navajo' Task Force, considerably reinforced by a platoon of tank destroyers and an engineer company, held Petit-Thier solidly, and it was this hamlet that would serve as a springboard for the recapture of the ridge.

As for the 14th CG, the three days of battle during which it had not been able to hold its positions and the battle fatigue of its main commanders did not speak in its favour. The 7th AD's AAR was laconic:

The SS Panzergrenadier advance towards Poteau. (*Nara*)

The area is temporarily relatively calm. This M8 is used as a makeshift shelter to take a breather. (*Nara*)

The SS Panzergrenadiers
redeploy southwards.
(*Nara*)

*The only other contact with Corps HQ was a visit to Division HQ by the Corps Deputy Chief of Staff on the afternoon of the 18th. At the time of his visit, the picture from the Corps' point of view was blurred. At 13:45, he informed the Divisional Commander that the 14th CG would be attached to the Division from 13:00. (This order was confirmed by a letter of instruction from VIII Corps HQ dated 18 December 1944.) It was immediately ordered to concentrate near Vielsalm, assemble its stragglers and reorganise as quickly as possible. It was in a state of extreme disorganisation and badly needed rest and a chance to regain its footing.*[9]

Lieutenant Colonel Dugan, who had shown great bravery in battle, was in turn relieved of his command, and the group was ordered to merge all its elements to form a Cavalry Recon Squadron.

## CC A to the Rescue

On the morning of the 18th, the 48th AIB, supported by Shermans from C Company, 40th TB, formed a task force to occupy Poteau. Colonel Rosembaum confirmed the instructions given:

> On the *night of 17 to 18 December 1944, my command post was in a house in Beho. On 17 December, I received orders to go to my divisional headquarters in Vielsalm. On arriving at divisional headquarters, I was ordered to move my CC from its position at Beho to a position covering the left flank of our division and to secure the Poteau Road junction. I moved my CC during daylight hours and took up a position to cover the left flank of our division.*[10]

Given the strategic importance of the Poteau crossroads for the defence of the northern sector of Saint-Vith, it could not remain in German hands. Hasbrouck therefore ordered Colonel Dwight Rosembaum's CC A to retake the village, and so at 10:00, the armoured brigade left its assembly area at Beho with the aim of retaking Poteau. At 11:45, a task force set off in column from Maldange with a section of Shermans in the lead, followed by a section from C Company, 48th AIB, then two others from C Company, 40th TB.

The 48th AIB heads for Poteau. (*Nara*)

The rest of the column was made up of the balance of C Company of the 48th AIB, A Company, the staff, and finally B Company, which closed the march. The column passed through Braunlauf, Crombach, Neundorf, Saint-Vith and Sart-Lez-Saint-Vith, from where it headed north-west towards Poteau, having established its command post in the village.

The attack did not get off to a good start, according to the Combat Interview with Lieutenant Reeves, leader of 1st Platoon, C Company, 40th TB:

The SS observed the arrival of the column of the 48th AIB from Poteau Wood. (*Nara*)

*The column passed through St Vith and headed west towards Poteau. Leading the column was the first platoon of C/40 in the following order: Sgt Truman L. Van Tine, Sgt Milan K. Alpeter, Lt Reeves, and Lt Gayle H. Spencer. When the lead tanks reached the clearing in the woods about 1,000 yards south of Poteau,[11] the column halted while the two lead tanks crossed the open space and reconnoitred ahead of them. As these tanks crossed the clearing, they came under fire from enemy self-propelled guns across the railway trench. None of the tanks was hit and they continued through the woods and into the open. As they came across open ground south of Poteau, the tanks received small arms fire from the houses near the bend south of the village.[12]*

*The tanks commanded by Van Tine and Alpeter withdrew into the woods and radioed the situation. Colonel Rosebaum then arrived at the head of the waiting column to assess the situation. He immediately ordered the C/48 to dismount and advance two platoons to the left to approach the southern edge of Poteau from the west. The remaining section of the C/40 was to move due north through the woods to the corner of the woods south-west of the town, where they were to establish a fire base. The infantry should radio as soon as they have a foothold in the town and the first tank platoon should dismount.*

*As the infantry advanced, Lieutenants Reeves and Spencer crossed the clearing and entered the woods to the west. At this point, however, Colonel Rosebaum's half-track was hit. When word came that the infantry had reached the edge of the town, Lieutenants Spencer and Van Tine moved their tanks towards the buildings on the edge of town. They discovered that only part of the infantry had reached these buildings. Lieutenant Spencer's tank took up position covering the west, while Van Tine crossed the road and covered the north and east. As Van Tine moved into position, he received bazooka fire from the house opposite (the one behind which Lieutenant Spencer had placed his tank). Lieutenant Spencer found himself facing a nest of MG 42s, which he quickly eliminated. Meanwhile, as Van Tine manoeuvred to take cover from the bazooka fire, his gun, rotating eastwards, hit a tree, temporarily immobilising his turret. At this point, he received a considerable amount of small arms fire from the house directly in front of him. Unable to get through the turret, Van Tine extricated himself from the tank, grabbed the 50-calibre machine gun and fired from the rear platform. He was almost immediately hit by a sniper. His driver, sensing that Van Tine was seriously wounded, reversed the tank and went to the rear to get medical assistance.*

*As Van Tine's tank returned to the road, Lieutenant Reeves and Sergeant Alpeter entered the town and fired cannon at the buildings. Shortly afterwards, Lieutenant James L. Sparing, leader of 2nd Platoon, brought his tank down to replace Van Tine.*

Orders were issued on the German side to hold firm to Poteau. (*Nara*)

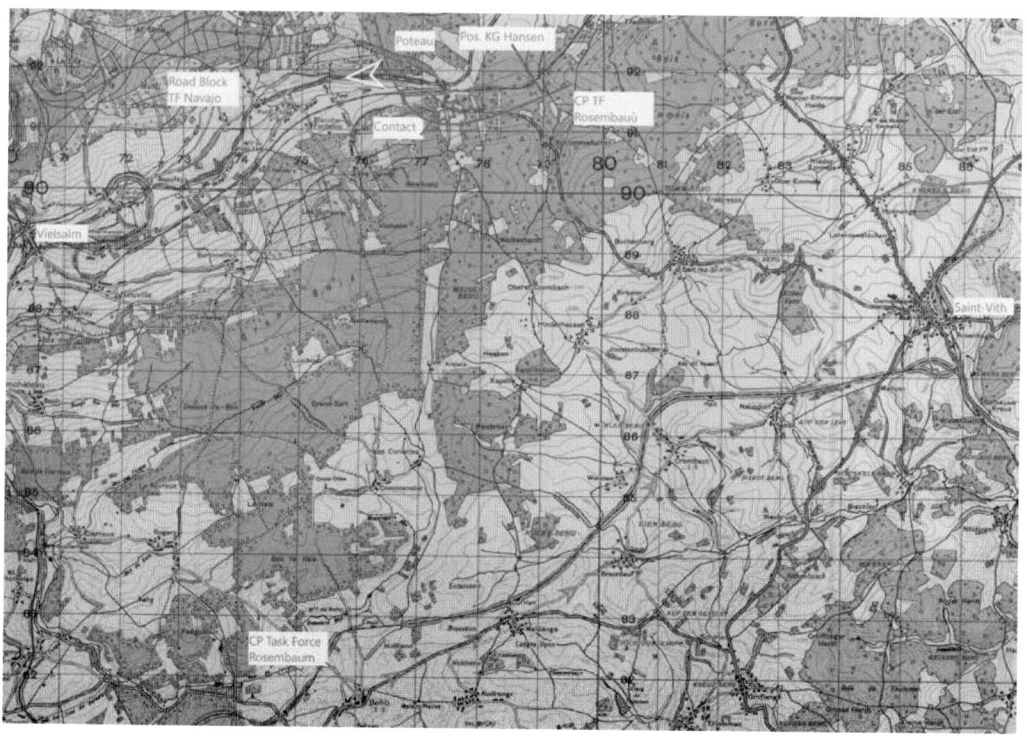

The Shermans of the 7th AD advanced in a column towards the objective. (*Nara*)

*Meanwhile, the infantry had been unable to advance because of intense machine gun fire from the edge of the woods to the south-west of their position. However, they were finally able to move around these positions and silence the machine guns. They then moved towards the buildings around which the tanks were huddled, and soon afterwards the sniper fire was silenced. The infantry quickly moved in around the tanks to provide them with the necessary protection for the approaching night.*

*At about the same time as the tanks moved into the southern end of Poteau, enemy guns (it is not known whether they were tanks or self-propelled guns) apparently moved their positions, and very soon afterwards the enemy began to fire large numbers of armour-piercing shells and machine gun bullets into the street of Poteau and the buildings at the southern end.*

*As soon as the C/40 had consolidated its positions around the tanks, the A/48 entered the town, but shortly afterwards received orders to move eastwards into the woods and then towards the canal where it was to establish its positions on the opposite bank. This move was successfully executed. The B/48 was then sent to link up with the right flank of the A/48. This line of infantry was to protect the column on the Sart-Lez-Saint-Vith*

The mechanised infantry dismounted to fight more effectively. (*Nara*)

*road*[13] *and act as a flank guard. Later, C/48 moved a platoon to the left of the road towards Poteau, at the edge of the woods, but to the south of the railway ditch.*[14] *During these movements the enemy fired some small arms fire across the tracks, and there was a continuous stream of fire down the street, but there were no major enemy attacks, nor any successful attempts to infiltrate the tank positions.*[15]

*German resistance was strong and by 15:30, CC A had still not retaken the village. At 16:00, the division commander sent a message to Colonel Rosembaum: 'It is imperative that you take Poteau tonight and hold it.' Rosembaum specified the location from which he commanded the battle: I established my command post at the farm about 3 miles from Poteau (where a stream crosses the Poteau – St. Vith road). I maintained my command post* [an old mill at a place called Schlommefurth] *here from 18 December until the afternoon of 21 December.*[16]

It was not until 17:00 that the crossroads was finally recaptured. An hour later, the infantry set up positions there and solid defensive measures were organised on the avenues approaching the town. However, no contact was yet established between CC A and CC R further west, and the road between Petit-Thier and Poteau was not safe as it was still under enemy fire.

Fatigue was beginning to show on the face of this SS-Panzergrenadier in Poteau. (*Nara*)

# A Red-Hot Sector

The following day, 19 December, German resistance in the sector continued to be fierce, carrying out numerous counterattacks on the village, which did not appear to be completely in American hands. Hasbrouck nevertheless asked CC A to prepare plans for an attack on Recht, as well as plans for a withdrawal via Petit-Thier and Vielsalm. Assault cannon, tank and artillery fire began to fall on the locality at 08:50. And at 11:00, a concentration of heavy artillery also fell on the village. However, the situation remained unchanged, and CC A continued to improve its positions, clearing the woods to the east in the afternoon and setting up roadblocks at Sart-Lez-Saint-Vith at 16:15. At 17:30, CC A was warned to expect friendly units from CC R coming from the west, and at 18:50 physical contact between the two CCs was effectively established.[17]

On 20 December, the Germans made another attempt to regain control of the crossroads. In his account of the events, Reeves says:

> *Enemy assault guns continued to fire on the four tanks of C Coy of the 40th TB in Poteau. In fact, the enemy was making the situation so hot that the tanks could not move except at night. During the morning rumours spread that an enemy attack was imminent. Shortly*

The Germans defended the road to Recht and the village of Poteau. (*Nara*)

Some of the fighters are seen here dressed very lightly for the rigours of the climate. The cold had just set in, and the next few days would be freezing. (*Nara*)

*afterwards, the infantry officer on the top floor of one of the buildings saw five enemy tanks coming round the hill on the road to Recht. Sergeant Alpeter's tank was the only one able to fire, but the rest of the company, in position in the woods, were able to engage the enemy, and a total of four enemy tanks were captured before the others fled. Sergeant Edward L. Burris shot three of them. Other tanks were hidden behind the crest of the hill but did not venture forward.*[18]

These tanks supported the Aufklärungs-Abteilung of the 9. SS-Panzer-Division 'Hohenstauffen', which had just joined the I. SS-Panzer-Korps and was given the task of advancing towards Vielsalm to help KG Peiper, which had run out of fuel at La Gleize.[19] The Hohenstauffen only managed to bring a Grenadier regiment into the Recht sector, having arrived on foot due to a lack of fuel and been accompanied by an armoured battalion. It was only able to set off again after siphoning off the tanks of all the division's

All day on 20 December, fighting continued for the recapture of Poteau. (*Nara*)

other motorised vehicles. At first, its push towards Vielsalm made good progress, but the assault was cut short in the woods east of Poteau when the infantry was attacked vigorously and had to withdraw. In reality, the Panzers were of no help, being only able to manoeuvre on the road, which was constantly under flanking fire from American units to the south.[20]

On the night of 20 to 21 December, C Company, 48th AIB, moved down the road towards Poteau. The GIs saw that the enemy had abandoned the town, leaving only a house full of civilians and an SS soldier in civilian clothes. The civilians themselves hung the white flags as the Americans entered the town. The four tanks from C Company, 40th TB went into action and crossed the bridge at around 03:20. The men of the C/48 were in position about 150-200 metres in front of the tanks. During the day, a large amount of abandoned American equipment was brought out of Poteau by salvage units, including eight 8″ guns, jeeps, trucks, etc. Curiously, the Germans had not destroyed this equipment before withdrawing from the town.

Later that day, the armoured infantry was given permission to occupy the crest of the hill to the north of Poteau to hold the ground above the village. One section reached

When the SS withdrew, they did not take the precaution of destroying their equipment. (*Nara*)

341639

the top of the hill and surprised a group of Germans in American uniform. However, shortly afterwards, this section was itself surprised by a large German patrol and forced to withdraw down the hill. At the end of the morning, five more tanks from C Company, 40th TB, left their entrenched positions in the woods and arrived at Poteau, completely opening the road to Vielsalm. During the evening and night, little activity was reported in the town, but in the woods, the enemy bypassed Poteau from the south and attacked the original American positions. At least one German tank crossed the forest west of Poteau and moved up the road from Sart-Lez-Saint-Vith to Poteau. These elements were accompanied by infantry, who attacked the last three US tanks left in the woods. Two Shermans were damaged and attacked, with the crews being forced to withdraw. Captain Nelson, the company commander, returned to Poteau and was the last tank to leave the wood, and the Panzers then occupied the dug-in positions previously occupied by the American tanks. The town of Saint-Vith had meanwhile fallen into German hands as the American withdrawal towards Vielsalm was organised.

## The Führer Begleit Brigade on the Attack

The following day, 22 December, the pressure was stepped up on the defenders of the crossroads and, by extension, on those of CC A. However, Hasbrouck insisted that the positions be maintained, and that control of the Poteau – Vielsalm road be maintained at all costs. Of course, the Germans in the opposing camp would have none of it. This time, it was Oberst Otto Remer's Führer Belgleit Brigade that was in charge. The strike force assembled was considerable. The day before, the Nazi officer had taken up position at Nieder-Emmels, 7 kilometres east of Poteau and only 3 kilometres as the crow flies from Sart-Lez-Saint-Vith[21] on the road from Saint-Vith to Poteau. The location was ideal for an armoured assault as the terrain was mainly pasture and only a wooded ridge blocked the road, which had the advantage of masking the Germans' approach. Remer was going to be able to manoeuvre and he knew it. His armoured regiment was equipped with Panzer IVs, StuGs and a handful of Jagdpanzer IVs, meaning he was therefore more or less on an equal footing with the Shermans, but he also had the advantage of numbers. The aim of his assault was twofold. Taking Poteau would be too costly, and his tanks would have to approach from the east along a road under fire from American tanks. He did not want to repeat the mistake of Hohenstauffen and so he decided to cut the Poteau – Saint-Vith road and try to find a path through the woods to bypass Poteau to the south.

At 08:30, one of his infantry companies surrounded the position of B Company, 38th AIB. Remer learned that the road was heavily used and managed to capture seven American officers and, above all, their precious jeeps. The Grenadiers managed to infiltrate to 2 kilometres north of Commanster, nearly 5 kilometres east of Sart-Lez-Saint-Vith, without finding a road that could be used by their Panzers. It was a dead end and Remer's men turned back.

They had not gone unnoticed, however, and the Americans reacted accordingly. C Company, 38th AIB was instructed to move nearby to the slope west of Schlommefurth

Although the ambush on the road from Poteau to Recht was a tactical success, the SS Panzergrenadiers were unable to convert the attempt. The Poteau outlets remained in American hands. (*Nara*)

The FBB soldiers attacked south of Poteau through the woods to find a possible route to Saint-Vith. (*Nara*)

and patrol the wooded area to the north and east. A platoon from B Company, 40th TB, was sent to the vicinity of Sart-Lez-Saint-Vith to repel German infiltration south of the town, and the Shermans began their engagement from the north-east of the sector at 09:45. Remer then received the opposite order: to take Sart-Lez-Saint-Vith and push westwards to block the US lines of communication between Saint-Vith and Vielsalm. As it fell back, the vanguard of the Führer Begleit Brigade came across an American artillery position at Hinderhausen. A furious battle ensued, but the Germans managed to return to Sart-Lez-Saint-Vith. However, they lost a precious booty when they were forced to return the twelve American jeeps they had captured in order to motorise the Führer Begleit Brigade's cycle reconnaissance battalion. Remer reorganised his troops, forming three Kampfgruppen around his three infantry battalions. One battalion, reinforced by twenty-five Panzers, was to attack north of Sart-Lez-Saint-Vith, where Rosembaum's CC A HQ was located. A second Kampfgruppe, also supported by Panzers, would approach Sart-Lez-Saint-Vith from the east. Between these two armoured Kampfgruppen, a third made up entirely of infantrymen attacked the village from the north.

At 11:00, the battle began. A platoon from B Company, 40th TB, and a platoon from A Company engaged sixteen Panzers in the vicinity. The tank destroyers were requested as

Civilians had to leave Sart-Lez-Saint-Vith, which had been devastated by the fighting. (*Nara*)

North of Poteau, the SS had to hold their positions. (*Nara*)

Poteau was a success that destroyed the cohesion of the 14th CG. (*Nara*)

reinforcements. Near Rosenbaum's HQ, the area of the vehicles of C Company, 48th AIB, was infiltrated by Remer's KG North, and the Panzer units of KG South eventually gained control of Sart-Lez-Saint-Vith. A message from the division announced a strong enemy attack to the south-west of the village and asked CC A to take steps to delay the flank of the enemy advance. Inside and to the north-west of Sart-Lez-Saint-Vith, the company platoon and the two Sherman platoons were still holding out, causing heavy losses to the KG in the centre. The latter, which had no armoured vehicles, was unable to assert itself. However, the vehicles of B Company and the 48th AIB train were destroyed by the northern KG. The remaining vehicles were withdrawn to Petit-Thier, 4 kilometres to the west on the road to Vielsalm. CC A's plan was to establish a new line from Poteau southwards for 2 kilometres from 16:45. Rosembaum's CC A evacuated his base from 16:30 to set up in Petit-Thier.[22]

South of the post, eight Panzer tanks from KG North approached this time. When these tanks came into sight, they were the target of combined Sherman fire. The US tankers claimed to have destroyed four of them, while the others withdrew behind the crest of the hill, but reappeared from time to time to harass the defenders. At this point, the American tankers began to run out of ammunition, and the available shells were redistributed between the machines so that each tank had an equal quantity. Withdrawal plans were now being drawn up and the infantry had to withdraw under a barrage of smoke. As the tanks began to pull back, the German infantry approached from the north. But a barrage of smoke and artillery fire held them back until the rearguard of CC A had successfully withdrawn to Vielsalm.[23] Poteau finally fell into German hands after five days of fierce fighting. Yet the fall of the crossroads was of little importance, as the 7th AD and its attached units had already evacuated Saint-Vith.

## Chapter 8

# A Dark Day for the US Army

### German Pressure Intensifies

During the night of 18 to 19 December, both sides tested their positions with sustained patrols. The crossroads were systematically shelled by the German artillery in order to hinder the movements in the pocket forming around Saint-Vith as much as possible. The northern flank, held by CC B of the 7th AD, was subjected

Two regimental combat teams were surrounded in the Schnee Eifel. Each regiment of the 106th ID was supported by a battalion of 105mm artillery. (*Nara*)

The Volksgrenadier gradually increased their pressure towards Saint-Vith. (*Private collection*)

The 7th AD held its positions firmly, but its losses were mounting. This medic is providing first aid to an armoured infantryman wounded by a bullet to the upper part of his left arm. (*Nara*)

to several attacks by KG Hansen, composed mainly of the SS-Panzer-Grenadiere Regiment 1. The SS tried to identify weak points in the US position, but without any convincing success and were relieved in the afternoon by SS-Aufklärung-Abteilung 9 of the 9 SS-Panzer-Division under Hauptsturmführer Recke. It was Recke who attempted to take Poteau on 19 December, but who also failed in the face of American tenacity and instead decided to dig in and wait for the rest of his division. The delay was used by the

CC R of the 7th AD, located to the west in the village of Petit-Thier, to reorganise by incorporating the remnants of the 14th CG. Together they formed Task Force Wanke and protected the north-western flank between Poteau and the River Salm. It was extended eastwards by CC A, which still held Poteau firmly. The east and south of Saint-Vith were held by the 7th and 9th AD CC Bs respectively. The system was flexible and the two commanding generals coordinated their efforts in the sector, with General Hoge having this to say on the subject:

> *At 12:15, opposite my CC B, 9th AD, an infantry and armoured attack was being prepared. Even before it started, we managed to neutralise three panzers, which aborted the attempt. During the afternoon I went to Crombach to discuss with General Bruce C. Clarke about the vulnerability of my positions along the river and railway. If St. Vith fell, we would be cut off, as there was no way back except through here. General Robert W. Hasbrouck had given us carte blanche, so Bruce and I teamed up without trying to find out who was in command. By mutual agreement, we drew up a plan to be executed by nightfall. Just as the move began, a weak attack was launched against our right wing. It was neutralised by mortar, tank and cannon fire. By 24:00 my CC was in its new positions between the 424th Infantry Regiment to the south around Maspelt and CC B, 7th AD to the north. The infantry moved into the centre of our new sector, with part of my 14th TB on either side. The valley running south to the edge of the town was the boundary between our Combat Commands. We were both convinced that this area was particularly exposed and decided to place a platoon of tank destroyers there. My command post was at Neubrück, 2 miles from St. Vith, on the road to Grufflange. Throughout the battle, there was very close liaison and excellent cooperation between us.*[1]

## Golden Lions Attempt Breakthrough in Schönberg

With the German pressure on the 7th AD's position increasing, Jones had no other solution to save his two encircled regiments than to order them to reach Saint-Vith by their own means by attacking Schönberg from the east. The two regiments occupied a position 10 kilometres east of Saint-Vith on the heights of the Schnee Eifel. The American battalions were deployed along the road from Bleialf to Auw. The 422nd RCT occupied the northern wing near Schlaussenbach, while the 423rd RCT was in the south around Buchet. Colonel Descheneaux, in command of the 422nd RCT, was ordered to attempt the breakthrough during the night. When he learned of this instruction, the officer sobbed and expressed his thoughts in these terms: '*My poor soldiers, they are going to be cut to pieces.*' The 423rd RCT was ordered to withdraw at 07:30 on the morning of the 18th, the orders having been issued by 106th ID headquarters at 02:15. Their intentions were clear: '*A panzer regiment combat group is occupying the Schönberg – Saint-Vith road. Mission: to destroy it by fire from buried positions south of the Schönberg – Saint-Vith road. Ammunition, food and water will be dropped. When the mission is accomplished, move towards Saint-Vith.*'[2]

The infantrymen of the 106th ID were ordered to attempt a breakthrough. (*Nara*)

Schönberg was firmly held by the 18. VGD. (*Nara*)

The orders were certainly intelligible, apart from the fact that an attack on Schönberg from the south had become impossible – the village was solidly held to the south by GR 293 and to the north by GR 295 of the 18. VGD.

At 09:00 on 18 December, orders to withdraw towards Schönberg were issued to the three battalions of the 422nd RCT. The units were to move on foot, take their heavy weapons and all the food and ammunition they could carry, and destroy the rest of their equipment with as little noise as possible. The II/422nd RCT had to go first, the I/422nd

At 09:00 on 18 December, the orders to withdraw towards Schönberg were distributed to the three battalions of the 422nd RCT. (*Nara*)

The columns of the 106th ID set off to extract themselves from the cauldron. (*Nara*)

The Germans were waiting with bated breath for the GIs. (*Nara*)

RCT followed, and finally the III/422nd RCT closed the march; a logical order insofar as the lines of the III/422nd RCT formed a screen to protect the withdrawal of the other two. Orders were distributed by carrier to prevent the Germans from realising too quickly that the GIs were listening in on radio transmissions. Even the telephone lines were considered insecure because of intrusions into the wire network during the previous twenty-four hours. The II/422nd IR picked up in time but missed the I/422nd which followed, thus creating a gap in the lines. The III/422nd stalled behind the II/422nd, leaving the I/422nd at the rear of the column. The movement proceeded very slowly as no reconnaissance of the withdrawal route had been carried out, so map adjustments were multiplied to avoid getting lost.[3] The units then regrouped to attack Schönberg, which was the only possible withdrawal route.

The instructions given to the battalions of Colonel Cavender's 423rd RCT were similar. They were to set off at 10:00 in the direction of Schönberg, leaving some covering forces behind. The guns of the 590th FAB were to follow in quick succession. The withdrawal took place in good order until the approach to the Bleialf – Radscheid road at around midday. The 18. VGD was determined not to let the GIs out of the trap in which it had cornered them, and so Cavender's battalions came under heavy fire and attacked, only to be halted 800 metres further on.[4]

Further north, battalions of the 422nd RCT prepared to storm Schönberg. The village was just as vital for the Allies as it was for von Manteuffel, with the latter perfectly aware that the encircled regiments would try to rally their lines via the village, which he now held firmly. The position awaiting the GIs was a veritable mousetrap: armoured vehicles and anti-aircraft machine guns were set up in the woods, at a bend in the road, to catch the infantrymen who had to cross the road in enfilade during their dispersed advance towards the hamlet. The GIs were completely unaware of the German set-up.

In the early afternoon, the three battalions prepared to assault Schönberg, I/ on the right wing, II/ in the centre and III/ on the left, where it tried to maintain contact with the 423rd RCT. The direction of the attack was supposed to follow the north-west axis until about 1,000 metres from Schönberg, when it was to change direction and attack to the west. I/422nd 's mission was to cross the Schönberg – Andler road and attack to the south-west. The attack zone was bounded on the left by the same road and on the right by the River Auw. In the event of the III/422nd being pincered by the 423rd IR attacking to the south, it would follow the II/422nd and be ready to attack in the area of the other two battalions.

The battalions had to move individually across the terrain, using their compasses to guide them to the final assembly areas. There were frequent stops to allow the patrols to search the front area for enemies before moving on, thus giving the men, who were exhausted, a chance to rest. Since the start of the march, they had been carrying their heavy weapons and all the ammunition they could carry, and although they were tired, cold, and hungry, their morale and their spirits were high.

It was around midnight when the battalions finally arrived at their starting points for the assault on Schönberg. The companies were allocated sectors, and each was responsible

The GIs ready for action. (*Nara*)

for its own. As this patch of woodland was very small, barely big enough for a company to spread out, let alone a battalion, there was no difficulty in coordinating security. No foxholes were dug, as the men were too tired to undertake the excavations, so they slept on the ground without any protection. The size of the area left little room for dispersal and instead the men huddled together. The battalions were on their own and fought independently, with no communication between each other or with the regiment. The order to attack was given at around 00.45: the attack on Schönberg was to begin at 07:30 on 19 December, and the battalions were ordered to seize this part of Schönberg in their departure zone and continue the attack south towards Saint-Vith.

In the I/422nd, the attack took place in column by companies. The attack was to head north-east until the leading elements crossed the Schönberg – Auw road, then southeast towards Schönberg itself. The II/422nd was on the left of the I/422nd. The men were warned to use the little food and water they still had sparingly, as there were no supplies left at the time.

After coordinating, the two battalions went on the attack as ordered at 07:30. C Company of the I/422nd came out of the woods, its leading elements advancing about 400 metres before they were blocked by machine gun and rifle fire from a house about 150 metres to their right. D Company's machine gun section was positioned at the edge of the wood and opened fire on the house. The enemy fire stopped and a dozen German soldiers came out of the house and disappeared on a ridge to the rear. C Company, meanwhile, continued to advance.

On the left, the II/422nd also attacked and advanced towards an open ditch on its front. This trench was quite deep, providing good cover on the flanks. No shots were fired during this initial phase and it was only when C Company resumed its advance that the II/422nd came under enemy fire. The US battalion nevertheless managed to clear Skyline Drive, a road running north to east from Radscheid. At this point, the leading elements of C Company crossed the road and contacted the II/422nd. The C Company commander, using his SCR 300 radio, reported to the I/422nd commander that he had contacted the 2nd Battalion and was continuing his advance.

The last elements of C Company had just left the assault zone when four German tanks came down Skyline Drive on its right flank and opened fire on the rest of the I/422nd in the wood. The GIs were caught off guard, having not bothered to dig in. They were huddled together because of the smallness of the wood, which served as an assembly area. In view of this situation, the officers decided to withdraw their companies and try to advance to the junction that the II/422nd had taken. This option had the advantage of providing good cover and more space for dispersal.

The battalion, minus C Company, withdrew and began to advance along the ditch. The lead elements had just crossed Skyline Drive when tanks arrived from behind and opened fire. The tanks on the right flank moved down the road and opened fire from the right flanks. A section of heavy machine guns from D Company moved into position and began firing at the infantry accompanying the tanks. They fired for around thirty seconds before being neutralised by Panzer fire. A rocket launcher team, with only two rounds

A Stug intervenes along the road that the Golden Lions have to cross. (*Nara*)

The US machine guns were brought into action to support the attempted breakthrough. (*Nara*)

of ammunition, tried to get into firing position but was immediately neutralised by the tanks. The riflemen returned fire as best they could, but their small arms were no match for the Panzer. The exchange of fire continued for around twenty minutes and caused many casualties. The carnage would have continued until the entire battalion was wiped out if someone had not waved a white handkerchief and started walking towards the tanks. The firing slowed down, and more men surrendered. The battalion commander and his staff fled via Skyline Drive. They were captured two days later defending another small patch of woodland with the remnants of several other units.[5]

In the wake of the first regiment's surrender, events began to take their toll on the infantrymen of the 423rd RCT, commanded by Colonel Cavender. Ammunition ran out just as quickly and the situation became desperate. There was nothing more to be done and Cavender ordered them to lay down their arms at 16:30. That day, around 3,000 GIs surrendered to the Germans, one of the most bitter defeats suffered by the American army in the Western European theatre of operations and the biggest mass surrender of the campaign, with Major General Jones being unfairly blamed for the surrender of his

Only a few soldiers managed to get out of the pocket, and were clearly severely affected by the fighting of the last few days. (*Nara*)

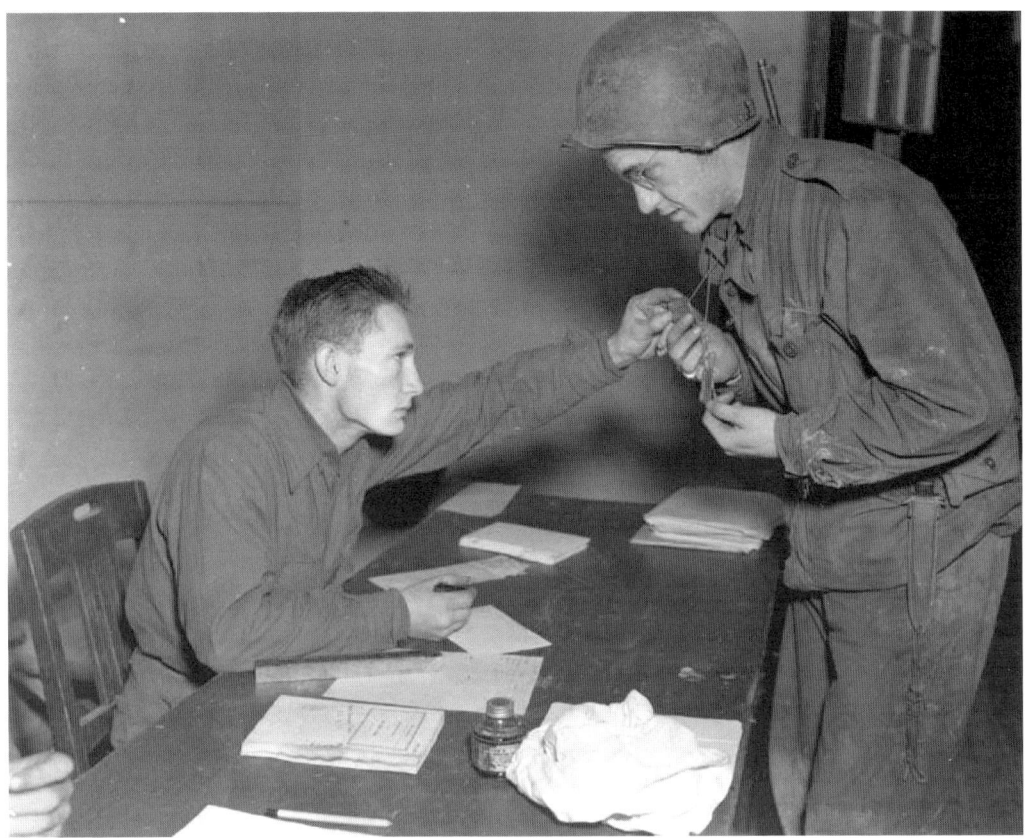

GIs from the 106th ID who joined their lines were carefully screened to prevent German spies from joining the ranks. The psychosis of Skorzeny's men was everywhere. (*Nara*)

two regiments. Five hundred men under the command of Major Ouellette held out until the morning of 21 December, but only seventy men managed to reach the Allied lines.

The cleaning of the pocket was mainly carried out by GR 293 of the 18. VGD. In the eyes of the Germans, the American resistance did not deserve much praise:

*Gradually, enemy resistance eased, and the groups surrounded in the Schnee Eifel surrendered. The men of the division's school unit broke through enemy lines on the Schnee Eifel ridges and began to sweep away resistance in the hills. Curiously, the enemy continued to show little initiative. The lingering impression was that the Americans, having been cut off from the rear, regarded further effort as hopeless. An inspection of enemy positions in the Schnee Eifel showed clearly that, despite the valour of the individual soldier, the Americans were fighting a rich man's war. Weapons and equipment were excellent, each improvised bunker had its own telephone and cooking facilities, while officers' suitcases contained uniforms for the Sunday walk.*[6]

## German Efforts Converge on Saint-Vith

On the German side, 19 December was reserved for preparations for the attack on Saint-Vith itself. No progress had been made against the American positions defending the town. The results that von Manteuffel had expected from his peak attack proved disappointing, as the infantrymen were not supported by their own heavy weapons, artillery or assault guns, while the Prümerberg road was firmly held.[7] The Americans were nevertheless feeling the pressure of the LXVI AOK. The AAR of the 7th AD stated:

> *At 09:30 on 19 December, an attack developed against CC B north of Hunningen. The attack moved west and then turned south. Shooting was difficult because of the fog, but by 13:00 the situation had calmed down. At 13:55, 17th TB and C Company of the*

The two American CCBs defending the east of Saint-Vith rearranged their positions with agility. M36 TDs took part in the action. (*Nara*)

*38th AIB, which were still south-east of Recht, were attached to CC B. At the same time, CC B was ordered to defend an area between CC B of the 9th AD on the right and the Recht – Sart-Lez-Saint-Vith road on the left. At 15:10, the 434th AFAB and two batteries of the 965th FAB were attached to CC B and moved into position. The only artillery support on 18 and 19 December, before the arrival of the 434th AFAB, was the 275th AFAB. The Corps artillery observers had left on the night of 17-18 December.*[8]

Two things should be remembered from this report. The first was that CC B of the 7th AD was tightening its forces in an arc facing west. Secondly, it received artillery

The medical teams did not evacuate the men from Hasnrouck who had been treated and were able to return to combat. The mission of the medical jeeps was to collect the wounded from the company dispensaries and transport them to the field medical facilities. (*Nara*)

support that would help it hold its positions. Lieutenant Colonel Robert C. Erlenbusch, CO of the 31st TB, described the brutality of the fighting and the feeling of pressure that must have been instilled in the US ranks the night before the assault on 19 December:

*Throughout the night of 18 to 19 December, from Recht, Born, Wallerode or Steinebrück, we heard the arrival of the enemy's reinforcements. He began to seriously harass the roads and crossroads, not only with his mortars but also, and this was the first time, with his artillery. He launched two night attacks, with infantry and armour, against the northern flank of CC B, apparently in the hope of capturing Hünningen. Both were repulsed by combined fire from the 31st TB, Armoured-Cars and small assault guns of the 87th CRS. Again, at 09:30, in successive waves, more than 500 infantrymen, supported by five tanks, rushed towards Hünningen, hoping to envelop the left flank of Bruce C. Clarke's left flank. Finally, at 13:00, they withdrew, leaving 150 corpses and one Panzer in flames. The other four, although damaged, managed to withdraw towards Nieder-Emmels. During the following night, a patrol of thirty-five men reached Neundorf, where the rear command post of my battalion was located. After brief but violent hand-to-hand combat, fifteen Germans had their throats cut and five were captured, while one of our men was seriously wounded and had to be evacuated and three others, after being bandaged, resumed their work.*[9]

In von Manteuffel's eyes, the situation remained very complicated, even though he no longer had the thorn in his side represented by the two regiments of the 106th ID that had just surrendered. The successes achieved by his 5. Panzer-Armee were impossible to exploit because of the huge traffic jam in Schönberg. In addition, the inexperience of the junior officers of the Volksgrenadier had disastrous consequences. The fighters stayed on the roads without trying to outflank their opponents through the woods, thus allowing the Americans to score some fine defensive successes. Passing through Heuem and the road branching off to the east of Wallerode-Mühle, von Manteuffel noticed at the end of the morning that only small sections of the FBB had reached the assembly area for the attack in the forest south of Medell, and therefore ordered that the attack be postponed until 20 December.[10]

## The CC B of the 9th AD Withdraws

In the 9th AD CC B sector, it became clear that a major attack was being prepared. On the afternoon of 19 December, a conference was held between the commanding generals of CC B of the 9th AD and the 7th AD. During this conference, it became clear that the position of CC B of the 9th AD was dangerous. It occupied a sector in front of the stream and a railway line to the south of Saint-Vith and its only possible exit was through the town. If Saint-Vith fell, this armoured brigade would be cut off from the world, so it was therefore agreed between Hoge and Clarke that CC B of the 9th AD would withdraw through Saint-Vith on the night of 19 to 20 December and occupy its

The Shermans of the various tank battalions involved in the Battle of Saint-Vith were a real powerhouse, working at full capacity. (*Nara*)

original zone behind the railway line and the stream running south of the town. This withdrawal was completed without difficulty,[11] with the two general officers cooperating admirably; a mutual respect seeming to exist between the two men.

The American withdrawal was the only success von Manteuffel was able to report on the evening of 19 December. He explained:

Many Stug IIIs were found in the Saint-Vith area after the battle. Without the presence of these machines, it is very likely that the tragedy of Saint-Vith would never have happened. (*Nara*)

*The enemy evacuated Gross Langenfeld during the night. GR 190 reached Dreihütten. The regiment on the left captured Elcherath and Hemmeres and crossed the Our near Steinebrück; it then advanced as far as Lommersweiler. According to divisional reports, at Brüssel Berg American tanks appeared for the first time in the defence of Steinebrück and enemy artillery and mortar fire was also stronger than in previous days. These weapons seemed to be near Grüfflingern and south of Neidingen. Contact with the 18. VGD was established at Setz. In addition to the bridge over the Our (now destroyed), the division intended to build an emergency bridge near Steinebrücke station, which was completed on 20 December.*

*To support the neighbouring corps on the left (LVI Panzer Corps), the 62. VGD was ordered to attack on 20 December through Grüfflingen towards Maldingen to block the St. Vith – Beho-Gouvy road. I thought that the abandonment of the attack on St. Vith, which was because this division had not attacked in the direction of Neundorf as previously ordered, would justify the risk in view of the reports and my own impressions of the enemy, namely that the combat effectiveness of the Führer Begleit Brigade would be quite adequate to support the attack of the 18. VGD. Moreover, the attack of the 62. VGD against Maldingen created favourable conditions for the continuation of the attack after the capture of St. Vith towards the crossing of the River Salm. Apart from the 62. VGD,*

'The plan is to eat away at their armour, stopping it with massive artillery support and then knocking out the Jerries' tanks at short range with our Shermans…' (Nara)

*the result on 19 December in this corps sector was disappointing overall. I mentioned that the enemy had taken advantage of this to strengthen their position near St. Vith. In my opinion, the lack of success was not so much due to the enemy's strength in numbers and equipment, but rather to the fact that neither on 18 December nor on 19 December did we manage to pull together from the attack and obtain the combined use of all forces in this sector. The conduct of the Panzer forces was excellent.*[12]

By the evening of the 19th, Saint-Vith was still in Allied hands. They had just received a reinforcement that would prove to be of vital importance for the future: the divisional artillery was now at work in the salient. The batteries of the 434th AFAB, equipped with 105mm guns, together with two other armies of 155mm howitzers from the 965th FAB, were to prove highly effective against the Panzers. Lieutenant Colonel Richard Chappins commanding the 48th AIB described the tactics to be employed in a very colourful way: '*The plan is to nibble away at their armour, stopping it with massive artillery support and then knocking out the Jerries' short-range tanks with our Shermans.*'

## An All-out Defence

Meanwhile, the 7th AD received all sorts of reports indicating that the enemy was advancing on all sides of its position. The I. SS-Panzer-Korps was advancing to the north, its leading edge, KG Peiper, having crossed Stavelot and passed Trois-Ponts, with the remainder of the 1. SS-Panzer-Division Leibstandarte Adolf Hitler following in its footsteps. The enemy was also reported in force to the south, at Houffalize, La Roche-en-Ardenne, Samrée and to the south-east, east and north-east of Saint-Vith. The town was not yet encircled, but a continuous defence in all directions was necessary to monitor the division's lines of communication. Saint-Vith had become a stronghold.

As a result, A Company, 33rd AEB, and D Company, 40th TB – elements of CC A that had hitherto been left on the southern flank – were ordered, shortly after daybreak, to take the Cherain and Gouvy outposts. At Gouvy, they found an army rations depot containing 50,000 rations that had just been set on fire by army quartermaster personnel to prevent its capture by the enemy, who were already threatening with small arms fire. D Company, 40th TB, repelled the assault and extinguished the fire, which had caused little damage, and began distributing rations to all the division's units. At Gouvy, the 7th AD also came across an abandoned enclosure containing more than 700 German POWs, guarded only by an officer and eight military policemen. These prisoners were successfully evacuated by the division.

D Troop of the 87th CRS was relieved of all missions in favour of CC A at 08:00 and was ordered to move immediately to Salmchâteau, then west, dividing into two columns to the north-west at the points with the mission of protecting the division's northern flank in its rear up to the general line Basse-Bodeux – Vaux Chavanne until relieved on orders or until repulsed by enemy action. To replace D Troop of the 87th CRS in the south-east, Task Force Lindsey was created from the 14th CG, consisting

Saint-Vith became a stronghold. This mortar team belonged to the 106th ID. (*Nara*)

Gouvy was occupied in force. This photograph was taken there on 21 December. These civilians improvised a stretcher to evacuate soldiers killed in the fighting. (*Nara*)

Task forces were created to plug the holes and try to create a relatively watertight defensive system. These US fighters are preparing to leave on missions. (*Nara*)

of eleven armoured vehicles, eleven light tanks, six assault guns and 236 men. It was placed in positions at Gruflingen, Thommen and Espelier with the task of protecting the division's south-eastern flank. In assigning this position to Task Force Lindsey, the divisional commander had in mind the problem of the lack of depth of the defensive position of the 424th RCT, the last regimental combat team of the 106th ID to be able to fight in the east.

Two other security groups, Task Force Hawks and Task Force Wanke, were formed from the 14th CG. The first, with five light tanks, a reconnaissance team and thirty men, set up a roadblock at Bovigny, far to the rear, and the second, with vehicles and eighty men, was attached to CC R for additional security on the northern flank between Poteau and Vielsalm. In addition to the above, a section of destroyer tanks with a reconnaissance section was sent out at 10:30 to eliminate an enemy tank reported to be harassing traffic at Houffalize. This force, however, met an unfortunate fate; not only did they fail to find the enemy tank, but on their return, they were ambushed at Sommerain and lost a tank destroyer, three jeeps, two officers and five GIs.[13]

## Lost Children as Back-up

Another major reinforcement now joined the defenders of Saint-Vith: the 112th RCT belonging to the 28th ID, from which it had been cut off in the early days of the German attack. Like the rest of the American front line, the GIs of the 112th IR were attacked on 16 December from their positions to the north of their division when the 116. Panzer-Division broke through to the south of their sector and isolated them from the rest of their division. On 17 December, the 112th IR was ordered to withdraw northwards to hold a defensive position along the west bank of the Our between Beiler and Weiswampach. It held this position all day on 18 December, but the sector was far from calm and the Germans tried to sweep them away. Early in the morning of 19 December, under cover of thick fog, the infantry regiment and its artillery battalion set off in good order for Huldange, without encountering any opposition from the enemy. The III/112th IR took up position there around noon and by 13:30, all its elements were in place. During the afternoon, an infantry attack was repulsed with virtually no casualties. One of L Company's sergeants recounted the skirmish:

*The company left at 13:30 and marched to woods outside Huldange where defensive positions were set up. The company ran out of ammunition and patrols were sent out. One patrol entered Huldange. There were three of us on the patrol that went into Huldange: Staff Sergeant Eipperdan, Staff Sergeant Delvis and me. We went to see if there were any Boche in or near the town. A woman beckoned us into her house, and we were sceptical about going in, but we decided to see what she wanted. Two of us went in to investigate, with Sergeant Davis providing cover. The woman seemed friendly, but her sinister words made us wary. I interpreted the French she spoke. She told us there were no Germans around, only an enemy tank she had seen two days ago. She then asked us if we wanted to eat and placed the most delicious roast duck dinner imaginable in front of us. We were starving and almost tempted to accept when suddenly Sergeant Delvis asked us to run away. He had seen a child running down the hill in front of the house. We took off immediately and just in time. No sooner had we reached our positions than a company of the enemy arrived in column of twos, led by two civilians who indicated our positions. All hell broke loose and our anti-tank guns, which were in position to the rear, opened fire in force directly at the centre of the column. From where we were, we could hear the screams of the wounded and see them scattered in a hedge. Staff Sergeant Peik then called in the artillery and targeted it perfectly. The shells formed a perfect frame at the end of the hedge and then formed an equally perfect frame going down the hedge. And that was the end of that company of Boche. When the operation was over, the three of us looked at*

A regiment of 28th ID was isolated in the snow a few kilometres south of the 106th ID sector. They were going to provide sub-total reinforcement to the defenders of Saint-Vith. (*Nara*)

The movement orders were greeted with relief by the men of the 112th IR. (*Nara*)

*each other, completely stunned, and congratulated ourselves on not having stayed for the duck dinner.*[14]

It is clear from this account that the soldiers were starving; they had been on the front line for three days without supplies. At around 14:00, Colonel Gustin Nelson, in command of the regiment, received the order to return to the positions he had occupied the day before! He described his reaction to this counter-order:

*Faced with this flagrant contradiction, I took the bull by the horns and drove to Vielsalm to meet General Alan W. Jones. No sooner had I finished explaining my problem than he said to me: 'Colonel, your regiment is now attached to my division, and I take full responsibility for it.' Truly relieved, I stood at attention and saluted, saying from the bottom of my heart: 'Thank you, Sir!' My new boss explained that he wanted my unit on the right of the 424th IR, but I asked him if it wouldn't be better to occupy the hills around Leithum and Beiler and keep contact between the two regiments by patrolling through the woods. He immediately agreed. On returning to Huldange, I noticed that after the incessant flurries of melting snow that had soaked the uniforms of my little lads, the wind had changed, bringing an almost Siberian cold. More worried about my men freezing than being hit by a bullet, I ordered fires lit so they could dry their bonnets.*[15]

At 17:45, Jones attached the regiment to his division and informed VIII Corps, which approved his initiative. This decision solved two problems. Firstly, Jones had additional elements to secure his southern flank, and secondly that the problem concerning the 112th RCT, which was no longer supplied and could not fight indefinitely as an independent unit.[16] After what could be described as an odyssey, these infantrymen were exhausted and had already suffered heavy losses. Nonetheless, they formed a veteran unit that was a welcome addition to Jones' force. The news was excellent for Hasbrouck, who had to dig deep to watch over his threatened rear. The AAR of the 7th AD made no secret of the fact:

> *In addition to the many reports continually coming in of enemy activity in the area, very encouraging information about friendly troops was received about 10:30 on the 19th. Officers of the 112th RCT visited Divisional HQ and reported that their unit had lost all contact with the rest of 28th ID, and that the regiment, on the initiative of the commanding officer, was taking up a defensive position on the southern edge of the woods about a mile and a half south of Holdingen. They knew nothing of our own dispositions or those of other friends at the time. Fortunately, this placed the 112nd RCT on the southern flank of the 7th AD, although there was a gap between the 112nd and the right flank of the 424th IR. From 16:00 on 19 December, the 112nd RCT was attached to the 106th ID and the following day it was moved to its left to close the gap.[17]*

The two units had reorganised, and the moment of truth was approaching. These SS-Panzergrenadiers will continue their advance north of the Saint-Vith salient. (*Nara*)

# Chapter 9

# Evacuating Saint-Vith

On 20 January 1945, the 7th AD returned to Saint-Vith after a difficult recapture. (*Nara*)

## Bradley Loses his Troops

On 19 December, at his staff meeting in Verdun, Eisenhower took a decision that would ultimately have a major impact on the Allies' counterattack plan. The German offensive had split Bradley's 12th Army Group in two, and as a result, Bradley found it extremely difficult to communicate with Hodges at the head of the First Army on the northern shoulder of the salient. To solve this problem, Eisenhower placed the northern part of the Ardennes front under General Montgomery's command.

Hodge left Bradley's fold to take orders from Montgomery. (*Nara*)

In practice, this meant that Hodges' American troops, who had previously been under Bradley's direct orders during the Battle of Normandy, found themselves under the British commander. The demarcation line was also placed very far to the south, passing through Givet, a French town on the Meuse.

Before Montgomery arrived, Hodges had sent his troops ahead of the German advance to slow it down. He succeeded in withdrawing Collins' VII Corps from its positions in front of Düren to the east of Aachen and turning it into a counterattack force designed to strike at the German flank. Montgomery preferred to regard Collins as a reserve rather than a counterattack force and so ordered Collins to assemble further to the

Layton J. Collins (pictured here in 1948 with his four-star general's uniform) was the most aggressive of the US corps commanders. (*Nara*)

Ridgway was a respected and experienced general. He knew both Patton and Bradley from his time in Sicily, but fifteen months later, the situation had changed dramatically. Patton now depended on Bradley, who had risen in rank, and Ridgway commanded an airborne corps. (*Nara*)

rear, on the plains of Marche, as a reserve force. Hodges and Collins both argued that the plains of Marche was too far west, and that Collins' mission should be to counterattack as soon as possible. Collins was one of the most aggressive American commanders and, over the next two days, continued to ask for permission to counterattack. For Montgomery, the main aim was elsewhere, believing it was important to stabilise the front and build up a mass of manoeuvres. In this, he was simply obeying Eisenhower's instructions, which he had received on the evening of the 19th: plug the gaps, hold the line and act like an anvil against which the Patton hammer would strike the German salient from the south.

This decision had repercussions on the ground in the Saint-Vith sector. The XVIII Airborne Corps, under General Matthew B. Ridgway, came under the aegis of the First Army. Ridgway was given responsibility for Saint-Vith and the troops there and decided that the remnants of the 106th ID should come under Hasbrouck's command.

In this line of defence that Montgomery had to build, there was an outgrowth to the east, the Saint-Vith salient, which after four days of battle and many initial setbacks was still resisting the blows of the 5. Panzer-Armee's north wing. Montgomery did not attach much importance to the defence of Saint-Vith, believing that the crisis lay elsewhere and was likely to develop further south. Keeping the salient in place unnecessarily

Two cavalrymen from VII Corps lead a reconnaissance mission. They were Montgomery's trump card. (*Nara*)

lengthened the lines and consumed units that were needed more elsewhere. He knew that, if necessary, when the pressure was too great, he could order the armoured units defending the town to retreat to a more easily defensible position behind the River Salm.

On the morning of 20 December, the G2 of the 7th AD gave his chief, General Hasbrouck, an update on the situation. It was not very encouraging. The American division was on the verge of being surrounded. From north to south, the German units identified were the 1. SS-Panzer-Division, the 18. VGD, the 62. VGD, the 2. Panzer-Division and, finally the 116. Panzer-Division. It should be noted that, in reality, the elements identified as 2. Panzer-Division were not intended for the attack on Saint-Vith, but for the attack on Bastogne, which continued to resist fiercely. The G2 report indicated a change in tactics and the arrival of new German units in contact:

*The enemy was determined and less concerned about saving manpower. For the first time, there was an attack led by armour alone; generally, until now, the fighting had been led by relatively small forces of infantry with armour support or, more often, infantry with no support other than assault guns and organic armament. The action intensified in the south of the zone, with an infantry attack from the heights south of Gouvy at midday. In*

An M36 from the 7th AD took up position in a scrolling formation. Its armour was light, so the crew did their best to take advantage of the terrain. (*Nara*)

*this case, the infantry was supported by mortar fire and some artillery fire. However, the positions were not penetrated, and heavy losses were inflicted on the enemy. It was from this contact at Gouvy that the appearance of a new division came to light, as well as, thanks to captured documents, some of its intentions. This was the 560. VGD [...] A prisoner at Gouvy also reported the arrival of another, incidentally expected, division in the salient force – the 2. SS-Panzer-Division, one of the combat formations of the vaunted 6. SS-Panzer-Armee.[1] The identification was not substantial, but it was at least an indication of the division's early appearance. The prisoner, according to his own statements, was part of the advance party, sent on reconnaissance to find quarters for members of the command. As the prisoner was a member of the Engineers, and as this function is normally considered to be the responsibility of the Engineers, the reasoning behind it was logical.*

*A prisoner captured in the vicinity of Poteau pointed to another formation that had made contact with our forces. This was the Gross-Deutschland Division.[2] At the time, it was thought strange that this identification should be made on this front. All the enemy's orders of battle indicated that the division was engaged on the Russian front. The identification was puzzling; further evidence was needed to confirm the division's appearance on this front. In addition to the above identifications, a further identification was made of the divisions previously in contact from the thirty-six prisoners interviewed during the day. The developments of the day gave food for thought on the artillery problem. Artillery fire increased during the day; medium-calibre concentrations were received during the day at several points on the eastern front of the sector. Movements of vehicles, particularly armoured vehicles, were again recorded on the front, generally in the same areas as before. The enemy still seems to be massing his forces along the perimeter of our positions for an assault in force, obviously with strong armoured support.[3]*

## First News From Saint-Vith

Intelligence reports available to Hasbrouck also indicated that German units were continuing to bypass the knot of resistance formed by Saint-Vith and were digging in both to the north and to the south. The general of the American armoured division could not extend his position indefinitely on his flanks; he was clearly aware of the risk of seeing the two B CCs of the 7th and 9th ADs encircled in the town. His headquarters moved from Saint-Vith to Vielsalm. Cut off from VIII Corps, he knew that to the north it was still possible to pass through the Spa region. In desperation, he sent a liaison officer to the First Army headquarters. This letter, which arrived safely, is very revealing of the situation of the 7th AD:

*My division is defending the line including Saint-Vith and Poteau. CC B of the 9th AD, the 424th Infantry Regiment of the 106th Infantry Division and the 122nd Infantry Regiment of the 28th Infantry Division are on my right and hold from Saint-Vith to Holdigen. The two infantry regiments were in bad shape, my right flank was wide open, and the sector was patrolled only by reconnaissance. Tank Destroyers and isolated*

Priest M7 105mm self-propelled howitzers in position ready to support their brothers in arms. (*Nara*)

Hasbrouck was always on the edge as his division's situation gradually became more precarious. Here he is photographed in Germany a few months after Saint-Vith, eating from a bowl on the bonnet of his jeep. (*Nara*)

*units that we had assembled and organised into defence teams held the road centres to the rear as far as Chérain. Two German divisions, the 116 Panzer Division and the 560 Volksgrenadiere-Division, have just started to attack north-west with their right flank at Gouvy. I may be able to hold them off for the rest of the day, but I will be cut off from the rear tomorrow. VIII Corps has ordered me to hold, and I will, but I need help. An attack to the north-east from Bastogne would save the situation and by turning would cut the bastards off from their rear. I also badly need air support. I have lost contact with the VIII Corps, so I am sending this letter to you. I understand that the 82nd Airborne Division is coming north and that my northern flank is not critical.*[4]

The message came as Montgomery proposed abandoning the Saint-Vith salient. In his eyes, the crisis was already developing much further west and keeping this corner in the German lines meant maintaining large numbers of troops, which were needed elsewhere. Hodges, for his part, preferred to envisage the establishment of a Malmedy – Saint-Vith line thanks to the arrival of the 82nd Airborne Division.[5]

During the day of 20 December, German pressure on the bastion did not ease. The divisional artillery made twenty-one attacks in all, and each time it was called upon to

The infantrymen of the 7th AD held on to their positions. (*Nara*)

provide fire support. There were 300 attacks that day. Despite instructions to conserve ammunition, no fewer than 6,815 rounds were fired. It was at Gouvy, to the south of the US front, that the pressure was strongest during the day. There were several repeated assaults by the 116. Panzer-Division in conjunction with elements of the 560. VGD. By the end of the day, only a corridor barely 10 kilometres wide remained between Vielsalm and Gouvy to supply the town, and the levels of food and ammunition stocks were beginning to worry the commanders there. Another highlight of the day was when seventy men from the 106th ID[6] managed to reach the lines. They belonged to the regiments that had surrendered the previous day and after being cared for and restored, they were placed in reserve to intervene if the worst came to the worst.

On the German side, the order of battle also changed. Sepp Dietrich's 6. Panzer-Armee had not managed to break through the Elsenborn ridge and the 5. Panzer-Armee had scored some successes in the south, so von Manteuffel was to be reinforced, as the main effort was in his sector. The fact that the roads in the north were completely congested weighed heavily in the balance. The German high command wanted to deploy the offensive potential of all its elite units as quickly as possible. Time was running out and the OKW was determined to avoid giving the enemy the chance to recover from

On the Elsenborn ridges, the SS-Panzers could not break through and suffered heavy losses. (*Nara*)

the initial shock. The bulk of the 2. SS-Panzer-Division 'Das Reich' had not yet been committed. It was the first to change its sector of attack. Saint-Vith, as a road junction between the two Panzer-Armee, was the obligatory crossing point for units transferred from one to the other. As the pivotal point of the German offensive, the town took on an even greater importance in the eyes of the German commanders, and the pressure kept mounting on the besieged.

## A Day in Hell

During the night of 20 to 21 December, the defenders of Saint-Vith heard armoured vehicle movements coming from all directions. The Germans wanted to settle the problem caused by the fierce American resistance once and for all. In addition to the full-scale attack that was being prepared, small groups of fighters crept into the corridor leading to the town to set up ambushes with the aim of hampering communications and supplies.

The fighting raged on in Saint-Vith, and the 7th AD was severely tested. (*Nara*)

A line of defence was set up to collect the retreating fighters. (*Nara*)

Artillery preparations began at 11:00 to soften up resistance to the north and east of the town. It preceded the assault waves from Volksgrenadier, which would follow one another for two days. It was the B CCs of the 7th and 9th ADs that bore the brunt of the offensive. After two hours of uninterrupted shelling, Sturmgeschütze and Hetzer accompanied by infantry presented themselves in front of the US lines, which defended without weakening. Artillery fire continued to fall on the GIs throughout the day.

At 16:10, the 38th Armoured Infantry Battalion (AIB) came under attack from Volksgrenadier immediately after an artillery preparation. The attack was repulsed at 17:10, but pressure continued to be exerted by the Germans on the whole front of CC B of the 7th AD with a main effort on the right flank of B Company, 23rd AIB, which a concerted movement of German tanks and infantry finally penetrated. At 19:30, enemy elements appeared behind its positions and simultaneous attacks were launched along the Schönberg – Saint-Vith road against B Company, 87th Cavalry Reconnaissance Squadron (mechanized) and from the north-east against A Company, 38th AIB.

At 20:20, the US lines were breached in at least three points as German units entered the town via the Prüm road. Street fighting ensued and the battle continued until around 22:00, when the commander of CC B, seeing that part of his position was no longer tenable, gave the order to withdraw the centre of his line to the heights west of Saint-Vith. Its isolated elements east of the town were ordered to attack through or north of the town and join forces establishing a new line of defence. While this concerted effort was being made on the eastern flank, troops to the north were not heavily engaged, although there was a definite threat in the Ober Emmels – Nieder Emmels area. The plan was to anchor a defence west of Saint-Vith on this still-important northern flank and hold on to it. The principle was to withdraw the US troops to the west of Saint-Vith and establish a collection line for the elements to the east of the town, which is what was done.

Throughout the night of 21 to 22 December, stragglers reached the new American positions as checkpoints under the responsibility of officers were set up on all the roads to intercept the retreating men, send them to the Hinderhausen region and organise defensive positions with them. This enabled around 150 fighters to be assembled.[7] As night fell on 21 December, an enemy infiltration force entered Hinderhausen from the north through sector CC A west of Rodt. A light tank attack drove them into the woods in the early evening.

However, the order to withdraw came too late for A Company, 23rd AIB, which could not be warned in time. Nevertheless, the battalion commander, Lieutenant Colonel Rhea,

The 7th AD was repelled outside Saint-Vith. (*Nara*)

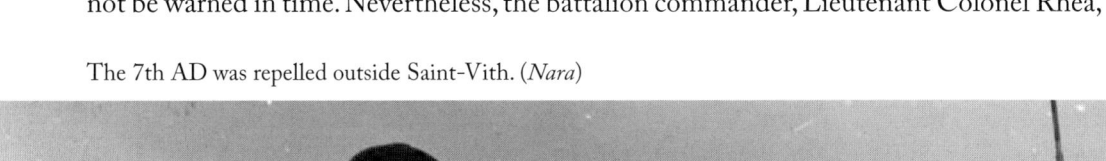

managed to maintain sufficient cohesion in the defence of the town to allow as many people as possible to reach the lines, ordering a platoon from the 814th Tank Destroyer Battalion to set up a barrage in the centre of the town. The decision paid off: at around 23:30, one of its guns managed to damage the track of a Panzer at the head of a column entering the town. The machine's crew tried to repair it, but to no avail and the wreckage caused an obstruction that the attackers had to get round. These twists and turns allowed the last defenders to evacuate the town unhindered.

The resistance in Saint-Vith had finally died out, but von Manteuffel had not yet achieved his goal. He now had to clear the exits from the town, which were still under fire from the Shermans of the 7th AD. This unit, although greatly reduced, retained sufficient defensive potential. The flexibility of its CC structure enabled it to adapt continuously to changing situations. In US Army doctrine, an AD is in no way designed for a defensive mission of this kind. This task is generally carried out by an Infantry Division reinforced by an Armoured Brigade.[8]

## The Saint-Vith Salient Must be Evacuated

Contrary to what Montgomery had told him about the possibility of a withdrawal, General Ridgway, who commanded the XVIII Airborne Corps, to which Hasbrouck was attached, refused to evacuate the Saint-Vith salient. As an airborne officer for whom

General Matthew Ridgway took over command of operations in the Saint-Vith - Vielsalm sector. (*Nara*)

Refuelling was beginning to pose a major problem for the 7th AD. (*Nara*)

fighting while surrounded was a normal tactical situation, he felt that not an inch of ground should be given up and so planned to create an abscess by allowing the armoured units to be encircled in a perimeter he called the 'fortified goose egg'. He planned to resupply the sector by air and only recommended evacuating the two infantry regiments belonging to the 106th and 28th ID.

For Hasbrouck, the order was tactical heresy and would place his division in an untenable defensive situation. The weather remained overcast and snowy and he had seen that, on 18 December, the Golden Lions could not be supplied by the C47s departing from England and that this logistical failure ultimately led to the fatal demise of the two infantry regiments. In addition, the engagement distance imposed by the compartmentalisation of the terrain and visibility was very short because the area was heavily wooded. The weather was miserable, with overcast skies, rain and melting snow reducing visibility, meaning the effects of the terrain and poor weather conditions combined to make the Volksgrenadier's task easier. Amply equipped with Panzerfauste, they were able to approach stealthily and have opportunities to destroy US tanks. Moreover, if the instruction was followed, petrol would soon run out and tanks that became immobile for lack of fuel would be irretrievably doomed. Lieutenant Colonel Erlenbush, the officer commanding the 31st Tank Battalion, accurately described the logistical difficulties of the day and everything that had been done to last as long as possible:

*We held a supply depot at Saint-Vith belonging to the 106th ID and used it until it was exhausted (8,000 rations and 10,000 gallons of petrol). Supply from the rear was extremely dangerous, as much of the enemy had bypassed St. Vith to the north and south. Because of these forces 'slipping in' on the flanks, our division's rear area was a mixture of friendly and enemy troops. Some Corps and Army ammunition supply points were in our hands, others were in enemy hands, others changed hands frequently, while other supply points were destroyed or evacuated by withdrawing friendly troops. The division's trains were at La Roche-en-Ardenne, where they were heavily engaged in the fight to avoid being overrun, and little help could be expected from there.*

*The problem of supply, therefore, was to drive lorries through miles of enemy-infested territory in search of friendly depots containing the type of supplies desired, and then back through miles of the same enemy-infested territory to deliver the much-*

Finally, the Germans were exhausted, allowing the 7th AD to withdraw in good conditions. (*Nara*)

*needed supplies to the fighting elements. The service facilities of the CC B units were pooled, and the maintenance sections were all grouped under the direction of Captain La Fountain, Maintenance Officer. The 31st TB set up a small workshop. Any of our vehicles that could be evacuated to this workshop were repaired there. At the same time, this group recovered many vehicles and weapons that had been abandoned in the area by retreating units prior to the arrival of the 7th AD. This equipment was repaired or, if beyond repair, 'cannibalised' to obtain parts for use in the repair of other vehicles and equipment. Often this combined maintenance section was operating under artillery fire, and often had to abandon its work and engage in a small battle with enemy patrols entering the area. In one case a four-man team lost a man before they could withdraw from the combat zone.*[9]

While Hasbrouck was considering withdrawing west of the River Salm, an instruction to the contrary reached him orally at 01.53 on the night of 22 to 23 December via the XVIII Airborne Corps Chief of Staff:

*General Ridgway believes that the enemy forces identified in the vicinity of Limmerlé are the 2. SS-Panzer-Division. In view of the loss of St. Vith, he considered it unsafe to hold the 424th and 112th Infantry Regiments in their present positions. He ordered the withdrawal under cover of darkness of the 106th ID and 7th AD to positions along the general railway line Bovigny, Beho, Maldingen. The exact positions on the ground are agreed between the Commanding Generals of the 106th and 7th Armoured Divisions. The following towns must be cleared of friendly troops before 07:00 this morning for an air mission: Sterpigny, Cherain, Rettigny, Gouvy, Limmerle, St. Vith. A covering force along this line (generally east of Gouvy) is to be left in place to cover the withdrawal.*[10]

Hasbrouck was aware of the enormous losses suffered by his CC B, which was now down to half its strength. He knew that the ridge line to the west of Saint-Vith imposed by Ridgway's order would not withstand a new German thrust, so told Ridgway that if the 'fortified goose egg' plan was adopted, there would soon be no 7th AD. Probably disturbed by this strong-headed response, Ridgway ordered Hasbrouck's armoured division to be placed under the command of General Jones.[11]

Ridgway explains in his memoirs that on the afternoon of the 22nd he went to Hasbrouck's and Jones' HQs and could only observe that the infantry general had a detached attitude to the dramatic situation facing his men.[12] Ridgway changed his mind

Ridgway's orders were to withdraw behind the railway line, but Hasbrouck was not happy with this decision. (*Nara*)

and Hasbrouck was reinstated at 18:53. He was also placed in command of all troops in the salient.[13] The new commander-in-chief of the salient ordered the withdrawal behind the Salm at 00:15 on the night of 22 to 23 December.

## Picking Up Under Fire

The situation was a tactical nightmare; the withdrawal had to be carried out during the day, during an enemy offensive, with exhausted troops lacking everything. All that remained were three roads across the bottleneck behind Saint-Vith and two intact bridges across the Salm: at Vielsalm and Salmchâteau. The communication routes were under threat from enemy infiltrators who ambushed the convoys. Liaison officers travelling between the besieged town and the headquarters in Vielsalm had to use light tanks to make the journey. For several days, Hasbrouck had ordered his division's train to hunker down at Marche-en-Famenne for obvious protection reasons, while the lorries supplied the front lines via the 82nd Airborne Division.

To organise the withdrawal of his armoured unit, the American general had to solve two problems. The first was to ensure a final logistical rotation to facilitate the withdrawal of troops without abandoning vehicles in order to maintain his division's offensive capability. Supply convoys were organised, with cooks and administrative staff, hastily armed, taking their places on the GMC platforms to escort the lorries. They managed to bring the petrol needed for the withdrawal into the salient and the cargo also included 5,000 rounds of 105mm ammunition, which would prove very useful in covering the evacuation by calming the enemy's ardour. The second challenge was to coordinate the operations in a coherent way, despite the exhaustion of the combatants and the difficulties in transmitting orders. To be on the safe side, each unit would be sent two vans carrying a message indicating the time of the drop.

General Hoge, commanding CC B of the 9th AD, described the excellent organisation of the stall:

*Headquarters in Vielsalm had planned for my CC B to stall first at 03:00. But at 01:25, we were up against the 62. VGD at Neundorf, Neubrück, Grüfflange and Thommen, in such a way that, to avoid disaster, I was forced to temporarily postpone our withdrawal.*

*At 05:00 Bob Hasbrouck sent this message to Bruce and me: 'The situation with the 82nd Airborne Division is such that if we don't join them soon, the opportunity will be lost. It is essential that we withdraw, whether the circumstances are favourable or not, if we are to evacuate with the vehicles! Inform me of the situation as regards breaking off and stalling.'*

*Finally, I was able to report that, all along the arc of the circle, the fighting seemed to diminish in fierceness; ten minutes later, the engines began to whirr, rumble and roar. Shortly afterwards, their caterpillar tracks were churning up the dirt roads.*

*A company of tanks was left as a rearguard, north of Maldingen, preventing the Germans from arriving from their Galhausen assembly area, while a small cavalry*

The artillery went first. (*Nara*)

The forced evacuation of Saint-Vith was a bitter blow for the 7th AD, but it recaptured the town a month later. (*Nara*)

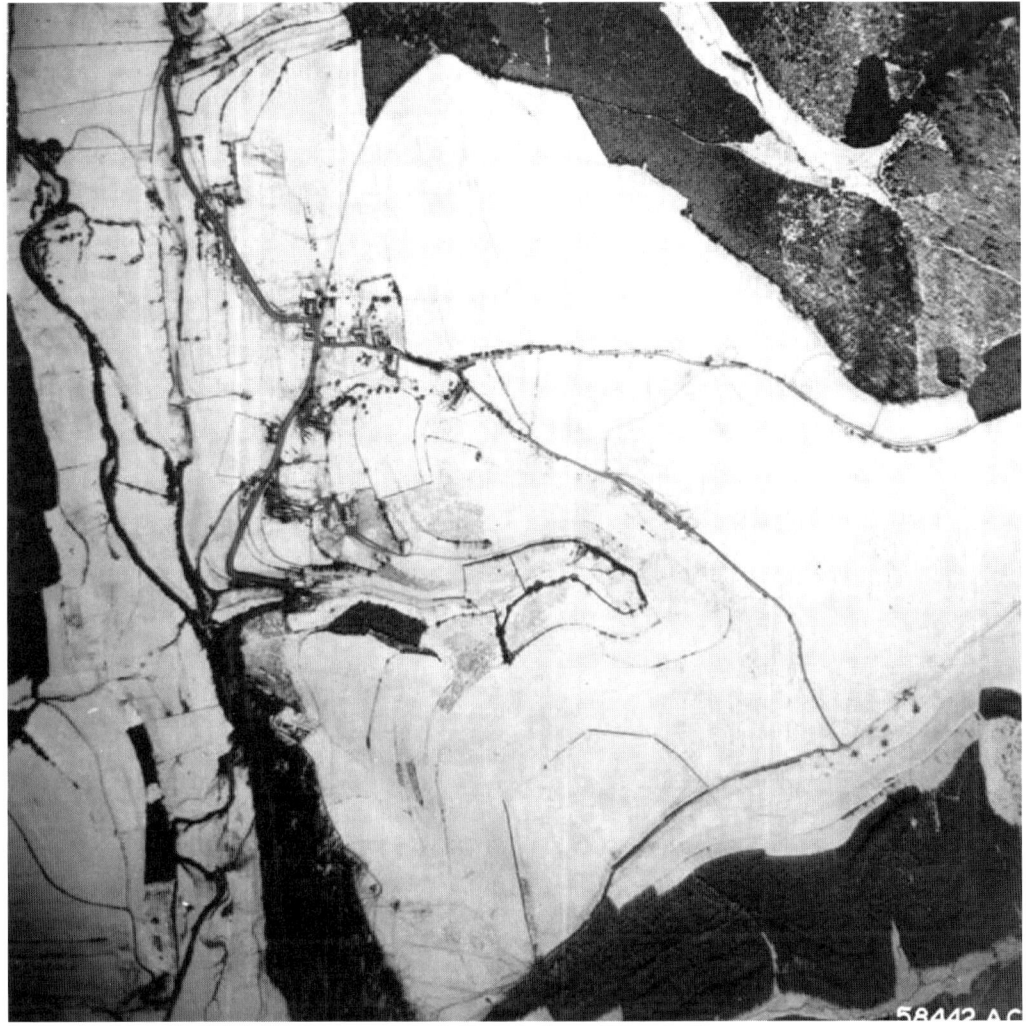

Aerial photograph taken on 23 December, showing a column of 237 vehicles evacuating Saint-Vith. (*Nara*)

*detachment under Captain Franklin P. Lindsey remained all morning at the other end of the village. The evacuation was successfully carried out with almost mechanical precision through Beho, Salmchâteau, Lierneux and Malempré, where my CC arrived at about noon. Thank God the enemy reacted only slowly, and only two tanks were lost. We were immediately followed by Task Force Wemple.*

*Although our men were exhausted, by mid-afternoon they were in position near Lansival and Manhay, attached to the 82nd Airborne Division.*[14]

The conditions for the evacuation were ideal throughout the sector. The Germans, too happy to have a breather after taking the town, did not realise the scale of the withdrawal that was taking place before their eyes and let the division escape without reacting. Although far from intact, the evacuated units would considerably harden the 82nd Airborne Division's front line.

A 7th AD fighter has just been seriously wounded. His survival depended on the medics intervening quickly. (*Nara*)

## Responsibility for the Decision to Evacuate Saint-Vith

The decision to withdraw from the Saint-Vith salient was the only thing to do given the precarious logistical situation of the 7th AD and the losses suffered. While consistent with Montgomery's desire to build a strong line of defence further west, Chester Wilmot's version that it was the British officer who gave the authoritative order to abandon the position seems exaggerated, to say the least. The decision was taken by Hasbrouck and assumed by Ridgway, his direct superior in the battle, because of the dramatic circumstances and tactical realities. It was therefore a completely American decision. It seems that Ridgway opposed Hasbrouck's initial decision to withdraw, only to change his mind when he saw the gravity of the situation for himself.

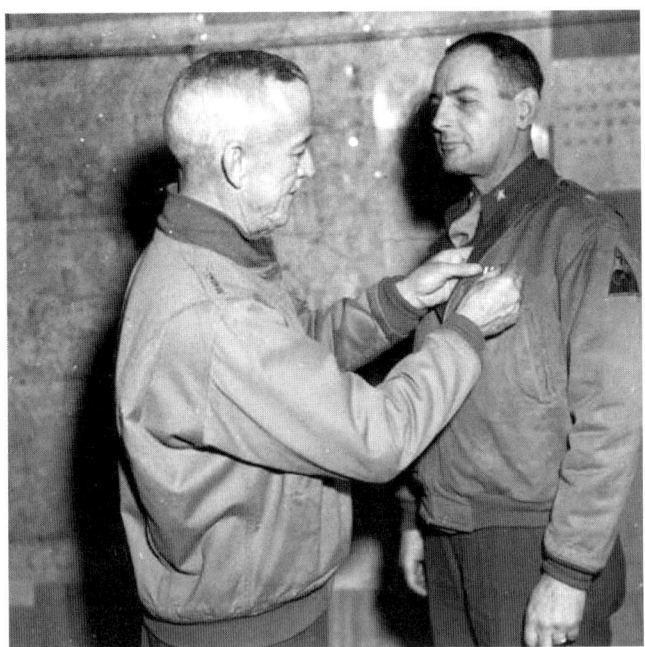

After the battle, Hasbrouck was decorated for the exemplary conduct of his division. (*Nara*)

The town was bombed by the American air force and the RAF after it had been evacuated and could no longer serve as a rail hub for the enemy. (*Bastogne War Musuem*)

A Tank Destroyer M10 on the prowl: it was not just in Bastogne where victory came at a price. (*Nara*)

Conclusions

# Bastogne and Saint-Vith – the Same Battle?

# A Front Line of Cowards?

The analysis of the first day of the engagement shows that the command of the 106th ID made no mistakes and that its men fought like lions. The unit suffered a full-scale attack and had to deal with a balance of power that was heavily against it.

As for the 14th CG, given the weakness of its anti-tank capabilities, it could do nothing other than resist the enemy to gain time before fading away. This formation could not be criticised, as it had resisted well in the face of the forces attacking it. This obliteration allowed the Volksgrenadier to break through Major General Alan W. Jones' left wing. When he received his first armoured reinforcements, he made the right decision to use them, and it was the erroneous information of the rapid arrival of the 7th AD that led him to divert his reinforcements to his other wing, which

After careful analysis, the infantrymen of the 106th ID did not deserve the opprobrium heaped on the division and its general after the battle. (*Nara*)

was just as threatened. On this first day of the German assault, the element of surprise had a considerable impact on the American system. In such situations, the fog of war and friction so dear to Clausewitz combine to make the conduct of the battle unintelligible. Major General Jones' unfortunate decision, however logical, resulted in the loss of his two regiments to the north of his position, who found themselves isolated and were forced to surrender.

However, it has to be said that the volume of fire that could have been devastating for the attacker was clearly not used enough. When the 7th AD arrived, only three unfortunate batteries of corps artillery continued to support the sector, twelve guns out of the ninety-six from the departure, in fact, of the only Corps battalion left in place, those of the 965th FAB.[1] Moreover, the resistance of the regiments of the 106th ID collapsed relatively quickly. Faster in any case than other units in similar conditions, with lack of experience probably being a crucial factor in the unfavourable evolution of the situation.

# Did the 14th Cavalry Group Fall Short?

Two years and half years after the event, in June 1947, General Robert Hasbrouck, commanding the 7th Armoured Division, recommended a presidential citation for all the units that had fought in the Saint-Vith salient during the first week of the German offensive, except for Devine's 14th CG because in his opinion, the unit had lacked discipline and had withdrawn without order. Admittedly, the skirmish and the emergency evacuation of Poteau had caused a crisis, the consequences of which had nevertheless been limited by Whiteman's initiative and the major delays caused by the appalling traffic jams in the German camp. In reality, if the 14th CG did indeed let go, it only did so after two days of fighting with very weak resources, particularly anti-tank resources.

We should also point out that the start of the Wacht am Rhein offensive was characterised by a powerful frontal assault on the positions of the 14th CG. The formation found itself engaged in a series of complicated manoeuvres, which were made possible by the mobility enjoyed by a cavalry unit. Withdrawal orders were dictated by the need to occupy road junctions. Each time, the cavalrymen set out to defend the villages where these important crossroads were located by using their firepower, which was ideally suited to deal with an infantry attack. Each time, they forced the Germans to deploy to win the day. Very often, Devine's men retracted before their opponents were able to develop their attack.

An M3A1 half-track belonging to a mechanised infantry unit of a US armoured division. These infantrymen had much more armoured support than the 14th CG. (*Nara*)

The cavalrymen of the 14th CG extracted themselves on foot from the villages where they were surrounded to continue the fight. (*Nara*)

Despite the difficulties, on the first day of the German offensive, the troops of the 18th CRS held out in places until nightfall and tried to use the darkness to rejoin the main body of the unit at Manderfeld. By the time they began to retreat, it was too late. German forces had infiltrated to the north and south of this collection position, which in turn had to be abandoned. During this first day of fighting, the cavalrymen fought very well, holding out for almost an entire day, delaying the enemy and suffering minimal casualties. Given the disproportion of their numbers, this was almost more than the US command had any right to expect from their men, who were in a position that was too stretched and too lightly armed. Their first day's action could be described as heroic, to the extent that three medals were even awarded for these operations. The fierce resistance of troops A and C of the 18th CRS, which were surrounded and did not surrender until they had used up all their ammunition, is an example of how well the unit held up in battle during the first few hours, when it still had all its cohesion. The cavalrymen were not really at fault; they carried out their mission within the limits of their resources and their weapons and their numbers being far from sufficient to stand up to the enemy's armoured rush. What is more, the survivors later joined the 7th AD, where they performed satisfactorily in combat. In any case, the resistance of the 18th CRS cavalrymen considerably hampered German movements. The 18. VGD did not realise that the horsemen's positions had been abandoned during the night and prepared full-scale assaults for the following morning. Considerable precious time was lost at a time when the element of surprise was losing its impact on the conduct of operations. This resistance to the east of the north–south ring road also enabled the 7th AD to reach Saint-Vith. Moving administratively, the American armoured division would not have been able to withstand the shock of a German attack on its flanks; the cavalry screen played its role to the full.

However, the 17th TB, which was supposed to hold Recht, did not fully carry out its mission. It was content to hold the direction of Saint-Vith and did not prevent KG Hansen from advancing westwards and it was Hansen who came upon the 14th CG traffic jam by surprise. Responsibility was shared at least equally between the tankers and

After the battle Hasbrouck gave a very negative report on the 14th CG. No doubt Devine's battle fatigue had influenced his judgement of the unit's behaviour. (*Nara*)

The 275th AFAB was not perfectly coordinated with the 14th CG, causing Devine additional problems. (*Nara*)

the cavalry, especially as the column of light tanks hampering the 14th CG's movement towards Recht appeared to belong to the 17th TB. It was the presence of these fugitives from the 7th AD's armoured unit that stopped the column of cavalrymen and facilitated the success of the famous Poteau ambush.

From an organisational point of view, the binomial composition of the cavalry groups could be called into question. One of the two squadrons was in the process of being reorganised after having fought during the autumn, which left Devine with only half of his elements to hold the position at the time of the shock. A traditional three-unit organisation would have kept a third of the strength in reserve, while a sufficient force could have held the line with greater cohesion.

However, the account of the events highlights several shortcomings in the foresight of the American command at several levels. The army group left a unit tested by recent fighting, temporarily reduced to half its strength, to hold a point on the front of vital interest: the Losheim Gap. This was a key invasion route, used every time since 1914 by the Germans attacking the sector. What is more, it was where two army corps met; a point in the system classically considered by all command manuals to be systematically a weak point on the front because of the difficulties in coordinating the units that joined hands there. However, not only was this point of junction of operational importance, but it was also defended by a workforce that was both too weak and ill-equipped. In a nutshell, the VIII Corps' plan to defend Saint-Vith was completely flawed due to the lack of manpower allocated by its higher echelons. This weakness pointed the finger at the 12th Army Group, which had preferred to gather its forces north and south of the Ardennes to go on the offensive.

At divisional level, Jones and Devine did not have time to coordinate. According to the manuals, cavalry could be used in defence provided it was sufficiently reinforced. The emergency counterattack plan provided for by 2nd ID was not reactivated when the cavalrymen came online, and they were left virtually alone until the arrival of the 7th AD. In addition, the lack of cohesion between the supporting units was particularly glaring. The anti-tank artillery was unable to communicate with the troops in the front line and the 105mm howitzers were not used to their full potential even though they were available, much to the dismay of Lieutenant Colonel Clay. Arguing that there was a lack of information about the position of the units once again underlines the lack of use of the resources Devine had made available to him. More so as one of the assets of US cavalry units was the power of their radio communication networks, guaranteeing a great capacity for remote control. Thanks to this, losses were minimal compared to the debacle of the first three days: 28% of his personnel and 35% of his equipment. It should be noted that the problem of organic anti-tank capability was only partly resolved from February 1945, with the arrival of the M24 Chaffee armed with a 75mm cannon to replace the M5A1.

## A Word on Colonel Devine's Condition After the Battle

Colonel Devine was withdrawn from the firing line due to battle fatigue, but better known today as post-traumatic stress disorder (PTSD); a physical and psychological reaction to the fear and fatigue resulting from a combat situation. Soldiers suffering from PTSD are now considered to be psychiatric casualties insofar as they become incapable of fulfilling their role in combat for reasons other than injury or illness.[2] This was not officially the case in 1944.

The number of cases of combat fatigue in American units during the Second World War reached a level that could be described as staggering. More than 504,000 soldiers were taken out of action due to 'psychiatric collapse', a term used early on to describe reaching breaking point. The number of men lost represents the equivalent of almost fifty infantry divisions lost to the war effort. Many more men were rendered unfit to fight in the Second World War than in any previous war, mainly because the battles were longer and more sustained.[3] Research carried out by the US Army after the Second World War showed that it was the unwillingness and inability of commanders to turn units into and out of combat, to re-equip and reconstitute them, that led to a high number of psychiatric casualties. Numerous studies show that frequent breaks away from the front, with hot meals and hot showers, prevent combat fatigue and solve many minor problems so that soldiers can return to their units. Such breaks were not frequent during the Second World War[4] and were totally impossible to implement in the crisis situation that characterised the first days of the Battle of the Bulge. In the case of Colonel Devine, it could be argued that this psychological collapse occurred very quickly. However, similar cases are not uncommon. For example, the shock of combat during the 1973 Yom Kippur War in Israel demonstrated the brutal nature of modern mechanised combat. In some cases, units lost soldiers to battle fatigue in less than 24 hours.[5]

Devine was exposed to this intense front-line stress. The First US Army neuropsychiatrist who examined him on 21 January 1945 took his account of the first

The GIs of the 106th ID who continued the fight after Saint-Vith behaved honourably. This patrol of the 106th brought back German prisoners. All they needed was a bit of rest to recover their energy. (*Nara*)

The heavy artillery also abandoned its equipment in front of the enemy. However, they were not punished. (*Nara*)

two days of the battle, and it was clear that the officer was experiencing the battle from the front line:

> *On the morning of 16 December, he was thrown to the ground by a mortar or the explosion of a shell. He had to be helped to his feet and suffered a slight laceration to his right hand, which was treated by the 18th CRS surgeon. In the afternoon he was knocked unconscious by a shell fragment that pierced the window of his command post. He must have been unconscious for a moment, as he remembers someone kneeling beside him as he lay on the ground. He spent a sleepless night at 106th ID headquarters. The following day he was still very active, trying to solve the critical problems of the moment. On the night of 17 December, he tried to assemble his staff at divisional headquarters. While en route, he was informed by radio that the roads were held by the enemy and in his attempt to rejoin his squadron, he came under enemy fire. He had to reach his command post through the countryside, through mud and torrents. He was cold and shocked when he arrived. He was looked after by the 14th CRS surgeon. On the morning of the 18th, he handed over his command to his executive officer and found himself in a dispensary in Vielsalm. He was sedated and given a coffee. He was evacuated to a medical unit at La Roche and on the morning of the 19th, he demanded to be released.*[6]

The colonel's misadventures did not end there. In the small village of Rendeux, he found himself in traffic, completely disengaged, wearing hospital pyjamas under his officer's coat. He struggled to send units on their way to the front as they tried to withdraw from the Saint-Vith sector, adding to the terrible traffic jam. His attitude was described as totally incoherent by the commander of A Company, 820th TD, who said: '*He was waving at the girls and shouting just as we passed.*'[7] He was brought before a doctor who immediately diagnosed extreme exhaustion. The colonel said he wanted to do his duty and return to Manderfeld to drive the Germans out, only to jump from one thing to another without following through on any of his ideas. Unbeknownst to him, he was given a strong dose of sedative in his coffee and fell asleep while talking. He was evacuated again to the rear[8] and ended up in Hotton, where the dispensary also came under German artillery fire. He was again evacuated to a field hospital, arriving there on Christmas Eve and finding himself caught in a bombardment. The doctor who examined him a month later found him still very agitated because of what had happened at the front. He felt that he could return to service but could not be sent to the front line where, once again subjected to stress, albeit less severe, there was a risk that he would suffer the same problems again[9].

Research into human factors also points out that the surprise effect has four direct and essentially physiological effects. These are increased physiological arousal, uncertainty, loss of attention and cessation of current activity. The surprised person often cannot remember what they were doing or thinking immediately before the event. This is known as an 'attentional blink', a form of protective detachment that inhibits too intense a risk. It was a syndrome that also seemed to strike General Jones when Ridgway arrived at the

Losses through injury were not the only ones that need to be treated; PTSD was not really taken into account during the Second World War. (*Nara*)

HQ at Vielsalm and decided to put Hasbrouck in charge of the sector. In close combat, these four effects generally only last a few seconds, depending on the scale of the threat. During this period, the individual is unlikely to take part in the fight, which can last long enough for casualties to accumulate. At the highest level of the organisation, the effects of surprise on a commander and his staff are at the level of 'blindness' and a tendency to carry out tasks normally devolved to lower echelons, which produces undesirable organisational effects. These may not appear for several hours and are behavioural responses to stimuli. Physiological questions apply mainly to individual participation in combat. Perception questions are more relevant to low-level commanders, generally at section, company or perhaps battalion level. Organisational effects occur at the level of the command battle group but are more perceptible in large collective headquarters removed from the immediacy of the battlefield operating at higher echelons.[10]

So not all stresses are the same, and the body's response varies according to the individual. However, it necessary to point out that Devine was not supposed to be fighting on the front line, but instead was supposed to be leading an engagement. The American colonel found himself simultaneously exposed to several types of combat stress, which acted on him with a cumulative effect, the result of which was akin to an avalanche of stimuli. Every man has his limits, and no one would have envied Colonel Devine's place on the front line.

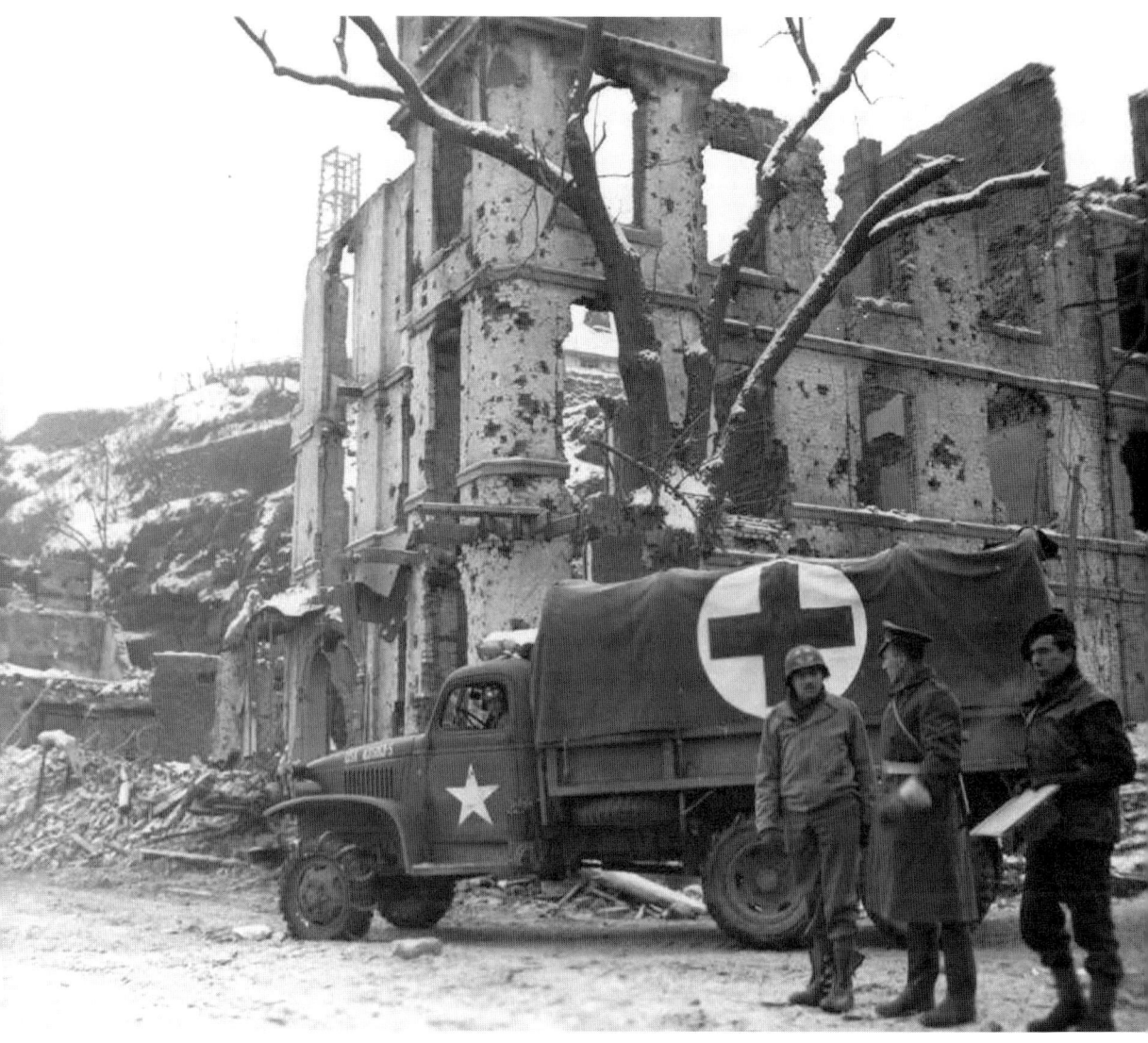

A GMC from the 106th ID evacuated the wounded to the rear. (*Nara*)

## Differences and Similarities

If you compare the terrain in front of Saint-Vith and Bastogne, you cannot help but notice that the lay of the land is quite similar, with steep slopes, wide wooded areas and so few roads that holding them was practically equivalent to holding the whole sector. The vital importance of Saint-Vith was measured by the number of American forces projected there. The Saint-Vith sector was reinforced from the start of the battle with twice as many armoured troops as those sent to hold the Clervaux – Bastogne axis. Saint-Vith received an entire combat command and an armoured division, i.e., four armoured brigades, whereas in the south there were only two.

SPW destroyed in the Luxembourg village of Heiderscheid. There are many similarities between the two sectors: whoever held the villages through which the roads passed, held the sector. (*Nara*)

The 28th ID sector on Skyline Drive was attacked by three Panzer divisions and a VGD, while the 106th ID was attacked by just two VGDs. The resistance of both divisions collapsed in two days. The 28th ID suffered enormous losses, most of them in combat, while the 106th ID saw two of its three regiments captured. In the case of the 28th ID, its essential role was practically eclipsed by that of the 101st Airborne Division. The Golden Lions would go down in history for having surrendered, but the fate of the 14th CG is perhaps worse; although it fought fiercely, collective memory retains only Devine's battle fatigue and the Poteau affair. It has been amply demonstrated here that if Jones had been correctly informed of the time of arrival of the armoured reinforcements, his decision making would have been different and a withdrawal such as at Clervaux would probably have occurred. In addition, it has been pointed out that the 14th CG was plugging a hole in an unfavourable sector without having the means to do so and that it had conducted itself honourably. The two crossroad towns remained in American hands for a time and the situation was similarly critical. In both cases, it was the flanks that gave out. The choice of encirclement or evacuation was linked solely to the nature of the troops there and to a calculation of risk.

American positions of the 99th Infantry Division in the sector north of Saint-Vith. (*Nara*)

## One Man Makes the Difference

At Saint-Vith, the front came under the command of the very methodical British officer Marshal Montgomery, who acted in accordance with the strictest military orthodoxy and ordered the evacuation of the Saint-Vith salient. He did more than strictly obey Eisenhower's instructions, however, and immediately thought of the battle in terms of crisis management. His first objective was therefore to build a solid line of defence while ensuring that the Mosan ditch was guarded. He quickly achieved his first objective and then succeeded in reducing to nothing the only real threatening breakthrough that managed to line the river at Dinant. He then reconstituted a mass of manoeuvres to go on the offensive from 3 January. It should be remembered that, with the notable exception of Bastogne, the whole of the rest of the stalemate was fought under British command: Saint-Vith, Vielsalm, Manhay, Hotton, Marche and Dinant were victories won under Montgomery's command with American troops. It was in this sector that the 5. and 6. Panzer-Armeen gave everything they had in terms of best troops and reserves.

On 26 December, Patton's thrust reached Bastogne with difficulty, having had to revise its initial axis of attack towards the north-east. Moreover, the troops of the lively general struck in a flank covered by less well-equipped units topped by a 7. Armee without Panzer.

We must also compare like with like. Montgomery's hierarchical equivalent in the Allied organisation chart was Bradley, with both men being at the head of an army group. While the Englishman held the reins firmly and skilfully commanded a front stretching from Zeeland to Givet at the heart of the battle, his American counterpart saw his power reduced to shreds and the only delicate operation in his sector was entrusted to the care of his subordinate and former superior, George Patton. The latter acted with complete independence of action, meaning the Battle of the Bulge, at its most critical moment, was led by two men who had been rivals since the Sicilian campaign: the Methodist Montgomery and the aggressive Patton. The most critical sectors rested on the shoulders of one man: Monty!

## Should Monty Stay or Should He Go?

Saint-Vith was defended by twice as many amoured elements as Bastogne. In Bastogne, they had been partially crushed to gain the time needed for the paratroopers to arrive in the town. The number of tanks and armoured vehicles requiring fuel to fight was therefore considerably lower. The town would be defended mainly by infantrymen and their fire support. The decision to lock in and resist the town was taken by a brigadier general acting as divisional commander, meaning an immense amount of latitude was left to a subaltern level of decision-making.

At Saint-Vith, the decision fell to Montgomery, who decided based on a much broader overview. The decision to evacuate the Saint-Vith salient was endorsed as necessary by the lower echelons. The defenders of Saint-Vith absolutely needed fuel to fight, as an immobilised tank was a dead tank. The supply difficulties were more than enough to justify the withdrawal of the 7th AD from the salient, which was threatened with encirclement.

Saint-Vith was not, however, a defeat. It is certain that this essentially defensive battle had as much, if not more, influence on the German failure as the stubborn resistance in Bastogne. The fact that the road junction had not fallen on 17 December had catastrophic consequences for the course of the offensive on the German side. In much the same way as a boxer unable to develop his full reach by suddenly paralysing his right jab means he loses his match, Sepp Dietrich's armoured fist became stuck in a monstrous traffic jam in the Eifel. Stronger-than-expected resistance on the Elsenborn ridge completed the bogging down of the German front. However, the overcast weather and the element of surprise, the other two conditions for the success of the offensive, were indeed present. The 62. VGD's lack of drive on the first day meant that it missed the opportunity to take the crossroads town before it was reinforced. The flexibility of the American military organisation came into full play, upsetting even the most pessimistic German planners as to the speed of the allied reaction. The speed of action of the 100% mechanised 7th AD did the rest. On the evening of 17 December, Saint-Vith no longer had any chance of falling like ripe fruit into German hands.

It was McAuliffe who decided to lock himself in Bastogne, Middleton having left him the choice. His paratroopers had to fight surrounded by the enemy for six days. (*Nara*)

These paratroopers of the 82nd Airborne Division went on the offensive in January 1945 - a counterattack made possible by Montgomery's good crisis management. (*Nara*)

## Was the Defence of Saint-Vith the Cause of a German Failure?

General Troy Middleton, commander of VIII Corps at the time of the Battle of the Bulge, wrote after the conflict:

*Two of the most important tactical locations in the 140 kilometres held by VIII Corps in the Ardennes Forest at the start of the Battle of the Bulge on 16 December 1944 were Bastogne and Saint-Vith. Through these towns passed road junctions which, if held, would disrupt the entire plan of any aggressor. Bastogne was an important communications centre and was worth the dice thrown for its defence. Its garrison wrote a brilliant chapter in history by holding the town against its adversary, so much of the commentary on the Battle of the Bulge has focused on this characteristic stretch of ground. As a result, the importance of Saint-Vith and its courageous defence by elements of the Corps troops, the remnants of the 106th Infantry Division and CC B of the 7th AD were largely overlooked. Aware of the importance of Saint-Vith to the American forces, the VIII Corps commander sent the commanding general of CC B of the 7th AD to place himself under the command of the commanding general of the 106th ID division, which had established its headquarters there, to assist in the defence of this important road centre.*

The resistance of the 106th ID on Skyline Drive on the first day, facilitated by artillery support that hampered German movements, had a considerable impact on the Battle of Saint-Vith and consequently on the results of the offensive. (*Nara*)

*In my opinion, it was the CC B that influenced the subsequent action and caused the enemy so much delay and so many casualties in and around this important area. Although the armoured weapon was not designed primarily to play a defensive role, the operation of the CC B was nevertheless a good example of how it can assume that role in an emergency. Its aggressive defensive measures completely disrupted the enemy's plan in the Saint-Vith sector.*[11]

This view was fully endorsed by General von Manteuffel at several conferences, when he stated that for the German counter-offensive of December 1944 to be successful, at least three things had to happen:

a) The German attack was supposed to be a surprise.
b) The weather conditions had to be such as to prevent Allied aircraft from hitting the German columns crossing the Ardennes.
c) The progress of the main German effort through and beyond Saint-Vith had to be rapid, not delayed.

The fall of Saint-Vith meant that logistical continuity could not be restored, as the rail hub was completely destroyed. (*Nara*)

The town of Saint-Vith reduced to a pile of rubble. Woe betide civilians in a strategic city in wartime! (*Nara*)

The first two requirements were met, while the third was not due to the defensive and delaying action of the 7th AD and the troops that joined it in the sector from 17-23 December.

In a history written for the US Army, von Manteuffel clarified his predictions on the eve of the battle:

*I expected the right Korps to capture St. Vith on the first day of the attack and hoped that by the evening of the second day of the attack its advanced detachments would be committed west of the Salm River and the bulk of its forces at Vielsalm. The question of whether the LXVI. Armee Korps should continue its advance westwards or should, in whole or in part, divert through Houffalize to protect its southern flank depended on the resistance which the armoured divisions had met so far, the situation on the southern wing of the 6. Panzer-Armee, and the resistance which the Korps expected in front of its own spearheads and had to be decided by these factors. That's what I always thought at the time, and my Chief of Staff had the same ideas. In my opinion, it considered the state of the troops, the terrain and the difficulties produced by the season, and after the capture of the line of resistance, it did not assume a powerful enemy in front of the Army for the first four days of the attack.*[12]

The German plan was therefore to capture Saint-Vith at 17:00 on 17 December, yet the town was not taken until the night of 21 December and the Saint-Vith area was not under full German control until 23 December, when CC B withdrew. On 22 December 1964, at a press conference in Watertown, New York, General von Manteuffel said: '*On the evening of 24 December 1944, I recommended to Hitler that the German army abandon the attack and return behind the West Wall.*' He also stated that the reason for this recommendation was the time lost by his 5. Panzer-Armee in the Saint-Vith area. Hitler

After the battle, American engineers, who were much better equipped than their enemy, retraced roads through the rubble. (*Nara*)

It was not possible to rebuild the town and so the stumps of buildings still standing were demolished. (*Nara*)

did not accept von Manteuffel's recommendation, however.[13] It should be noted that the commanders at the lower tactical echelons were not informed of their missions until the last minute. This was particularly the case with the 18. VGD, whose commander immediately organised a Kriegsspiel, which led to the conclusion that the town could not be taken before the 18th. Consequently, even before it began, the German plan to take Saint-Vith on the evening of the 17th was completely flawed.

By imposing an operational plan from above, without considering the enlightened opinion of the men on the ground, the German operational plan was constructed by a rear staff completely unaware of the realities faced. The theoreticians imposed their plan on the tactical commanders and the result was an operational plan that was certainly well thought out in terms of its aims, but poorly calculated in terms of available resources, timing and fuel allocations – a major flaw in the Wacht am Rhein plan as a whole.

In fact, it can be concluded that a large part of the German failure in the Ardennes was due to the relentless defence of the town. Indeed, the fact that the road junction had not fallen on 17 December would have catastrophic consequences for the progress of the offensive on the German side. The stronger-than-expected resistance on the Elsenborn ridge and the huge traffic jams had completely bogged down the German front in the 6. Panzer-Armee sector, but the overcast weather and the element of surprise, the other two conditions for the success of the offensive, were indeed present.

## A 7th Armored Division That Could Have Been More Effective From the Outset

In the case of Saint-Vith, there was no denying the remarkable responsiveness of the US Army and the exemplary fighting spirit of the 'Lucky Seven'. Without wishing to be pessimistic, the unit saved a desperate situation that would have been much less desperate had it not been for several flaws in VIII Corps, which in turn led to the rapid collapse of this part of the front.

The masterly error that led to the tragedy was the false information given to Major General Jones about the arrival of the 7th AD. Middleton assured him that the division coming to his rescue would be operational by 07:00 on 17 December, but CC B was 135 kilometres away and was due to leave at 03:30. Worse still, it was delayed and did not actually set off until 04:30. The Ninth Army estimated that the head of the western convoy would arrive at 14:00 on 17 December and its last vehicle at 02:00 on the 18th,

Going into battle in administrative order meant a delicate redeployment. (*Nara*)

This intelligence officer analyses documents left on the battlefield in February 1945. (*Nara*)

but the corrected information was not transmitted in time and thus influenced Jones' judgement in deciding to maintain his position on Schnee Eiffel. It is difficult to justify Lieutenant Colonel Slayden's silence in this matter.

However, several facts show that VII Corps was aware of the importance of the Saint-Vith sector and the weakness of its defences there:

1. Middleton installed substantial artillery support behind Saint-Vith.
2. The secondment of Lieutenant Colonel Slayden from VIII Corps headquarters to support Jones in his decisions.
3. The fact that Middleton very quickly reinforced the 106th ID, with a strength equivalent to what he did for Bastogne: a CC from the 9th AD and another complete armoured division.

All these factors indicate that VIII Corps headquarters feared the fragility of this untrained troop, which was thrust into the front line as soon as it landed. Yet Hasbrouck and Clarke were clearly not informed that a battle was in progress at Saint-Vith. All the indications were that orders were being carried out swiftly, but there was no sense of crisis. It got to the point where, at the outset, their movement towards Bastogne, their first announced destination, was carried out in an administrative manner. They did not form task forces ready for action but moved in column with the armoured artillery assembled instead of being dispersed in battalions for possible support. By moving towards Saint-Vith, the 7th AD was not behaving like a division that was going to attack, but like a unit that was changing sector and then being engaged after loosening up. Going to meet the enemy without being deployed to fight an encounter would cost it a great deal of time. Without these mistakes, it might have been possible to arrive in time to save the 422nd and 423rd RCT and the 106th ID. A mistake that was not made by the 101st Airborne Division, which started a little later and knew it was in for a nasty surprise. This highlights the fact that on 16 December, Middleton was not yet aware of the scale of the crisis he was

The 7th AD quickly went back on the attack after reorganising. (*Nara*)

The 7th AD had a brilliant campaign in Germany. This Tiger II was destroyed well after the Battle of the Bulge. (*Nara*)

about to face. He acted quickly, of course, but seemed to lack prudence in his analysis of the situation and was therefore guilty of overconfidence.

Let us imagine that the 7th AD had been better informed about the seriousness of the situation. That instead of taking an administrative movement configuration, it had approached the battle in a shock-ready configuration with its cavalry screen deployed to avoid any surprise encounters, its CCs advancing in concert on their axes of progression with their artillery support battalions correctly distributed within its three battle groups. It would not have moved any faster but would have been able to move more quickly into action on the northern flank of the 18. VGD. Here again, the blame should not be placed on Hasbrouck and his staff, but rather on the higher echelons who had failed to grasp the gravity of the situation in time. Adopting the right tactical deployment would have been possible when the march orders in Holland were drawn up before the division began its projection towards Saint-Vith. The impact of this poor choice of command, which led to the adoption of an administrative move, was considerable. Once again, a mistake was made at 12th Army Group level.

## Overwhelming Responsibilities at the Top

Remember, it is always the leader who loses the battle, never the soldier![14] In the order of causes of defeat, a general loses a battle because he has been misinformed, either through his own fault, that of his superior or that of the enemy. Jones and Middleton were both misinformed. If a general has been well informed, then if he loses it is because he has made the wrong decision. Neither Jones nor Devine committed any errors of command on 16 and 17 December. If the general decides well, he can lose if he is badly served by his subordinates. Most of the subordinates obeyed the orders given to them, which followed from the implacable consequences of the balance of forces. There were still two causes of defeat: decisions taken too late or bad luck. The units on the front line had only one thing to do: hold out until reinforcements arrived. The withdrawals orchestrated by the

Bradley did not assess the scale of the German assault until the second day of the battle. This failure of his intelligence service led to a cascade of disasters caused by a lack of precaution. (*Nara*)

14th CG corresponded to this scenario, as the cavalry unit was well-equipped with means of transport and was therefore able to use the fluidity of its organisation to act. It should also be noted that its greatest losses occurred at Poteau, where it was immobilised. Jones commanded an infantry division; he knew his positions were under threat but expected to receive reinforcements quickly. No decision was taken too late. Does this mean that there was a form of bad luck, as Hasbrouck asserts when talking about Jones? No, except that he found himself in the wrong place at the wrong time in a configuration that was inappropriate for the tactical situation. Once again, this was due to a lack of intelligence at the highest levels of the Allied system. It is true that he was surprised, but surprise has a leverage effect on the battlefield.

Jim Storr argues that surprise normally has a greater impact than a 10-to-1 balance of power, pointing out that the creation and exploitation of surprise was at the heart of German tactics during the Second World War and during the opening phase of the Battle of the Bulge. This largely explains the difference in performance on the battlefield between the German and American armies described at the opening of the offensive. The German army wanted to capitalise on the surprise effect; to achieve a lightning breakthrough as far as the Meuse before the US command had time to react. For them,

The 7th AD was able to extricate itself from the Saint-Vith sector and take up a rear position. (*Nara*)

The 82nd AD arrived just in time to set up a collection position at Vielsalm. (*Nara*)

mobility and manoeuvre were simply the means to achieve this in both time and space. The statistics of military history show that surprise occurs in only 40% of battles. However, when it does occur, it increases the chances of success and reduces losses, and is more effective than any balance of power. Surprise is therefore extremely important and commanders must go to great lengths to achieve it and exploit its results. There are few other things they can do that are as effective in terms of tactical success. In the battles studied, the probability of achieving surprise in a single attack was only around 40%. It is important to note that the probability of achieving surprise in several separate attacks can be much higher, this observation stemming from a simple simulation in which the attacker launched four simultaneous low-level attacks on separate axes. This simulation showed how the probability of obtaining a certain surprise varies according to the probability of surprise in one or more other given attacks.[15] The German army attacked over a front width of almost 100 kilometres, if its resources were concentrated in the area of the First US Army alone. There were several separate operations at Armee-Korps level and this multiplication of assault sectors had a cumulative effect on the extent of the surprise within the US system.

In war, lost time is never recovered. On the contrary, it tends to have a snowball effect. This is one of the components of the famous friction so dear to Clausewitz. The stubborn resistance of the defenders of Saint-Vith had the leverage effect of allowing the 82nd Airborne Division to build a powerful defensive line behind the Salm, a defensive front that allowed the Allies to reorganise in a coherent manner in line with the developing situation. After a week of indecision, on 23 December the initiative changed sides, and the Gods of War did the same, starting by allowing the Allied air force to take off.

As we have seen, the fatal error of judgement was above all linked to a problem of coordination between two armies in the context of a lack of understanding of the seriousness of the situation at 12th Army Group level. The difficulty of coordination at the junction of two systems is a classic example of theoretical tactical trials. When there is a lateral transfer, which was the case with the 7th AD at Saint-Vith, passing from one army to another, it is the higher echelon that must take responsibility, because it is at this level that the problem of coordination is theoretically played out. It was therefore 12th Army Group that was responsible for the loss of the two regiments of the 106th ID.

## Delicate Communication

The crisis that developed in the Ardennes resulted in a bloody battle that ended in a draw. This posed a real communication problem for Eisenhower and Marshall (the Chief of Staff of the US Army) and occurred precisely at a time when it was important to maintain morale in the rear during the battle. The resistance at Bastogne, the hole in the doughnut and McAuliffe's thunderous '*Nuts!*' were a godsend. If Patton managed to rescue the Screaming Eagles in time for Christmas, the communication battle was won. On the other hand, to assume that the crisis in Saint-Vith was such that it must be abandoned to the enemy shows the true scale of the problem. In effect, this meant that control of

On the outskirts of Bastogne, the paratroopers were waiting for Patton. This .50 was fired by an airborne artilleryman from the 907th GFAB, if the tactical sign on his helmet is anything to go by. (*Nara*)

the situation in the north-eastern sector was so problematic that it was preferable to withdraw command from the American Bradley and hand it over to a Briton. Such an admission of weakness would undermine the morale of the American population at the height of the festive season. The press would go wild, the Senate would call for heads, and some would surely roll. Bastogne was so much more presentable publicly that it became the tree that hides the forest of a disaster that was barely contained.

After the war, the triumphant United States faced two problems. Communism had to be contained at a time when the ideological heartland of European populations was swaying between liberalism and communism. At the time, no one doubted that while the Americans were liberators, it was the Russians who had broken the Wehrmacht and enabled victory in the end. The man in the street was still too uninformed about the deleterious effects of Stalinist communism and what was really happening in the East. The Marshall Plan filled people's bellies, and communism gradually receded as the horrors of Stalinism transpired in the West. The Russian Bear became a scarecrow. The Red Army was now equipped with an admirable, very powerful armoured machine that was battle-hardened in the depths. Its potential was well proven; its ten successive offensives, which in the space of a year took the T34s from the USSR border to Berlin, and the Manchurian offensive, where it proved capable of crossing 400 kilometres of virtually untamed steppes in one leap in eleven days, were more than enough to demonstrate this. The German offensive in the Ardennes was led by two powerful and experienced armoured units. The choice was made to present it as an attempt that had failed miserably in the face of a curtain of GIs taken by surprise as they prepared for Christmas. It was a demonstration, as romantic as it was dazzling, that the US Army stationed in Europe used, among other things, to appear to be the best possible bulwark against a tide of red armour.

Is it still necessary to present a major crisis in the European campaign as a victory? Historiographers of the US Army are at liberty to focus public attention on the Battle of the Bulge, the strictly tactical defensive victory that was the siege of Bastogne. The early stages of the battle of Saint-Vith were marred by errors, just as they had been at Bastogne. What was different was that at Saint-Vith, the American soldiers were inexperienced. They were up against quality Volksgrenadier divisions. Mistakes were costly and paid for in cash. In Bastogne, the effective resistance of the 28th ID delayed the enemy long enough to slow the operational tempo and there was a little more space to trade for time. This was enough to make the difference, giving the US commands a breathing space.

On 12 October 1944, General Marshall visited the Elsenborn barracks, which served as headquarters for the 28th ID. (*Nara*)

An armoured infantryman from the 4th Armoured Division escorts three German soldiers. This photograph, like many others, presents the battle as a great American victory. In reality, however, it was more akin to a draw. (*Nara*)

After the battle, the 106th ID was reconstituted for combat. (*Nara*)

So, if one is going to talk about the battle, you might as well focus on where it ended well. Bradley and Eisenhower would take the same route in their memoirs, and neither have been caught in a lie. People's beliefs are never more than matters of opinion. However, it must be admitted that it was easier for them to talk abundantly about their successes than about their mistakes. The difference is such that it has distorted reality. The Battle of the Bulge is said to have been an Allied victory when it was, at best, a draw.

One statistic tells the whole story. During the Battle of Normandy, an offensive operation that was theoretically more costly for the attacker, the Third Reich lost 325,000 men,[16] while the Allies suffered 219,000 casualties.[17] This meant that one Allied soldier was sacrificed for every 1.5 Germans.[18] During the Battle of the Bulge, German losses were estimated at between 81,000 and 103,000 combatants. The level of Allied attrition, meanwhile, was 82,395 soldiers,[19] i.e. approximately one soldier lost on both sides for one lost on the opposing side. The only difference between the belligerents here was that the Allies could afford such a high cost, whereas the Third Reich could not.

# Notes

## Chapter 1

1. Dragon's teeth.
2. Delaval, M., *Saint-Vith, during Hitler's final Blitzkrieg,* Vielsalm, 1984, p.37-8.
3. Washington, Nara, RG 338, Foreign Military Studies, B 688, p.23.
4. An Abteilung corresponds to a battalion.
5. /cac2/CGSC/CARL/nafziger/944GXAJhttps://usacac.army.mil.pdf accessed on 25/3/2015.
6. In his report, it seems von Manteuffel had reversed the figures, as the 26. VGD was to operate under the XLVII. Panzer-Korps, further south in the Bastogne sector.
7. Delaval, M., op. cit., p.38.
8. Fort Leavenworth, Ike Skelton Library, N-17500.1033-2, MSB 151, pp.109 and 148.
9. Washington, Nara, MSB 688, p.1-22.
10. Prohüber, K-H, *Volksgrenadier-Divisionen*, Aachen, 2018, p.216.
11. Washington, Nara, RG 338, Foreign Military Studies, SB 688, pp.1-2.
12. Dietmann mentions Volksliste 3, German citizens on probation. They could serve in the ranks but could not be promoted beyond the rank of private first class.
13. Fort Leavenworth, Ike Skelton Library, N-17500.1033-2, MSB 151, p.109.
14. Dupuy, T., *Hitler's last gamble,* Shrewsbury, 1994, p.444.
15. Fort Leavenworth, Ike Skelton Library, N-17500.1033-2, MSB 151, pp.146-8.
16. Edwards, R., *German Airborne Troops*, London, 1974, p.137.
17. Rusiecki, S., *The Key to the Bulge*, Mechanicsburg, 2009, pp.20-1.
18. Student, K., *Generaloberst Kurt Studen und seine Fallschirmjäger*, Friedberg, s.d. [1980], p.495.
19. Washington, Nara, MSB 688, pp.28 -9.
20. The officer was appointed General Major on the following 23 December when he was awarded the Ritterkreuz for his leadership of operations. https://www.lexikon-der-wehrmacht.de / Personenregister/K/KittelF.htm consulted on 23/7/2023.
21. Washington, Nara, MSB 028, pp.1-4.
22. Kriegsspiel (war game) was originally a complex pawn game developed by the army of the Kingdom of Prussia in the nineteenth century to teach officers combat tactics. It enabled German officers to test battle plans on maps and learn from them to avoid certain potential problems.
23. Washington, Nara, RG 338, Foreign Military Studies, B 688, pp.32-3.

## Chapter 2

1. Whiting, C., *Death of a Division, in the hell of the Schnee Eifel in December 1944,* Jalhay, 1992, p.195.
2. Fort Leavenworth, Ike Skelton Library, N-12472, Order of battle of the United States Army, vol. 2, p.421.
3. Massart, A., *Saint-Vith,* Jalhay, p.79-80 and Coles, H., *Ardennes, the Battle of the Bulge*, Washington, 1965, p.171 (for the exact list).
4. US Army, *The 106th, the Story of the 106th Infantry Division*, n.d., 1945, pp.3-4.
5. McDonald, C., *Commandant de compagnie, combattants américains dans la bataille d'Europe*, Brussels, 1990, p.88.
6. Fort Benning, USAIS Library, Jones, A.W. Jr., *The Operations of the 423rd Infantry (106th Infantry Division) in the Vicinity of Schonberg During the Battle of the Ardennes, 16-19 December*

*1944*, Advanced Infantry Officers Course, 1949-1950, p.6. The author of this study is the son of General Jones, commander of the 106th ID. He took part in the battle in the ranks of the division commanded by his father as a lieutenant on the staff of the 423rd Infantry Regiment. He can be considered a first-rate witness. However, in terms of historical criticism, it must be borne in mind that his point of view could hardly be neutral. It can be assumed that in writing his memoir, he was keen to defend the honour of his family and his brothers in arms. His account has been kept, however, because it is corroborated by McDonald, who commanded one of the companies of the 2d ID in this sector.

7.   McDonald, C., *Noël 44, la bataille des Ardennes*, Brussels, 2004, pp.122-3.

8.   Fort Leavenworth, Ike Skelton Library, AAR, *612th Tank Battalion*, report dated 4 January 1945.

9.   Yeide, H., *The Tank Killers, a history of America's World War II Tank Destroyer Force*, Drexell Hill, 2007, p.144.

10.  Fort Benning, USAIS Library, Horton, J., *The Operations of the 820th Tank Destroyer Battalion in a Retrograde Movement during the Counteroffensive in the Ardennes*, Advanced Infantry Officers Course, 1948-1949, p.8.

11.  Fort Benning, USAIS Library, Keyes, L., *Operations of the 106th Infantry Division in the Battle of the Bulge, 15-22 December 1944*, Staff Department Infantry School, 1949-1950, p.3.

12.  https://www.benning.army.mil/armor/earmor/content/issues/2014/oct_dec/Howard.html, consulted on 7/9/2022.

13.  https://14cavalrygroup.files.wordpress.com/, consulted on 7/9/2022.

14.  Coll, *Cavalry in the Gap: the 14th Cavalry Group and The Battle of the Bulge*, p.1, consulted on 31/12/08.

15.  Quoted in Delaval, M., op. cit., p. 84.

16.  Coll, *Cavalry in the Gap: the 14th Cavalry Group and The Battle of the Bulge*, p.3, consulted on 31/12/08.

17.  Ibid., p.4, accessed 31/12/08.

18.  Self-propelled engines on Light Tank M5A1 chassis.

19.  Hummel, l., 'The Military US Geographical Agent: The Case of Cold War Alaska', *Geographical Review*, Vol. 95, No. 1 (Jan., 2005), pp.47-72.

20.  Fort Leavenworth, Ike Skelton Library, N-12472, *Order of Battle of the United States Army*, vol 1 and 2, pp.18 and 421.

21.  Fort Leavenworth, Ike Skelton Library, N-12472, *Order of Battle of the United States Army*, vol 1, p.112.

22.  Washington, Nara, RG 407-Ent 427A-Box 19014-Folder CI 329A-14 Cav Gp Ardennes, Group Interview with 32nd CRS, p.3.

23.  Yeide, H., *Steeds of Steel: A History of American Mechanized Cavalry in World War II*, Minneapolis, 2008, pp.228-35.

24.  Washington, Nara, RG 407-Ent 427A-Box 19014-Folder CI 329A-14 Cav Gp Ardennes, Group Interview with 32nd CRS, p.4.

25.  Washington, Nara, RG 407-Ent 427A-Box 19014-Folder CI 329B-14 Cav Gp Ardennes, 18th CRS Staff Narrative, p.1.

26.  Washington, Nara, RG 407-Ent 427A-Box 19014-Folder CI 329B-14 Cav Gp Ardennes, *AAR 14th CG*, entry of 11/12/1944.

27.  Fort Leavenworth, Ike Skelton Library, AAR 820th TD, entry dated 10-15/12/1944.

28.  It was equipped with M18 Hellcats in early 1945.

29.  Gabel, C., *Seek, Strike, and Destroy: U.S. Army Tank Destroyer Doctrine in World War II*, Fort Leavenworth, 1985, p.47.

30.  Bastogne, Bastogne War Museum documentation centre, Fonds Kraft de la Saulx, A0138, 14th Cavalry Group (Mecz), account of events after investigation by Lieutenant Jack Shea, annex: Captain Nash's interrogation report, 10/1/45.

31.  The 106th ID depended on the VIII Corps and the 99th ID on the V Corps.

32. Dimarco, L., *The US Army's Mechanized cavalry Doctrine in World War II*, Fort Leavenworth, 1995, p.83.
33. Fort Leavenworth, Ike Skelton Library, War Department, *FM 2-30, Cavalry Reconnaissance Squadron Mechanized*, 28/8/1944, p.55.
34. Washington, Nara, RG 407-Ent 427A-Box 19014-Folder CI 329B-14 Cav Gp Ardennes, 18th CRS Staff Narrative, p.1.
35. An American armoured division is divided into three Combat Commands (the British equivalent of brigades). It represents one third of a division's strike force, comprising a tank battalion, an infantry battalion, an artillery battalion and any support elements.

## Chapter 3

1. Fort Benning, USAIS Libray, Jones, A.W. Jr., *The Operations of the 423rd Infantry (106th Infantry Division) in the Vicinity of Schonberg During the Battle of the Ardennes, 16-19 December 1944*, Advanced Infantry Officers Course, 1949-1950, pp.12-13.
2. Washington, Nara, MSB 688, p.37.
3. An American infantry division is divided into three Regimental Combat Teams. This is often a combination of an infantry regiment and an artillery battalion.
4. Delaval, M., op. cit., p.39.
5, Delaval, M., op. cit., pp.61-2.
6. The V1 flying bomb was called the Buzz bomb by the GIs because of its characteristic vibrato. They were fired from fixed booms aimed at Liège and Antwerp. Their flight therefore generally followed a virtually similar corridor during the attacks. This corridor is called Buzz Bomb Alley.
7. Washington, Nara, RG 407-Ent 427A-Box 19014-Folder CI 329B-14 Cav Gp Ardennes, narratif de l'état-major du 18th CRS, pp.4-6.
8. Washington, Nara, MSB 688, p.34.
9. Washington, Nara, RG 407-Ent 427A-Box 19014-Folder CI 329B-14 Cav Gp Ardennes, Narrative of Troop A, 18th CRS, pp.5-8.
10. Washington, Nara, RG 407-Ent 427A-Box 19014-Folder CI 329B-14 Cav Gp Ardennes, *AAR 14th CG*, entry of 16/12/1944.
11. Bastogne, Bastogne War Museum documentation centre, Fonds Kraft de la Saulx, A0138, 14th Cavalry Group (Mecz), account of events after investigation by Lieutenant Jack Shea, pp.15-16.
12. Washington, Nara, MSB 688, p.40.
13. Bastogne, Bastogne War Museum documentation centre, Fonds Kraft de la Saulx, A0138, 14th Cavalry Group (Mecz), account of events after investigation by Lieutenant Jack Shea, pp.16-17.
14. Washington, Nara, MSB 688, p.37.
15. Bastogne, Bastogne War Museum documentation centre, Fonds Kraft de la Saulx, A0138, 14th Cavalry Group (Mecz), account of events after investigation by Lieutenant Jack Shea, p.18.
16. Washington, Nara, RG 407-Ent 427A-Box 19014-Folder CI 329B-14 Cav Gp Ardennes, narrative of Troop C of the 18th CRS, pp.1-5.
17. Washington, Nara, MSB 688, pp.35-8.
18. Washington, Nara, RG 407-Ent 427A-Box 19014-Folder CI 329A-14 Cav Gp Ardennes, Group Interview with 32nd CRS, p.6.
19. Washington, Nara, RG 407-Ent 427A-Box 19014-Folder CI 329B-14 Cav Gp Ardennes, *AAR 14th CG*, entry of 16/12/1944.
20. Ibid.
21. Cuppens, G., *Massacre à Malmedy*, Bayeux, 1989, p.27.
22. The Tigers made their way south and were engaged at Schönberg. Schneider, W., *Tiger in Combat*, t.1, Mechanicsburg, 2004 , p.274.
23. Macdonald, C., op. cit., p.318.
24. Delaval, M., op. cit., p.87.
25. Ibid., p.58.

26. Bradley, O., *Histoire d'un soldat*, Paris, 1952, p.439.
27. Delaval, M., op. cit., pp.61-2.

## Chapter 4

1. Gillie, M.H., *Forging the Thunderbolt, Mechanicsburg*, 2006, p.216.
2. Fort Leavenworth, Ike Skelton Library, N-12472, *Order of Battle of the United States Army*, vol 2, pp.480-3.
3. Delaval, M., op. cit., p.86.
4. Washington, Nara, RG 407, After Action Report 7th AD summary of operations.
5. *The Battle at Saint-Vith 17-23 December 1944, An historical example of Armor in the defence*, US Army Armor School, 1966, p.4.
6. Washington, Nara, RG 407, After Action Report CC B 7th AD, entry dated 16/12/1944.
7. Washington, Nara, RG 407, After Action Report 40th Tank Battalion 7th AD, entry dated 16/12/1944.
8. Delaval, M., op. cit., p.61.
9. Ibid, p.89.
10. Fort Leavenworth, Ike Skelton Library, FM 7-10, Armored Force Manual, Tactics and Technics, March 1942, pp.140-1.
11. Massart, A., *Saint-Vith*, Verviers, 1995, p.214.
12. The unit was attached to the division from 13 August 1944 and remained so until 9 May 1945. Fort Leavenworth, Ike Skelton Library, N-12472, *Order of Battle of the United States Army*, vol 2, entry for *7th AD*.
13. Washington, Nara, RG 407, AAR CC B 7th AD entry dated 16/12/1944.
14. Delaval, M., op. Cit., p.87.
15. *Washington, Nara, RG 407, AAR CC B 7th AD* entry dated 17/12/1944.
16. Delaval, M., op. cit., p.89.
17. Delaval, M., op. cit., pp.88-9.
18. Bradley, O., op. cit., pp.426-40.

## Chapter 5

1. Trad: fast detachment, a battalion of the regiment had bicycles to move around quickly.
2. Freiburg, BA, MS B 734 pp.19-20.
3. Fort Benning, USAIS Library, Jones, A.W. Jr., *The Operations of the 423rd Infantry (106th Infantry Division) in the Vicinity of Schonberg During the Battle of the Ardennes, 16-19 December 1944*, Advanced Infantry Officers Course, 1949-1950, pp.15-18.
4. Delaval, M., op. cit., p.71.
5. Freiburg, BA, MSB 151a, p.16.
6. Delaval, M., op. cit., p.98.
7. Washington, Nara, RG 407, AAR *CC B* 7th AD entry dated 17/12/1944.
8. Delaval, M., op. cit., p.87.
9. Washington, Nara, RG 407, *AAR CC B 7th AD* entry dated 17/12/1944.
10. Washington, Nara, RG 407, *AAR CC B 7th AD* entry dated 17/12/1944.
11. Washington, Nara, RG407, AAR 17th TB, 7th AD, entry dated 17 and 18/12/1944.
12. Washington, Nara, RG 407, 14th cavalry group-Box 24108-Folder CI-329-2.
13. Bastogne, Bastogne War Museum documentation centre, Fonds Kraft de la Saulx, A0138, 14th Cavalry Group (Mecz), account of events after investigation by Lieutenant Jack Shea, pp.30-2.
14. Quoted in Delaval, M., op. cit., p.85.
15. Washington, Nara, RG 407-Ent 427A-Box 19014-Folder CI 329A-14 Cav Gp Ardennes, Group Interview with 32nd CRS, p.1.
16. Delaval, M., op. cit., p.116.
17. Bastogne, Bastogne War Museum, Fonds Kraft de la Saulx, dossier A0162, folder 7th AD, AAR 17th TB, entry dated 17 and 18/12/1944.

18. Washington, Nara, RG 407, AAR 7th AD, entry dated 17/12/1944.
19. Washington, Nara, MSB 688, pp.40-1.
20. Fort Benning, USAIS library, Jones, A.W. Jr., *The Operations of the 423rd Infantry (106th Infantry Division) in the Vicinity of Schonberg During the Battle of the Ardennes, 16-19 December 1944*, Advanced Infantry Officers Course, 1949-1950, pp.18-19.
21. Freiburg, BA, MSB 151a, p.17.

**Chapter 6**
1. Washington, Nara, MSB 688, pp.38-9.
2. Freiburg, BA, MSB 151a, p.35.
3. Underlined in the original text.
4. Freiburg, BA, MSB 151a, p.34.
5. Literally, the Führer's escort battalion.
6. They also incorporated some Panzerjäger IV l/70 (A) according to Longue, M., 'The "Chenogne-Rechival valley" Engagement', in *39/45 Magazine*, N°381, September-October 2023, p.53.
7. Washington, Nara, Ethint 80, pp.1-3.
8. Ibid. p.3.
9. Washington, Nara, MSB 688, p.42.
10. Bastogne, Bastogne War Museum, Fonds Kraft de la Saulx, file A0162, folder 9th AD, AAR 14th TB , entry dated 18/12/44.
11. Freiburg, BA, MSB 151a, p.36.
12. Delaval, M., op. cit., p.117.
13. Washington, Nara, RG 407, AAR 7th AD, entry dated 17/12/1944.
14. Freiburg, BA, MSB 151a, pp.36-7.
15. Washington, Nara, Ethint 80, pp.3-4.

**Chapter 7**
1. Reynolds, M., *Men of Steel 1 SS Panzer-Korps*, Staplehurst, 2005, p.95.
2. Captain Martin mentions bazookas in his report, which could be Panzerfaust or Panzershreck.
3. Washington, Nara, RG 407-Ent 427A-Box 19014-Folder CI 329A-14 Cav Gp Ardennes, Group Interview with 32nd CRS C Troop, pp.10-11.
4. Tiemann, R., *The Leibstandarte*, vol. IV/2, Winnipeg, 1998, pp.69-70.
5. Washington, Nara, RG 407-Ent 427A-Box 19014-Folder CI 329A-14 Cav Gp Ardennes, Group Interview with Captain North Commander HQ Troop 14th CG, entry dated 18/12/1944.
6. Gudgin, P., *Armoured Firepower*, Frome,1997, p.234.
7. Washington, Nara, RG 407-Ent 427A-Box 19014-Folder CI 329B-14 Cav Gp Ardennes, *AAR 14th CG* , entry dated 18/12/1944.
8. Washington, Nara, RG 407-Ent 427A-Box 19014-Folder CI 329A-14 Cav Gp Ardennes, Group Interview with Captain North Commander HQ Troop 14th CG, entry dated 18/12/1944.
9. Washington, Nara, RG 407, *AAR 7th AD*, entry dated 18/12/1944.
10. Bastogne, Bastogne War Museum, Fonds Kraft de la Saulx, file A0162, folder 7th AD, letter from Rosembaum dated 6/6/1967.
11. Lieutenant Reeves stated in his report that he was north of Poteau, but his description of the events and the map coordinates he gave were to the south-west of the village.
12. The map reference is 774912.
13. A small village called Rodt in US reports, here the French version of the place name has been used.
14. Coordinate 772917, Lieutenant Reeves mentions a canal, but it is actually the railway ditch.
15. Washington, Nara, RG407, Combat Interview 40TH TANK BN - C CO. LT GERALD E. REEVES, 1ST Platoon Ldr. Entry of 18/12/1944.
16. Bastogne, Bastogne War Museum, Fonds Kraft de la Saulx, dossier A0162, folder 7th AD, letter from Rosembaum dated 6/6/1967.

17. Washington, Nara, RG407, *AAR 7th AD*, entry dated 18 and 19/12/1944.
18. Washington, Nara, RG407, Combat Interview 40TH TANK BN - C CO. LT GERALD E. REEVES, 1ST Platoon Ldr. Entry dated 19/12/1944.
19. Washington, Nara, MSA 877, pp.37-8.
20. Delaval, M., op. cit., p.166.
21. The village is referred to as Rodt in American reports, which is what it is called today.
22. Washington, Nara, RG 407, AAR *CC A* 7th AD, entry dated 22/12/1944 and Ethint 80, pp.5- 7.
23. Washington, Nara, RG407, Combat Interview 40th TB C CO. LT GERALD E. REEVES, 1ST Platoon Ldr. Entry 19/12/1944.

**Chapter 8**
1. Delaval, M., op. cit., pp.139-40.
2. Fort Benning, USAIS Library Jones, A.W. Jr., op. cit., p.19.
3. Fort Benning, USAIS Library, Moon, P. Jr, *The Operations of the 1st Battalion 422nd Infantry (106th Infantry Division) in the Battle of the Bulge in the Vicinity of Schlausenbach Germany*, Advanced Infantry Officers Course, 1949-1950, p.18.
4. Fort Benning, USAIS Library Jones, A.W. Jr., op. cit., p.20.
5. Fort Benning, USAIS Library Jones, A.W. Jr., op. cit., p.20.
6. Washington, Nara, MSB 688, pp.42-3.
7. Freiburg, BA, MSB 151a, p.38.
8. Washington, Nara, AAR 7th AD, entry dated 19/12/1944.
9. Delaval, M., op. cit., p.136.
10. Freiburg, BA, MSB 151a, p.38.
11. Washington, Nara, RG 407, AAR 7th AD, entry dated 19/12/1944.
12. Freiburg, BA, MSB 151a, pp.38-9.
13. Washington, Nara, RG 407, AAR 7th AD, entry dated 19/12/1944.
14. Fort Leavenworth, Ike Skelton Library, N-11232 A, 3rd Bn 112th Infantry History, entry Coy L dated 19/12/1944.
15. Delaval, M., op. cit., p.131-2.
16. Fort Benning, USAIS Library, Atkins, E., *The Operations of the 28th Infantry Division) in the Bulge, 15-26 December 1944*, Advanced Infantry Officers Course, 1949-1950, pp.29-32.
17. Washington, Nara, RG 407, AAR 7th AD, entry dated 19/12/1944.

**Chapter 9**
1. The report refers to an SS-Panzer-Armee, even though it was still only a Panzer-Armee. This anachronism suggests that the archived report may have been written a relatively long time after the event.
2. The elements of Gross Deutschland identified actually belonged to the Führer Begleit Brigade, the Führer's escort brigade under the command of Otto Remer, whose ranks included elements from Gross Deutchland who still wore the forearm stripe identifying the elite unit on their sleeves.
3. Washington, Nara, RG 407, 7th AD AAR dec 1944 entry dated 20/12/1944.
4. Merriam, R., *Dark December,* Chicago-New York, 1947, p.156.
5. Macdonald, C., op. cit., p.467.
6. Washington, Nara, RG 407, 7th AD AAR *CC B* dec 1944 entry dated 20/12/1944.
7. Washington, Nara, RG 407, 7th AD AAR CC B Dec 1944 entry dated 21/12/1944.
8. Delaval, M., op. cit., p.176.
9. Fort Leavenworth, Ike Skelton Library, *Saint-Vith: an historical example of armor in the defense,* US Armor School, 1950, p.26.
10. Washington, Nara, RG 407, AAR 7th AD, entry dated 22/2/1944.
11. Washington, Nara, RG 407, AAR 7th AD, message from Ridgway arrived at 06:35 on 22/12/1944.
12. Martin, H., *Soldier: the Memoirs of Matthew B. Ridgway,* New York, 1956, p.120.

13. Washington, Nara, RG 407, AAR 7th AD, message from Ridgway arrived at 18:53 on 22/12/1944.
14. Delaval, M., op. cit., p.219.

## Conclusions

 1. Coles, H., *Ardennes, the Battle of the Bulge*, Washington, 1965, p.275.
 2. Dale, F., *Battlefield Stress: Causes, Cures and Countermeasures*, These de maitrise, US Army Command and General Staff College, Fort Leavenworth, 1985, p.12.
 3. Shultz, D., *Combat Fatigue: How Stress in Battle was Felt (and Treated) in WWII*, https://warfarehistorynetwork.com consulted on 14/7/2023.
 4. Kearnes, M., *Lessons in Unit Cohesion: from the United States Army's COHORT (Cohesion, Operational Readiness, and Training) Experiment of 1981 to 1995*, US Army Command and General Staff College, Fort Leavenworth, 2022, pp.26-36.
 5. Ibid, p.2.
 6. Bastogne, Bastogne War Museum documentation centre, Fonds Kraft de la Saulx, A0138, 14th Cavalry Group (Mecz), account of events after investigation by Lieutenant Jack Shea, appendix: report of examination of Colonel Mark Devine by Major Philips Wagner of 21/1/45, 45th Evacuation Hospital.
 7. Bastogne, Bastogne War Museum documentation centre, Fonds Kraft de la Saulx, A0138, 14th Cavalry Group (Mecz), account of events after investigation by Lieutenant Jack Shea, annex: Captain Nash's interrogation report, 10/1/45.
 8. Bastogne, Bastogne War Museum documentation centre, Fonds Kraft de la Saulx, A0138, 14th Cavalry Group (Mecz), account of events after investigation by Lieutenant Jack Shea, appendix: interrogation report by Captain Clrk, medical officer of the 820th TD Battalion, 10/1/45.
 9. Bastogne, Bastogne War Museum documentation centre, Fonds Kraft de la Saulx, A0138, 14th Cavalry Group (Mecz), account of events after investigation by Lieutenant Jack Shea , appendix: report of examination of Colonel Mark Devine by Major Philips Wagner of 21/1/45, 45th Evacuation Hospital.
10. Storr, J., *The Human Face of War*, Birmingham, 2009, pp.84-6.
11. Introduction by Troy Middleton, VIII Corps Commander, in *The Battle at Saint-Vith 17-23 December 1944, An historical example of Armor in the defence*, US Army Armor School, 1966.
12. Fort Leavenworth, Ike Skelton Library, N-17500.1033-2, MSB 151, p.109.
13. Fort Leavenworth, Ike Skelton Library, *The Battle at Saint-Vith 17-23 December 1944, An historical example of Armor in the defense*, US Army Armor School, 1966, p.4.
14. Yakovleff, M., *Tactique théorique*, Paris, 2009, pp. 216-17.
15. Storr, J., op. cit., p.86.
16. Total broken down into 35,000 dead, 105,000 wounded and 185,000 prisoners.
17. Americans: 26,000 dead, 91,000 wounded and 8,000 prisoners (total 125,000 men) and Commonwealth forces: 17,000 dead, 62,000 wounded and 5,000 prisoners (total 94,000 men).
18. Lopez, J. (dir) et al, *Infographie de la Seconde Guerre mondiale*, Paris, 2018, p.133.
19. American figures taken from the battlebook dedicated to a senior staff ride for senior officers in the US Army.

# Bibliography

## Sources

Among the plethora of books devoted to the Battle of the Bulge, there are not many that deal with the Battle of Saint-Vith. Two sectors have received the most attention: Bastogne and the sector of the 1. SS-Panzer-Division from Malmedy to La Gleize. A few rare books mention the disastrous fate of the 106th Infantry Division, with the two most comprehensive works on the subject being published at the time of the fortieth anniversary of the battle: Maurice Delaval's *Saint-Vith au cours de l'ultime Blitzkrieg de Hitler* and Colonel Alexandre Massart's *Saint-Vith*. Both books are of a very high quality.

Delaval's is a fantastic edition of eyewitness accounts from the belligerents at the time, some of which have been used in this book to illustrate points in a more vivid and immersive way. Colonel Massart's book, meanwhile, gives pride of place to American sources but does little to explore German accounts.

Since the publication of these two books, a large number of documents have been declassified, including the After Action Reports of the American units, which have been used extensively here. Despite research, the German archives of the divisions involved have not been discovered, and the archives at corps level are not precise enough. Consequently, the reports written by commanders at tactical level and collected by American historians have been used. Taken together, these provide an interesting corpus of sources. True to form, it is preferable to return to the archives sooner rather than reword what has been read in the works of this book's illustrious predecessors.

**Archives**
Washington Nara
*Ethint*
  N° 80 Führer Begleit Brigade in the Ardennes
*Foreign Military Studies*
  MSB 028 (62. VGD)
  MSB 688 (18. VGD)
*RG 407*
14th Cavalry Group
  *AAR 14th CG*
  Group Interview with Captain North Commander HQ Troop 14th CG
  Group Interview with 32nd CRS
  Narrative of Troop A of the 18th CRS
  Narrative of the 18th CRS staff
7th Armored Division

AAR 7th AD
7th AD AAR CC B
AAR 17th TB, 7th AD
Combat Interview 40th VF
Freiburg Bundes Archiv
MSB 151a
MS B 734
Bastogne Documentation Centre of the Bastogne War Museum (Fonds Kraft de la Saulx)
A0138, 14th Cavalry Group (Mecz), account of events after investigation by Lieutenant Jack Shea
A0162, binder 7th AD
A0162, binder 9th AD
Fort Leavenworth, Ike Skelton Library
*The Battle at Saint-Vith 17-23 December 1944, An historical example of Armor in the defence*, US Army Armor School, 1950
FM 2-30, Cavalry Reconnaissance Squadron Mechanized, 28/8/1944
FM 7-10, Armored Force Manual, Tactics and Technics, March 1942
N-11232 A, 3rd Bn 112th Infantry History
N-12472, Order of battle of the United States Army, vol. 1 & 2
N-17500.1033-2, MSB 151
AAR, 612th Tank Battalion
Dale, F., *Battlefield Stress: Causes, Cures and Countermeasures*, These de maitrise, US Army Command and General Staff College, Fort Leavenworth, 1985
Gabel, C., *Seek, Strike, and Destroy: U.S. Army Tank Destroyer Doctrine in World War II*, Fort Leavenworth, 1985
Kearnes, M., *Lessons in Unit Cohesion: from the United States Army's COHORT (Cohesion, Operational Readiness, and Training) Experiment of 1981 to 1995*, US Army Command and General Staff College, Fort Leavenworth, 2022
Fort Benning, USAIS Library
Atkins, E., *The Operations of the 28th Infantry Division in the Bulge, 15-26 December 1944*, Advanced Infantry Officers Course, 1949-1950
Horton, J., *The Operations of the 820th Tank Destroyer Battalion in a retrograde movement during the counteroffensive in the Ardennes*, Advanced Infantry Officers Course, 1948-1949
Jones, A.W. Jr., *The Operations of the 423rd Infantry (106th Infantry Division) in the vicinity of, Schonberg during the Battle of the Ardennes, 16-19 December 1944*, Advanced Infantry Officers Course, 1949-1950
Moon, P. Jr, *The Operations of the 1st Battalion 422nd Infantry (106th Infantry Division) in the Battle of the Bulge in the Vicinity of Schlausenbach Germany*, Advanced Infantry Officers Course, 1949-1950

**Published works**
Bradley, O., *Histoire d'un soldat*, Paris, 1952
Coles, H., *Ardennes, the Battle of the Bulge*, Washington, 1965
Collective, *Cavalry in the Gap: The 14th Cavalry Group and The Battle of the Bulge, s.l., n.d*
Cuppens, G., *Massacre à Malmedy*, Bayeux, 1989
Delaval, M., *Saint-Vith during Hitler's Final Blitzkrieg*, Vielsalm, 1984
Dupuy, T., *Hitler's Last Gamble*, Shrewsbury, 1994
Edwards, R., *German Airborne troops*, London, 1974
Gillie, M.H., *Forging the Thunderbolt*, Mechanicsburg, 2006
Gudgin, P., *Armoured Firepower*, Frome,1997
Hummel, L., 'The Military US Geographical Agent: The Case of Cold War Alaska', *Geographical Review* Vol. 95, No. 1 (Jan., 2005)

Longue, M., 'The "Chenogne-Rechival valley" commitment', in *39/45 Magazine*, N°381, September-October 2023, p.53

Lopez, J. (dir) et al, *Infographie de la Seconde Guerre mondiale*, Paris, 2018

Macdonald, C., *Noël 44 la Bataille d'Ardenne*, Brussels, 2004

Martin, H., *Soldier: the Memoirs of Matthew B. Ridgway*, New York, 1956

Massart, A., *Saint-Vith*, Verviers, 1995

McDonald, C., *Commandant de compagnie, combattants américains dans la bataille d'Europe*, Brussels, 1990

Merriam, R., *Dark December,* Chicago-New York, 1947

Prohüber, K-H., *Volksgrenadier-Divisionen*, Aachen, 2018

Reynolds, M., *Men of Steel: 1 SS Panzer-Korps*, Staplehurst, 2005.

Rusiecki, S., *The Key to the Bulge*, Mechanicsburg, 2009

Schneider, W., *Tiger in Combat,* t.1, Mechanicsburg, 2004

Shultz, D., *Combat Fatigue: How Stress in Battle was Felt (and Treated) in WWII*, https://warfarehistorynetwork.com

Storr , J., *The Human Face of War*, Birmingham, 2009

Student, K., *Generaloberst Kurt Studen und seine Fallschirmjäger*, Friedberg, n.d. [1980]

Tiemann, R., *The Leibstandarte,* vol. IV/2, Winnipeg, 1998

Whiting, C., *Mort d'une division, dans l'enfer du Schnee Eifel en décembre 1944*, Jalhay, 1992

Yakovleff, M., *Tactique théorique*, Paris, 2009

Yeide, H., *Steeds of steel, A History of American Mechanized Cavalry in World War II*, Minneapolis, 2008.

Yeide, H., *The Tank Killers: a History of America's World War II Tank Destroyer Force*, Drexell Hill, 2007

**Webography**

https://www.lexikon-der-wehrmacht.de

https://usacac.army.mil